DANCING MANY DRUMS

A STUDIES IN DANCE HISTORY BOOK

DANCING MANY DRUMS

EXCAVATIONS IN AFRICAN AMERICAN DANCE

EDITED BY

THOMAS F. DEFRANTZ

THE UNIVERSITY OF WISCONSIN PRESS

The University of Wisconsin Press
1930 Monroe Street
Madison, Wisconsin 53711

www.wisc.edu/wisconsinpress/

3 Henrietta Street
London WC2E 8LU, England

Printed in the United States of America

Library of Congress Cataloging-in-Publication Data
Dancing many drums : excavations in
African American dance / edited by Thomas F. DeFrantz.
382 pp.   cm. — (Studies in dance history)
Includes bibliographic references and index.
ISBN 0-299-17310-0 (cloth: alk. paper)
ISBN 0-299-17314-3 (pbk.: alk. paper)
1. African American dance—History.
2. African Americans—Social life and customs.
I. DeFrantz, Thomas.   II. Studies in dance history
(Unnumbered)
GV1624.7.A34 .D38   2002
793.3'089'96073—dc21   2001001943

Publication of this volume has been made possible in part by a generous grant from
Richard A. Long in honor of Katherine Dunham's 90th birthday;
and by the generous support of the Anonymous Fund
of the University of Wisconsin–Madison.

Contents

This volume is a tribute to African American dance archivist Joe Nash. Its title comes from a 1976 article by Nash that under-scored the variety of expressive idioms danced by Africans of the diaspora.[1] That article—and the "many drums" of its title—sug-gested a continuous history of African American dance practice with commonalities that spanned movement idioms.

In many ways Nash can be viewed as a progenitor of the field of African American dance studies. Born in New York in 1919, Nash taught himself basic ballet positions from books he borrowed as a child from the library.[2] He met Pearl Primus at the National Youth Administration in the early 1940s and became her first dance partner, until he began formal study with Syvilla Fort and Katherine Dunham. After serving in the U.S. military, he danced in the 1946 revival of the musical *Showboat* choreographed by Helen Tamiris and began collecting programs, photographs, clip-pings, and other memorabilia related to African American dance artists. In the late 1940s and 1950s he appeared in a string of West End and Broadway musicals, including *Finian's Rainbow* (Lon-don, 1947), *Inside U.S.A.* (1948), *Bless You All* (1950), *Flahooley* (1951), and *My Darlin' Aida* (1952). He danced in the New York City Center Light Opera Company's production of *Carmen Jones;* was a founding member of Aubrey Hitchen's Negro Dance The-ater in 1953; and performed as a guest artist with the compa-nies of Primus, Charles Weidman, and Donald McKayle. All the while he kept adding to his collection, and he continued to collect memorabilia after he retired from performing. In 1982 he began teaching the dance history course at the Alvin Ailey American Dance Center. Five years later he became a senior consultant to

Joe Nash and Pearl Primus in Primus's *Haitian Play Dance,* on tour, ca. 1946 (Photographer unknown; Photographs and Prints Division, Schomburg Center for Research in Black Culture, the New York Public Library–Astor, Lenox and Tilden Foundations; reproduced with permission)

the African American Tradition in Modern Dance program at the American Dance Festival.

Eventually, Nash's priceless collection of memorabilia came to include some 2,000 items, which he divided between the Schomburg Center for Research in Black Culture, in New York City, and the Tallahassee Black Archives and Museum in Florida. His prescience and the passion he brought to his subject result in the creation of the first major collection about African American dance, and many of the photographs in the pages that follow come from the Joe Nash Collection at the Schomburg Center. Without Nash's committed effort to preserve the history, practice, and theory of African American dance, this volume could not exist.

The second part of the title derives from the sensation of archaeological recovery that permeates African American dance scholarship today. While Nash's collection is remarkably rich, it is also, necessarily, a fragmentary offering. It is hardly an understatement that the history of African American dance performance has been documented insufficiently. Combing through archives, newspapers, literature, and oral histories, the scholars here reveal materials neglected by traditional studies of American dance history. While the subjects scrutinized in these explorations of sacred, social, and concert dances may be unfamiliar to many readers, these same subjects represent verifiable "highpoints" for the few scholars working in the field of African American dance history. Although very much alive, this field operates very much on the margins of both African American studies and dance studies.

This volume was prompted by a Congress on Research in Dance Special Topics Conference, "African-American Dance: Researching a Complex History," organized by John O. Perpener III and hosted by the Department of Dance, College of Fine and Applied Arts, University of Illinois at Urbana-Champaign, 25–27 April 1996. That landmark event brought together artists, critics, and historians working within and around issues of historiography and identity associated with African American dance practice. Over three days, the participants explored the process of dance scholarship as it intersects with African American studies. Among the conference highlights were a thorny panel discussion about generational affiliations within "black dance" by choreographers Ronald K. Brown, Ralph Lemon, and Bebe Miller; a reminiscence by Bella Lewitzky, whose company was in residence during the conference, about Lester Horton's interracial modern dance studio in Los Angeles in the 1940s and 1950s; and a final dinner in honor of Katherine Dunham, in which she spoke about her East St. Louis cultural and performing arts center.[3]

Eight of the twelve chapters included here have not been published before. Of these, three developed from materials presented at the conference. I commissioned several new essays and solicited various reprints to illumine the range of scholarly material presently available in the field. I hope that the diversity of analytic approaches will inspire new and probing studies of African American dance history, criticism, theory, and practice.

The volume is divided into three sections: theory, practice, and history. These are porous categories, and the source materials found among them certainly overlap. Still, I find the distinctions useful if only to remind the reader that scholarly *approaches* to African American dance history distinguish how work becomes categorized. The chapters in the theory section offer speculative analyses of dance events from fresh readings of extant documentation. Practice sits at the center of the volume, with its strong emphasis on oral history as a reminder that, in African American tradition, the act itself supersedes its discussion. The history section pays tribute—by way of thick description and analysis— to artists, companies, and works typically relegated to footnote status in other volumes.

The two exquisite James Van Der Zee photographs that are the cover and frontispiece (p. 2) of this volume complicate the notion of African American dance practice, theory, and history. The young girls captured here are students of tap dance, a hybrid form that drew on, at least, African and Irish traditions of percussive musicality. This pictorial evidence of tap dance being taught in Harlem studios in the 1920s and 1930s avoids easy assumptions of a "naturalized" history of dancing black bodies. These carefully dressed girls suggest a socializing feature of dancing lessons, and introduce implications of class and gender in the formation of African American dance history. For me, the photographs raise other practical and theoretical questions. Could these girls have become professional dancers? What sorts of roles would have been available to them? Who were their teachers? Do these images invoke a minstrel-era stereotype of cavorting, infantilized dancing black bodies? If not, why not? Does the "black lens" of photographer James Van Der Zee somehow mitigate the exoticism of black bodies in motion? These images, like the others that follow, invite this sort of speculative perusal.

My hope in bringing this volume to fruition is to inspire more focused explorations of African American dance. Few will dispute the importance of African-inspired music and movement to the world culture we now share; in terms of popular music and dance, the African American influence has been profound. This volume arrives at the millennium as the first scholarly anthology devoted to African American dance.[4] May many others follow, and may they plow even more deeply into its beautiful black ground.

NOTES

1. Joe Nash, "Dancing Many Drums," *National Scene Magazine Supplement* 4, no. 8 (September–October 1976): 2–3, 8–11.

2. Joe Nash, telephone interview with the author, 3 February 1999.

3. For a detailed report of the conference, see Naomi Jackson, "Report on the CORD Conference African-American Dance: Researching a Complex History," *Dance Research Journal* 28, no. 2 (fall 1996): 107–10.

4. *African Dance,* ed. Kariamu Welsh Asante (Trenton, N.J.: African World Press, 1996) offers a striking collection of Afrocentric essays detailing African dance practice on the continent and in diaspora.

Acknowledgments

This volume could not possibly exist without the superb editorial assistance and counsel of Lynn Garafola. Although she stepped down as editor of Studies in Dance History between the time this project was proposed and finished, she remained a sturdy, nurturing presence throughout. Her high standards and consummate professionalism as an editor and researcher cannot be overstated.

I was also fortunate to receive assistance from Claude Conyers, who graciously read and commented on portions of the manuscript. Elizabeth Aldrich, Linda J. Tomko, and Constance Valis Hill each provided much-needed encouragement along the way. Carol Martin and Joan Erdman, the previous co-editors of Studies in Dance History, have also been instrumental in bringing this project to fruition. I thank them for their sincere efforts.

Dr. Richard Long has been extremely supportive of this project since its inception. I thank him, as well as Philip S. Khoury, dean of the School of Humanities, Arts, and Social Sciences at MIT, who provided several grants that allowed me to complete research for this volume. I also wish to thank the staff of the Dance Collection, the New York Public Library for the Performing Arts, especially Phil Karg, and the staff of the Schomburg Center for Research in Black Culture, especially Antony Toussaint.

Finally, I thank the authors who gave of their time and energy to see this project through. An anthology such as this required much more work and focused attention than I ever imagined. The authors were right there with me from beginning to end, providing answers, clarifications, and fascinating ideas about how to tell this story of dance.

DANCING MANY DRUMS

"Dance Class, 1928" (Photograph by James Van Der Zee; copyright © Donna Mussenden Van Der Zee; all rights reserved; reproduced with permission)

African American Dance: A Complex History

Thomas F. DeFrantz

Scholars of African American dance history face a battery of unusual challenges. Reliable documentation of dance events predating the mid-twentieth century is slight; few research centers or major libraries contain specialized collections chronicling African American dance performance, and misreadings of racial separation and racist attitudes permeate early writing about African diaspora culture in America. Frustrated by the painful lack of focused research and criticism and the absence of credible source material, many historians interested in African American dance slip away from the field to the safety of literary studies, labor studies, cultural studies, or art-making. Finally, there is the issue of categorization, complicated by critics who variously refer to the broad spectrum of expressive idioms practiced by African American artists as "African American dance" or the equally amorphous "black dance." How has this happened?

WORD SLIPPAGE: THE B(L)ACKGROUND

Since the mid-nineteenth century, the term "race" has served as a shorthand for expressing variance from a preferred European norm. In the mid-1980s, when cultural historians and literary theorists began placing "race" in quotation marks, they attempted to undermine this long-uncontested social category.[1] Denying biological, critical, or even descriptive truth to "race" as an identity marker challenged rigid assumptions American critics had long held about "black art," including dance. "Race" is principally a means of labeling, a politically motivated system of assigning people of color to a position outside the hegemonic mainstream of (white) Western civilization.

Still, the use of "race" as an identity marker has not disappeared from the academy, nor have forms of racism abated simply because theorists have identified "race" as a construction. Instead, "race" has taken on more complex nuances of meaning and usage. For instance, in academic as well as in more general usage, "African American" and "black" now flourish side by side. I notice a contextual shift in my own usage of the words in writing and teaching. To black students I say "black" unless I'm trying to historicize an event, in which case I'll rely on the more ponderous term "African American." But if my class has international or white students, I tend to say African American exclusively. I like to think that the seven syllables, or two written words, indicate a stratification of inquiry that forces the listener or reader to consider the implications of cultural hybridity and invention. The words stop the eye, ear, and tongue. But in conversation with someone I do not know well, I always catch my slippage of using "black" to a person who is not African American. For me, "black" as a descriptive marker is reserved for conversation with those who might be able to imagine its implications in the United States, including a history of political and economic inequity, institutionalized social affliction, and spiritual resiliency. Like other African American scholars, I slip upon "black" to underscore an imaginary cultural coherency. I acknowledge that this impulse is in part sentimental, a romanticized sway toward the comfort of neat binary opposition: "black" as the polar opposite of "white." But I must confront this slippage in order to write about work made by African American choreographers, American social dance practice, and "black dance."

What is "black dance"? What does it have to do with race? Is it different from African American dance? Does the moniker matter? Is it about semantics? Can't we simply allow linguistic slippage between "black" and "African American" to imply complexity and leave it at that? Does it matter who is writing about "blackness" and to whom? If there can be "black dance," why is there no critical category of "white dance"? And why has "black dance" stuck when its etymological predecessors, such as "darky dance," "colored dance," and "Negro dance," have not?

Some answers to these questions can be found within the political metamorphoses of the 1960s. "Black dance" became a category of performance during this era, in large part because of the Black Arts movement and its collective attempt to define a "black aesthetic." Ironically, the term "black dance" seems to have been invented by white critics as a shorthand for work they felt uncomfortable with or ill-prepared to address.

The Black Arts movement inspired a heightened critique of American social order by African American artists.[2] These artists assumed an inviolable connection between art and politics and through their close association with the Black Power movement sought to create a coherent "black aesthetic" inspired by, about, and for black people. Committed to intensive community involvement, they espoused a model of art production that valued the participation of artists and audiences in the creation of an art that explicitly confirmed the well being of the group.

Not all African American artists working in this era aligned themselves with the Black Arts movement. But throughout the late 1960s and 1970s, many journalists routinely referred to all choreographic work produced by African Americans as "black dance."[3] The phrase was originally intended to mark difference from the mainstream of concert performance, and it was employed with divergent connotations in both the "black press" and the "mainstream press." For example, critic Marcia Siegel entitled a chapter of her 1972 collection of criticism, *At the Vanishing Point,* "Black Dance: A New Separatism." In a series of essays covering several years of work offered by African American choreographers, Siegel self-consciously probed the validity of "black art" from her vantage point as a self-described "serious white critic":

> I think we all at some time have asked ourselves whether we must adopt special positions from which to view black art. When people were hurling their hatred at us from the stage, we cowered in our guilty shoes and thought of "social relevance" as a possible stan-

dard. When we saw amateurish performances or half-finished ideas being cheered hysterically, we wondered if we could slip out of our telltale skins and see this art as black people see it, or if we should duck the problem and not try to cover it at all.[4]

Siegel's comment illustrates the cultural confusion and critical anxiety of the era that gave rise to the category of "black dance." While she recognizes that these performances satisfy imperatives understood by their artists and "target" audiences, she also assumes a (white) critical "we" unable to understand aesthetic motivations of "their" "black art."

Here, implications of a separate-but-equal (black) dance tradition peek out from behind the harsh words predicting the (white) critic's obsolescence. Of course, the work Siegel referred to *did* feel different from other work chronicled in her book of critical essays. Its political import as a tool of social and cultural coherency—evidenced by the "hysterically" cheering crowds she witnessed—confirmed an undocumented dimension of dance performance. That dimension, linking proscenium forms of concert dance to New World religious practices and contemporary experiences of African American people, developed outside the concert hall and the dance studio. Ultimately, it began in the cultural interchanges wrought on the slave ships crossing the Atlantic during the middle passage—the source of African American hybridity. In the 1960s, some concert dance made by African American artists for African American audiences intentionally dramatized the shared memories, experiences, and aesthetic values of African American people. These dances and their characteristic performance styles became known as "black dance."

ON BEING "BLACK"

According to art historian Richard J. Powell, many artists viewed the recuperation of "black" as a mark of identity during the 1960s as an "emphatic proclamation of an oppressed people's psychological reorientation."[5] In dance, this decidedly nationalistic reorientation emphasized connections between everyday experiences and art-making to embrace multiple movement idioms and a range of expressive approaches in the representation of "blackness." However, this strategy held consequences of essentialism for audiences, critics, and artists. For example, the half-hour television series *On Being Black,* produced for a single season by Boston's public television station WGBH, presented dramas by black writers that illuminated the "black experience" for a largely white audience. An episode telecast in May 1969 featuring the Alvin Ailey American Dance Theater in two contrasting works demonstrated the variety of creative strategies employed by choreographers as well as the competing ambiguities of "racial" identification during that era.[6]

The program begins with a single, silhouetted (black) male fighting and punching against a bright orange background as dissonant chords sound and the program's title flashes on the screen. The dancer stretches against imaginary chains around his neck and hands, his body racked in anger and pain. As if to enact the show's title, the man performs "being black" as an embattled solitary existence in which his body endures a purgatory of tortured muscular contractions and repels attacks by unseen oppressors.[7] From this opening sequence we understand "being black" at this particular moment in the 1960s to be about physically embodying barely suppressed rage.

Alvin Ailey appears briefly as the on-camera narrator for the program to remind the audience of his own choreographic intention to "project the essential dignity and beauty of men" through concert dance. The program then screens a filmed version of Talley Beatty's recent work *The Black Belt.* According to program notes of the stage version of this ballet, the Ailey company commissioned Beatty's piece in 1968 as an examination of "the realities of the black belt" or ghetto; its "ferment, paradox, conflict and dilemma"; its "aspiration for mobility"; and its "surge toward integration and assimilation into the mainstream of American Life."[8] *The Black Belt*'s carnivalesque depiction of a day in the ghetto includes scenes inside tenement apartments; a sequence in a storefront church, where a gang of marauding male rapists wearing white-face masks attack a female worshiper; an ambiguous crucifixion of a man stripped to his dance belt; a surreal scene of mourning by a mysterious group of hooded women; and a full-scale riot in the streets, complete with looting, fighting, and general mayhem. The dance ends when all of the rioters are shot by machine guns from offstage white policemen and the dancers are massed in a heap, smothered by useless stolen merchandise.

The Black Belt portrays ghetto life without purpose, hope, or apology. Its archetypal characters enact quirky individualistic rituals that, taken together, suggest a community unraveling at its seams. Beatty's choreography employs blocks of hyperkinetic movement phrases built from impossibly fast sequences of turns, leg extensions, leaps, freezes, and shifts of direction, all executed with a suffocating rhythmic precision. A surrealistic protest dance with obvious references to civil rights activism and the contemporaneous Black Arts movement, *The Black Belt* depicts an explosive rage and its narrative consequences in the streets of an urban ghetto.

On Being Black continues with a presentation of Ailey's *Revelations* (1960), which he introduces as a lyrical counterpoint to Beatty's work. On camera, Ailey calls the dance "a ballet" composed "to our own passionately beautiful spirituals." In this context *Revelations*, which by 1969 had been consistently heralded as a classic of the modern-dance repertory, represents the strength and faith held by mature African Americans involved in the struggle for political equity. Choreographed as a suite of dances representing African American religious practice in the rural American South, *Revelations* employs a limited palette of dance movements

Title sequence from *On Being Black,* WGBH television program, 1969

that emphasize fully stretched torsos, carefully articulated body isolations, and character-driven interactions enriched by details from the choreographer's memory.[9]

Although both *Revelations* and *The Black Belt* historicize aspects of African American experience, they employ emphatically different approaches to movement vocabularies, musical selection, and overall kinetic effect. Nevertheless, most critics and audiences considered both Beatty's protest dance, set largely to the music of Duke Ellington, and Ailey's traditionally shaped suite, set to spirituals and gospel music, to fall well within the era's amorphous definition of "black dance." The artistic range of these artists was thus diminished by a label that, while it had no aesthetic identity, seemed to refer to one.

The Alvin Ailey American Dance Theater stands at the center of any study of "black dance" because of its predominance at the moment when the term came into regular usage. Significantly, Ailey conceived his company and its operations as an unabashedly assimilationist project, with three goals he often recounted in interviews: to employ the scores of excellent black dancers in New York who had no performing homes, to give artistic voice to African American experience in terms of concert dance, and to assemble a racially integrated repertory company that could perform both modern dance classics and new works by Ailey and other young choreographers. His achievement of each of these goals is clearly demonstrated by the television program, where three of the thirteen bodies engaged in "being black" are white.

3   4

Ailey integrated his company to counter the "reverse chauvinism in being an all-black anything." As he explained, "I am trying to show the world that we are all human beings and that color is not important. What is important is the quality of our work."[10] This obvious echo of Dr. Martin Luther King Jr.'s 1963 speech that counterposed the "content of character" to the "color of skin" confirms the anti-essentialist stance Ailey assumed in relation to "race."[11] Ironically, if his intention was to demonstrate the ability of African American dancers as commensurate with their white counterparts, his company set the standard for "black dance."

For some critics, "black dance" came to be signified simply by the presence of African American dancers. Other critics and artists, including Ailey, realized that little could be accomplished by labeling work made by all African Americans as something intrinsically beyond the mainstream of modern dance, even if those artists' offstage lives remained bound by inescapable, everyday American racism.[12] Still other, typically younger African American artists, committed to the political need for a coherent "black aesthetic," viewed their own work as belonging to a category outside traditional structures of dance performance and synergetic with the emergence of Black Power.[13] These artists sought to invest "black dance" with the proclamation of self-representation, to use it as a tool of mobilization to create work relevant to African American audiences. An impasse of terminology and usage developed along this fault line, as the erratic articulation of "black dance" had to somehow satisfy its artists, its core audience, cultural outsiders, casual observers, disinterested critics, fans, and its own etymological birth as both a component of a vibrant political movement and a shorthand for "racial" difference.

For its practitioners the emergent "black dance" contained political import as a practice that engaged its audience, encouraged call-and-response participation, and communicated connections between art and contemporary political events. According to choreographer and author Carole Johnson, the issue of expressive freedom became central to the controversy surrounding the invention of "black dance": "Freedom is what all Black people are seeking. . . . 'Black dance' . . . does not preach a particular ideology. . . . Rather than a particular style of dance this expression 'Black dance' indicates the particular historical time and the conditions in which Black people currently find themselves."[14] Here Johnson predicted that "black dance" might become an inclusive category, able to encompass a range of expressive dance idioms so long as the work offered a political intervention that aligned it with contemporary "blackness." Surrealistic works, like Beatty's *Black Belt*, could be termed "black dance" in response to their musical selections, use of social dance movements, and archetypal characterizations with obvious culturally specific antecedents. Traditionally shaped dance suites, like Ailey's *Revelations*, mined ancestral memory through musical choices, an abstraction that underlined the representation of a pervasive spiritual dignity, and a narrative suggesting cultural advancement from despair toward triumph. Other successful works created by African American artists in this era included *Tangents* (1968), a precise, cool, abstract work by Rod Rodgers; *Las Desenamoradas* (1967), Eleo Pomare's tightly structured adaptation of Federico García Lorca's *The House of Bernarda Alba; Africa's Children* (1968), a full-length ballet employing Ghanaian dance forms created by the Philadelphia-based choreographer Arthur Hall; and various ballet works by Louis Johnson, including *Forces of Rhythm* (1972) for the Dance Theatre of Harlem. By the mid-1970s, "black dance" had come to be defined by its artists as work that was explicitly engaged in the act of black self-identification.[15]

JAZZ DANCE/BLACK DANCE

The first two sustained efforts to chronicle African American dance practice were published before and after the 1960s articulation of "black dance." Their differences in title, methodology, and achievement established lasting paradigms for African American dance scholarship. Originally published in 1964, the authoritative *Jazz Dance: The Story of American Vernacular Dance*, by Marshall and Jean Stearns, portrays history as a chronological series of biographical portraits of significant popular entertainers.[16] To research their subjects, the couple conducted a staggering number of personal interviews. Much of their documentation came from oral transcripts of these interviews augmented by research from the popular press. The achievement of their volume lies in the subtle way that they align personal testimony with scholarly research to construct a layered and compelling history of dance practice. Written with a wry, journalistic style that seems to underscore the esoteric parameters of their subject, the volume documents African American dance from the plantation through the 1960s in terms of its practitioners and their practices.

Lynne Fauley Emery's *Black Dance in the United States from 1619 to 1970*, first published in 1972, offers a sweeping chronological history of dance practice traced from the middle passage, through the islands of the Caribbean, to the plantations of the United States.[17] Inspired by the author's desire for a "dance literature with which [her] black students could identify,"[18] Emery conducted a painstaking review of the slim extant literature on African American dance and examined diverse sources such as travel diaries, journalistic accounts, short periodical articles, and critical reviews. Heavily illustrated, the volume described a trajectory of African-derived performance modes from the slave trade to the concert stage as a travelogue of African American presence in dance. Written in a fairly dry, "objective" tone, but with a palpable empathy for the historical difficulties encountered by people of color in America, *Black Dance* arrived as a bibliography transformed into prose to chronicle a history of dance defined by "race."

These two volumes created the mold for approaches to the field and remained the only book-length studies of African American dance practice for nearly two decades. Although each of these books became invaluable as reference works, each had clear limitations. Emery's travelogue approach struggles to document far too much in one volume, careening from slave festivals through nineteenth-century popular entertainments to "classical" twentieth-century forms.[19] Her attempt to be all-inclusive forces an encyclopedic stratification, in which certain "prominent" artists receive limited attention, others receive a cursory biographical paragraph outlining their training and "great works," while still others are reduced to footnote status. Worse, Emery fails to consider what links the dancers and dances she documents beyond "race." Her "slavery-to-freedom" format assumes an undiluted lineage of dance practice from African dance forms to contemporary modern dance and suggests an unfortunate narrative of "primitive" dance under segregation that gave way to preferred "classical" dance after the Civil Rights movement. In essence, "black dance" is defined here as "not-white dance," as a separate stream of performance that may be detached from (white) American dance history.

The Stearnses include white dancers in their study and define its parameters by aesthetic affinities ("jazz dance") rather than "race." But their critical assumption that jazz dance can only be considered a "vernacular" form threatens to overshadow the professional achievements of the artists they interview.[20] Surely many of the artists included here, such as Aida Overton Walker and the Nicholas Brothers, achieved transcendent mastery in their transformations of "vernacular" social dance structures for the stage. Were the Stearnses conceptually opposed to the identification of consummate technique *within* these African-derived expressive idioms? If not, why do they end their volume with a prediction that "art dance and vernacular dance will combine more and more effectively as time passes"?[21] Why was it not possible to consider the dances of the African diaspora they chronicled in their book as art?

Where Emery often reduces the history of African American dance to a story of racial disenfranchisement and victimization at the hands of powerful whites, the Stearnses' smooth portrayal of relations between black dancers and white audiences, including themselves, denies a relationship of dance performance to political strategy. Although researched and published in an era defined by shifting attitudes toward racial segregation, *Jazz Dance* ultimately seems curiously apolitical. The Stearnses offer a normative history of African American dance practice as the foundation of dance in popular entertainment; Emery proposes a corrective history of African American dances and dancers, positioned eternally outside the mainstream of American dance.

Another major distinction between the two volumes may be

found in their starting points. While Emery begins her chronicle in the middle passage, determined to arrive finally at "black dance" in the United States, the Stearnses begin their history with an easily overlooked section on African performative imperatives. Citing research conducted but not yet published by art historian Robert Farris Thompson, they compile a sequence of commonalities linking African dance traditions that survived the middle passage and contributed to "jazz dance." Thompson had conducted extensive fieldwork in a range of sub-Saharan cultures to arrive at his seminal articulation of pan-African dance and music performance eventually published in the 1966 article "Dance and Culture: An Aesthetic of the Cool." His analysis describes "the dominance of a percussive concept of performance; multiple meter; apart playing and dancing; call-and-response; and, finally the songs and dances of derision."[22] Thompson's work, extended slightly by separate research in the teaching primer *Modern Jazz Dance* by San Francisco–based scholar and choreographer Dolores Kirton Cayou,[23] predicted a third strain of African American dance scholarship that explored theoretical imperatives embedded within dance practice. The documentation of these qualities of motion provided critical linkage between obviously intertwined sacred and social traditions of African American dance performance. Each of these attributes could also be discerned in concert work made by artists involved in the Black Arts movement, although the final attribute—the songs and dances of derision—most clearly encompassed the political dimension of "black dance" performance. In this category, movement provokes metacommentary and suggests narratives outside the physical frame of performance. For many concert artists of the Black Arts movement, the ability of stage dance to refer to experiences well outside the proscenium frame provided the most important connections of their work to contemporary black experience.[24]

These performance characteristics indicated a continuity of aesthetic approaches to dance and music-making in line with the articulation of a "black aesthetic" in the 1960s.[25] Reconceived in the 1990s by cultural and literary theorists as "Africanist retentions" or "Africanisms," these hallmarks of African-derived performance provide a theoretical framework for the identification and interpretation of diasporic traditions of art-making.[26] Africanisms discernible in concert dance, for example, are qualities of design and execution based on insistent rhythmicity, angularity, percussive rupture of underlying flow, individualism within a group dynamic, and access to a dynamic "flash of the spirit" that simultaneously confirms temporal presence and ubiquitous spirituality.[27] These qualities are not particular movements so much as compositional strategies that may inform any given moment in a dance. As such, they are recurrent aesthetic imperatives that may be employed both by African diaspora artists and, significantly, by others following this tradition. While some scholars have resisted this theoretical approach because of its implication of a narrow and singular "African dance" idiom, the identification of these conceptual traditions has created the most consistent approach to documenting Africanist performance across generations and geographies of African American dancers and choreographers, as well as in work by others, including white Americans, Europeans, and Asians.[28]

Subsequent literature devoted to African American dance followed the three perspectives outlined above: the use of brief biographical narratives describing the practice of individual performers and companies, the documentation of historical narratives culled from research, or the articulation of theoretical principles of performance, usually in tandem with case studies. But as the literature expanded, the discursive category of "black dance" was rejected by many scholars, critics, and artists because of its controversial invention and frequent use as a condescending label by journalists in the 1960s and 1970s. Over time, the term disappeared and resurfaced clumsily, and rarely without apologia, in the titles of volumes of sweeping historical documentation following Emery, including Alice J. Adamczyk's useful *Black Dance: An Annotated Bibliography* (1989) and Edward Thorpe's highly inadequate *Black Dance* (1990).[29] Neither of these authors convincingly define their use of the category of "black dance" beyond its obvious implications of "race"; for me, this essentialist use insidiously compresses dance practice into an amorphous mass shaped by its variance to the dominant (white) histories of dance. Other scholars recognize this ambiguity. African American historian Richard Long titled his 1989 volume that documents more than a century of participation by African American artists in dance *The Black Tradition in American Dance*. This title suggests black presence coherent to American dance history. Long's technique incorporates Africanist compositional strategies, including the political implications of certain dances, within the biographical documentation of artists and artistic trends.[30]

By the late 1990s, some cultural theorists proposed a strategic reclaiming of "black" as a marker of cultural ubiquity.[31] From this perspective, "black dance" suggests a wide range of practices, from forms of Argentinian tango to South African gumboot dance and the *Creole Giselle* performed by Dance Theatre of Harlem. While this strategy underlines the increased presence of scholars exploring African-diaspora performance and predicts their collaboration across academic disciplines, it fails to acknowledge the peculiar history of the term in American discourse outlined in this essay. Ultimately, there can't be a singular idiom called "black dance" that contains a clear definition for all who invoke it. As I've argued, the category has to occupy several discursive spaces simultaneously, defined at least by who is speaking and to whom. Surely scholars have to be willing to define their use of the term if we are to move toward a more complex rendering of the material it may contain.

This volume and essay refer to "African American dance" in part because of the term's less problematic invention, but also to invite its readers to look beyond how "black" can be defined by its racial opposite "white." The black body in motion does not render itself as an alternative to anything; as Fanon writes, "it is."[32] While "African American dance" may seem as equivocal as "black dance," its linguistic origins are not so clearly politicized along the lines of white spectatorship of Africanist performance. I first became aware of the term in the 1990s as it was used by African American dance historians; to my mind these authors granted it a crucial elasticity of meaning.[33] Here I intend for the term to accommodate practice, history, and theoretical hallmarks of performance as they are realized by African diaspora dancers and others concerned with diasporic forms. Some of the authors in this volume are more forthcoming than I; they refer to "black dance" as a corporeal reality, a socially and politically circumscribed idiom of undeniable cultural coherency. Other authors write around the essentialist implications of "black dance" to describe particular Africanist aesthetic processes and dance practices. Ultimately, I appreciate the conceptual complexity suggested by the interplay between "black dance" and "African American dance" and the ways in which the two phrases suggest divergent audiences and critical strategies. Surely any dance made by African Americans is not automatically "black dance." But just as surely "black dance" exists, even if only in the United States as an echo of the fomentation of its 1960s genesis.

The chapters in this volume explore an array of theories, geographies, and historical periods of African American dance. Fifteen years separate the publication of the earliest essay from the most recent offering. I have not smoothed over their digressions in terminology or approach to "black dance." Instead, I intend for the tension between their assumptions to reflect the great flux of discursive and methodological strategies in African American dance documentation. Most of the authors included in this volume claim African ancestry, a fact that points to the formation of a vibrant literature steeped in an experiential understanding of black cultural processes. In all, this volume reflects the emergence of new critical and historical strategies that underscore the instability of ideas across different historical periods.

RESEARCH METHODOLOGIES: HISTORY— CHOOSING STORIES TO TELL

Dance history is created by the documents historians assemble. Because sustained inquiry into African American dance has come only in the past three decades, the field is unusually open to a range of methodological approaches. Until recently, however, many authors, including Arthur Todd writing in the 1950s and Joe Nash writing in the 1970s, anticipated or followed Emery in the burdensome task of tracing a comprehensive chronological narrative of African American dance practice.[34] Separated by decades, their writings arrived at crucial moments in the formation of the field and by the irrefutable breadth of their source materials confirmed that a range of unexplored subjects awaited documentation. But for too long, they remained among the few documents that did not question the viability or "historical accuracy" of African American dancers in professional American dance. This latter strain of critical writing, represented in two essays from 1944 by *Dance Observer* correspondent Lois Balcom, continued unabated throughout the 1960s, 1970s, and 1980s, especially in daily newspaper and weekly periodical pieces concerned with the "suitability" of African American dancers in ballet.[35] Another prevalent type of article, replicated by this Introduction, attempts to trace the history of "black dance" as a critical category. Among these, Julinda Lewis Williams (1980) and Zita Allen (1980) both acknowledge that the field is far too wide to be contained by a single designation.[36]

Recent historical scholarship offers in-depth exploration of single performances, careers, or events.[37] In this volume two pairs of essays detailing overlapping eras confirm the contemporary trend to complicate the rendering of African American dance history through close reading and political contextualization. Maureen Needham details the 1934 Asadata Dafora work *Kykunkor*. This seminal dance opera set a standard for the participation of African dance idioms on the American concert stage. Brenda Dixon Gottschild's documentation of the career of Norton and Webb during the same era offers insight into the construction of "high-class" popular entertainment by African Americans.[38]

Constance Valis Hill documents the intriguing history of what may be the lost masterpiece of Katherine Dunham's career, the 1951 ballet *Southland*.[39] Despite the dance's many merits, it was the creation of this work that tore the fabric of interracial trust that bound Dunham's dancers together. Valis Hill's essay connects the political dimension of performance, always palpable in Dunham's work, to the political intricacies of government sponsorship for dance artists during the Cold War era.[40]

In telling the story of the New York Negro Ballet on tour in

Great Britain, Dawn Lille Horwitz writes a chapter long missing in American ballet history. The African American presence in classical ballet, ultimately confirmed by the founding of Dance Theatre of Harlem in 1969, grew slowly alongside a waxing American interest in theatrical stage dancing.[41] Dance writer Zita Allen has separated the history of African American dancers in ballet into two categories—the individual dancers who struggled to take ballet classes long before there were dance companies of any sort, and the "all-black" ballet companies that served, often only temporarily, as vehicles for these dreamers.[42] The New York Negro Ballet provided a full-scale convergence of dancers and dance in the still-segregated America of the 1950s.

THEORIES OF AFRICAN AMERICAN DANCE

The implications of Africanist performance imperatives for African American dance have been extended in excellent scholarship in the 1980s and 1990s by Kariamu Welsh Asante (1985), Katrina Hazzard-Gordon (1990), Jacqui Malone (1996), and Brenda Dixon Gottschild (1996).[43] Each of these authors build upon Robert Farris Thompson's evocation of an abiding "aesthetic of the cool" linking performance practice to aesthetic hallmarks of the African diaspora. It may be useful here to offer a brief précis of these works to illustrate the complexity that has enriched the field in recent years.

In *Jookin': The Rise of Social Dance Formations in African American Culture*, Hazzard-Gordon replicates the chronological narrative of cultural causality suggested by Emery, tracing dance practice from Africa, the middle passage, and slave culture in the United States to the "jook joints" of Cleveland, the principal site of her research. Her text offers a reading of social dance history inflected by her interest in working-class black dance arenas. In *Steppin' on the Blues: The Visible Rhythms of African American Dance*, Malone follows the Stearnses to mine "African American vernacular traditions" but looks well beyond the proscenium stage to examine fraternity and sorority stepping, the Florida A&M University marching band, and dance in Mutual Aid Societies. Dixon Gottschild's groundbreaking study, *Digging the Africanist*

Presence in American Performance: Dance and Other Contexts, explores the obvious but unacknowledged presence of African performance elements in work by European Americans. The implications of her book suggest innumerable directions for further study of how African American performance practices saturate American dance idioms, whether or not black bodies are present.

The most common theoretical approach to African American dance history follows Asante's "Commonalities in African Dance: An Aesthetic Foundation" by invoking the omnipresent spiritual dimension that permeates African-diaspora performance traditions, including dance and music. In the present volume, P. Sterling Stuckey connects the relationship of dance to religion as a cultural imperative through an examination of their documentation in literature and music history.[44] His essay suggests a theoretical source of religiosity as the root of African American dance. As he points out, the compression of sacred and "secular" events in many African cultures contributes to a palpable sensation of urgency common to African-diaspora dance events. The importance of spirituality to the African American concert stage inspired a series of seminars begun in 1998 and sponsored by the American Dance Festival entitled "The Black Church, Spirituality and Modern Dance."[45]

While scholars have underscored the importance of minstrelsy and vaudeville to the establishment of the professional black performer,[46] the experiences of African Americans on public stages deserve greater scrutiny. Here Nadine A. George untangles a web of spectatorial ambiguities surrounding dance performance by the Whitman Sisters, a quartet of light-complexioned African American entertainers who worked at the beginning of the twentieth century. She argues that dance performances by the Whitman Sisters actively upset race and gender categories and challenged the expectations of audience members, producers, and theater owners, making the vaudeville stage an unlikely site of resistance.

The importance of music and dance in African-diaspora culture prompted the widespread assumption that all black people dance well. In truth, segregation in the first half of the twenti-

eth century allowed few cultural outsiders access to the process
of African Americans learning to dance. This process was further concealed by literature that featured fantastic accounts of
African Americans dancing and by the disproportionate visibility
of professional black entertainers who danced.[47] Marya Annette
McQuirter questions this erasure and the anxiety that surrounds
the public performance of social dance. Her depiction of *awkwardness* for African American dancers in the social realm provides
a long-deferred critique of stereotypical assumptions of how people achieve "vernacular" dance.

Studies that acknowledged the slippery nature of "race" in
dance began to appear in the 1990s with the publication of work
by Anne Cooper Albright, Sally Banes, Ramsay Burt, and Susan
Manning.[48] On the whole, these authors resist Emery's approach
by avoiding historical narratives that stratify African American
artists according to the prominence granted them by mainstream
critics. On the other hand, few African American dance artists
have received full biographical exploration. For example, Pearl
Primus figures unequivocally among the "pioneers" of African
American concert dance, but there has been no book-length study
of her life, career, or choreography.[49] But it is also true that the
impulse to document history through the work of an individual
artist runs counter to the collective imperatives of "black dance"
practice. Richard C. Green addresses this paradox in an essay that
gives a biographical account of the first part of Primus's career,
then challenges the current revisionist effort to canonize her. His
arch skepticism of a "new" literature of African American dance
history that reproduces existing paradigms of dance analyses reveals the complicity of dance scholars in constructing "race" as a
research methodology.

PRACTICE—WRITING "BLACK DANCE"

As Emery points out repeatedly, the development of journalistic criticism that can engage the complexities of "black dance" and
acknowledge its political dimensions has been slow to emerge.
The few African American critics sensitive to this task and published frequently in both the black press and national dance publi-

cations have included Zita Allen, Brenda Dixon Gottschild, Doris Green, Bernadine Jennings, Carole Johnson, Julinda Lewis, William Moore, C. S'thembile West, and Arthur T. Wilson.[50] Now, with arts criticism and column space in national decline, the additional task of chronicling performance while illuminating its cultural underpinnings poses a challenge few dance writers are seemingly prepared to meet.[51] In 1980, critic Zita Allen described the severity of this cultural divide in which "white critics seem so totally unfamiliar with Afro-American cultural heritage and history and ignorant of the processes of their interaction with, and influence on, their own" that they were "ill-equipped to either identify those roots or determine when they are being demeaned and denied or drawn from for inspiration."[52] Two decades later, this cultural divide persists.

Beyond education in African American cultural processes, alternative methods of documentation may also be useful in bridging this divide. In this volume, Marcia E. Heard and Mansa K. Mussa offer a photo essay that chronicles the history of African-dance practice in New York City. Their essay confirms the continuous and vital presence of traditional African dance idioms, practiced today by a host of American dancers. As Heard notes, African dance forms currently rank among the most popular idioms offered in college dance departments, but the artists and companies she documents here remain unknown to the public at large.

The close correlation between African-derived music and dance has enormous research implications for the study of African American musical idioms. Sally Banes and John F. Szwed suggest that dance instruction songs, buoyed by technologies of mass distribution, have served crucial functions in the formation of a syncretic American dance culture rooted in African-diaspora performance practice.[53] Their study of these tangible documents that lie well outside the traditional domain of African American source materials is indicative of the widening research strategies employed by dance historians.

Although videotape and film allow viewers to see the silhouettes achieved by dancers in the past, they are unable to contain the expressive essence of performance. Still, films provide glimpses of dance practice and individual performances long gone. Archivist Ernest Smith contributed a "Selected List of Films and Kinescopes" to the first two editions of the Stearnses' *Jazz Dance*. That detailed listing included important sources, from Hollywood footage of the late-nineteenth century through 1966.[54] Two other key documentaries of African American dance styles are Mura Dehn's six-hour opus *The Spirit Moves: Jazz Dance from the Turn of the Century 'till 1950* and *Dance Black America*.[55]

Unlike literature, painting, or music, whose texts are not limited to the moment of performance, dance studies must rely heavily on the memories of creators and practitioners to re-create the dance. Interviews and oral histories shed important light on the creative impulse and can prove more important to the subject than research gathered from secondary sources such as performance reviews. For example, African American dancers and choreographers were particularly forthcoming about their work at the crucial juncture preceding the emergence of "black dance," as is clear from choreographer Donald McKayle's 1966 essay "The Negro Dances in Our Time," the spring 1967 *Dance Scope* devoted to "Negro Dance," and the 1968 *Dance Magazine* feature, "Three Leading Negro Artists and How They Feel about Dance in the Community: Eleo Pomare, Pearl Primus and Arthur Mitchell."[56] Read in chronological order, these pieces outline a shift in attitude: from the multiracial, integrationist model of African American presence in American dance favored by postwar artists like McKayle, to the transitional moment that identified white aesthetic domination of concert dance practice (represented in the *Dance Scope* collection by Joan and Tom Hartshorne's "Jolly Black Minstrels Need Not Apply: A Report from Karamu"), to the need for a "black dance" mode that satisfied African American audiences, a position espoused by Pomare, Primus, and Mitchell.

In addition to statements by the artists themselves, the ephemera generated by conferences, performances, and festivals can be useful in recapturing and contextualizing the past. Besides articles that appeared occasionally in mainstream dance publica-

Booty Control

Thomas F. DeFrantz

Two years ago choreographer Jawole Willa Jo Zollar stood in front of a crowded panel titled "How Black Dance Is Perceived" at the 8th Annual Conference of the International Association of Blacks in Dance. She wanted to speak to the power of the butt. "Most young women I've talked to," she said, "have been through some very strong, traumatic, sexual abuse. I think there comes a way that you want to reclaim your sensual being through the dance. In Nigeria, shaking the butt is raised to a powerful level of artistry. We have to work with that energy here, and raise it to a higher level so that we can begin a healing cultural momentum."

Later that year Zollar premiered two versions of a dance that explored this theme: for Philadanco, she made *The Walkin', Talkin', Signifying Blues Hips, Lowdown, Throwdown;* for her own company, the New York–based Urban Bush Women, she premiered *Batty Moves.* (In a program note, the choreographer reminds us that "batty" refers to the buttocks in Jamaica. It is also a derogatory term for gay men, but Zollar didn't share this information with her audiences.) Each version cast Zollar's gauntlet onto the stage, exploring in dance terms the momentum of the booty as satire, da butt as a treatise for gender education, da backside as initiator of movement, as a source of heat, as fun, as a focal point of conversation and desire, and as a celebration; in other words, *the derriere* as a cultural aesthetic.

Three simultaneous solos open the Bush Women's version of the dance like a careful conversation a woman is having with herself. "Now where did I put my left cheek? Oh here it is, connected to my thigh and belly." The women allow their cheeks to slope toward the corners of the space; to support precarious balances on one leg; to bat against the air in syncopated skirmish with a sudden percussion burst. Each woman works it out in her own good time, sometimes circling her torso and breasts slowly, magnificently—as if to finally discover her anatomy in motion. Sometimes they drop to the floor and get nasty with "the butt-erfly"—a dirty dance done at parties when the good girls have all gone to bed. A song breaks in— "Big Mama Coming Down"—a signifying rhyme that promises much body, much attitude, and no regrets. These sisters will have their bodies, all of their bodies, and it will please them.

"Booty Control," an attempt at dance criticism that acknowledges African American cultural underpinnings in the choreography of Jawolle Willa Jo Zollar, read at "New Critical Voices," sponsored by the Dance Collection, New York Public Library for the Performing Arts, February 1997

In a second section, four women stir so slowly that you can feel the heat pulsing down from the hot Caribbean sun. They cross the stage in a hurry for no one, brimming with contempt for any notion quicker than a nod. Sometimes the quartet falls into step, moving through a brief unison passage phrased with the cleansing fullness of a complete exhalation. Mostly, they take their cp time—that's "colored people" time—working a turn with one leg held in attitude position to demonstrate how the gluteus maximus runs even that show.

Other sections feel like extended snapping contests. "Your butt's so big that when you bent over the roaches thought it was an eclipse" the seven women seem to say to us, dancing in a line stretched across the stage, backfields prophetically in motion before our gaze. Responding to a leader's calls, the women break the beat, shout, leap and play, shifting rhythmic modes in familiar blocks of eight-counts each. It's all big fun, like a sorority initiation where the women share party dances and test out very necessary steps such as the "four corners," "chillin'," and the eponymous "attitude walk." They call each other out as they move, and their banter takes our attention away from their bodies; it helps normalize the presence of the backside, 24-7. By the time the women answer a call to "go for what you know"—we begin to see how the bottom is shaping specific theatrical dance movement, how it informs pirouettes and battlements as much as shimmies, leaps, and rolls across the floor.

Last month I witnessed the dance as performed by Philadanco and the Urban Bush Women within a single week, and the differences were instructive. Where the Bush Women were hard and precise in the line dances, the 'Danco dancers asserted their individuality, filling the actions with the loopy logic of giddy adolescent play. Where the Bush Women fed controlled energy into the breakout sections, imbuing motion with careful fury, the 'Danco women treated the pure dance sections as fun release, as an animated conversation. The women of Philadanco, I thought, had a better time with the dance.

This onstage moment to exhale is, I think, part of what Zollar meant when she prescribed a rump-shaking cure. She means to heal the dancers and the dance by reminding us how our bodies are profound not just in the metaphors they inspire, but in the memories they contain. The end of Philadanco's *Walkin' Talkin' Blues* says it best: the soloist who began the dance works out in the center of the stage as we hear recorded singing. She moves her bottom as she did before; but now we see the motion more clearly. We see context for these movements, provided by her sisters who encicle her, witnessing her successes, teasing her missteps, cajoling her to strength. We understand these to be dances of presence and desire; movements that celebrate the power of the individual and challenge the realm of the social. They are movements of the bottom that inspire controversy and healing at the top.

Desiree Piña of Philadanco in Jawolle Willa Jo Zollar's *The Walkin', Talkin', Signifying Blues Hips, Lowdown, Throwdown* (Reproduced with permission of the Philadelphia Dance Company)

tions, small books originally produced to accompany festival programming may also be useful. Of these, *The Black Tradition in American Modern Dance* (1988), *Black Choreographers Moving: A National Dialogue* (1991), and *African American Genius in Modern Dance* (1993) meld interview with critical analyses of concert work and their underlying conceptual methodologies.[57] In this volume Veta Goler's essay takes this approach. Goler uses the idea of a "blues aesthetic" as a prism through which to explore the work of choreographer Dianne McIntyre.

WHERE WE DANCED

Clearly, a diverse body of scholarship reflecting the diverse body of African American artistry has emerged in the last decades of the twentieth century. This volume hopes to complicate the scholarly examination of African American dance: document that a vibrant literature is in the process of formation, while advancing the basic idea that dance, like its research, is something that black people *do*. As we recover and interpret details of these processes across historical eras and geographies, we pay homage to an ancestral legacy of direct participation in the arts, to the life-affirming choreographies that have sustained and nurtured African American corporeality.

For dancers and choreographers the most fruitful sites of discussion have been dance festivals. In a tradition begun even before the nineteenth-century "Congo Square" gatherings of New Orleans, African Americans convened frequently to celebrate and share movements, compete in dance challenges, and consecrate a common artistic heritage of dance.[58] In concert dance Edna Guy and Hemsley Winfield began a tradition of shared programming by African-diaspora artists when they organized the "First Negro Dance Recital in America" in April 1931; Guy extended this gesture in 1937 as organizer of the "Negro Dance Evening" with Alison Burroughs at the Ninety-second Street YM-YWHA.[59] Later important conventions of African-descent artists, each of which merit scholarly exposition, include the 1973 Congress on Black Dance at Indiana University, organized by the Modern Organization for Dance Evolvement and the Association of Black Choreographers; DanceAfrica, the annual festival of companies based in traditional and neo-African idioms founded by Chuck Davis in 1977; Dance Black America, presented by the Brooklyn Academy of Music in 1983; Black Choreographers Moving toward the Twenty-first Century, conceived and organized by Halifu Osumare in 1989; and the Sixth Biennale de la Danse, "Mama Africa," which took place in Lyon, France, in 1994.

Currently, the largest gathering of African Americans involved in professional dance occurs at the annual conference of the International Association of Blacks in Dance (IABD). Spearheaded by Joan Myers Brown, artistic director of the Philadelphia Dance Company (Philadanco), the IABD was founded as a clearinghouse organization where artistic directors of regional companies presenting modern dance and ballet in the African American grain could network. IABD conferences began in 1988 to showcase Philadanco and the companies of founding artistic directors Anne Williams (Dallas Black Dance Theatre), the late Jeraldyne Blunden (Dayton Contemporary Dance Company), Cleo Parker Robinson (Denver's Cleo Parker Robinson Dance Ensemble), and Lula Washington (Los Angeles Contemporary Dance Theatre). For these companies and their close affiliates the IABD fulfilled the promise of resource-sharing proposed at the First National Congress on Blacks in Dance held at Indiana University in 1973.[60]

More than this, IABD events function like family reunions. The conferences offer dance classes, scholarly panels, skill-building workshops for company directors, an annual awards dinner honoring individual contributions to the field, and a range of performance showcases.[61] Internationally recognized companies share the stage with local aspirants, and young dancers are introduced to elders in the dance community.[62] The idioms represented in performance have ranged from the African-inflected pointework of Atlanta's Ballethnic to African-inspired work performed by a host of companies, including Chicago's Muntu Dance Theater, as well as jazz dance soloists, modern dance groups, and experimental ensembles forging links between African and modern dance techniques. At these events the complex history of African American dance comes into contemporary focus, dramatizing issues of "black dance," cultural retention, personal style, dance technique, and spirituality. Like the chapters in this volume, the artists, critics, and scholars who attend IABD events attest to the fact of black people dancing many drums while drawing from the abundant wellspring of African diaspora culture.

TALKING DRUMS! *The Journal of Black Dance*

presents

The Pearl Primus Memorial Series - 1

"I HAVE DANCED ACROSS MOUNTAINS AND DESERTS, ANCIENT RIVERS
AND OCEANS AND SLIPPED THROUGH THE BOUNDARIES OF TIME AND SPACE."
- PEARL PRIMUS -
1920 - 1994

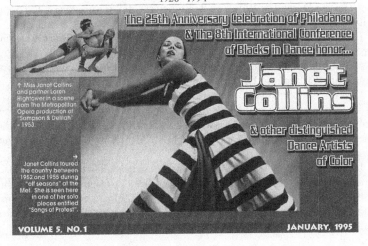

↑ Miss Janet Collins and partner Loren Hightower in a scene from The Metropolitan Opera production of "Sampson & Delilah" - 1953.

→ Janet Collins toured the country between 1952 and 1955 during "off seasons" at the Met. She is seen here in one of her solo pieces entitled "Songs of Protest".

The 25th Anniversary Celebration of Philadanco & The 8th International Conference of Blacks in Dance honor...

Janet Collins & other distinguished Dance Artists of Color

VOLUME 5, NO. 1   JANUARY, 1995

Cover, *Talking Drums! The Journal of Black Dance* 5, no. 1 (January 1995)

NOTES

I extend special thanks to Susan Manning, Carol Martin, and especially Lynn Garafola who commented on previous versions of this chapter.

1. The anthology *"Race," Writing, and Difference,* ed. Henry Louis Gates Jr. (Chicago: University of Chicago Press, 1986) includes several essays that demonstrate how "race" is a literary and political construction.

2. Thomas F. DeFrantz, "To Make Black Bodies Strange: Social Critique in Concert Dance of the Black Arts Movement," in *A Sourcebook on African American Performance: Plays, People, Movements,* ed. Annemarie Bean (New York: Routledge, 1999), 83–93.

3. Critic Walter Terry, who wrote at regular intervals about "Negro Dance" in his *New York Herald Tribune* column, titled a section of his collected essays published in 1971, "The Black Dance." Walter Terry, *The Dance in America,* rev. ed. (New York: Harper and Row, 1971), 156–64.

4. Marcia B. Siegel, "Black Dance: A New Separatism," in *At the Vanishing Point* (New York: Saturday Review Press, 1972), 137.

5. Richard J. Powell, *Black Art and Culture in the Twentieth Century* (London: Thames and Hudson Ltd., 1997), 121.

6. I thank Vladimir Stefanovic, footage manager for WGBH, for his help in discovering information about this series.

7. Certain movements in this video sequence seem to be inspired by Donald McKayle's 1959 work *Rainbow 'round My Shoulder,* a concert dance that details oppressive life on a Southern chain gang.

8. Alvin Ailey American Dance Theater program notes. The stage version of the work premiered at the Edinburgh Festival, 26 August 1968.

9. See Jennifer Dunning, "The Life and Times of an American Classic," *New York Times,* 3 December 1995, sec. 2, 1 for an account of the genesis and popularity of *Revelations.*

10. Anna Kisselgoff, "Ailey: Dancing the Dream," *New York Times,* 4 December 1988, 1.

11. Rev. Martin Luther King Jr. speech, 15 June 1963, at civil rights demonstration, Washington, D.C.

12. For example, in 1967 Ailey was arrested and held overnight in New York on suspicion of having murdered four policemen in Cincinnati. The police were looking for a black male with a mustache and beard; Ailey, like a million other black men, fit the description. See Ellen Cohn, "Alvin Ailey, Arsonist," *New York Times,* 29 April 1973, 33.

13. The dozens of choreographers and musicians affiliated with the black dance movement included Nanette Bearden, Chuck Davis, Syvilla Fort, Arthur Hall, Bob Johnson, Carole Johnson, Louis Johnson, Elma Lewis, Mike Malone, Joan Miller, Clyde Morgan, Walter Nicks, Eleo Pomare, Ronald Pratt, Rod Rodgers, Raymond Sawyer, and hosts of African dance companies across the country.

14. Carole Johnson led the published effort to define "black dance" in the short-lived journal *The Feet.* Carole Johnson, "What Is Black Dance?" *The Feet*

(July 1971): 2. Also, see DeFrantz, "To Make Black Bodies Strange: Social Critique in Concert Dance of the Black Arts Movement."

15. Of course, many other works and performances enlivened the era. These works number among those deemed successful by contemporary critics.

16. Marshall Stearns and Jean Stearns, *Jazz Dance: The Story of American Vernacular Dance* (New York: Schirmer Books, 1979; 2d ed., New York: Da Capo Press, 1994).

17. Lynne Fauley Emery, *Black Dance in the United States from 1619 to 1970* (Palo Alto, Calif.: National Press Books, 1972; 2d ed., Pennington, N.J.: Princeton Book Company, 1988).

18. Emery, *Black Dance in the United States,* ix.

19. A second edition, published in 1988 by Princeton Book Company, featured an ill-advised additional chapter, "Popular Dance in the Twentieth Century," by Brenda Dixon-Stowell. Burdened by an excess of source material and theoretical approaches, the addition underscored the impossibility of chronicling centuries of dance practice in a single volume.

20. The Stearnses define their use of vernacular to be "in the sense of native and homegrown" (*Jazz Dance* [1994], xvi); Jacqui Malone specifies her intention that the term "vernacular" "refers to dance performed to the rhythms of African American music: dance that makes those rhythms visible" (*Steppin' on the Blues: The Visible Rhythms of African American Dance* [Urbana: University of Illinois Press, 1996], 2).

21. Stearns and Stearns, *Jazz Dance* (1994), 361.

22. Robert F. Thompson, "Dance and Culture, an Aesthetic of the Cool," *African Forum* 2 (fall 1966): 88.

23. After defining common physical stances and approaches to movement in African dance forms she studied, Cayou extends Thompson's list to include "functionalism—becoming what you dance—the art of real life." Dolores Kirton Cayou, *Modern Jazz Dance* (Palo Alto, Calif.: Mayfield Publishing Company, 1971), 8.

24. See DeFrantz, "To Make Black Bodies Strange: Social Critique in Concert Dance of the Black Arts Movement."

25. The articulation of "Africanisms" offers a conceptual framework for the discussion of performative commonalities between West African cultures and Africans in diaspora. See *Africanisms in American Culture,* ed. Joseph Holloway (Bloomington: Indiana University Press, 1991) for essays that describe artistic traditions shared by Africans and Africans in diaspora; and Brenda Dixon Gottschild, *Digging the Africanist Presence in American Performance: Dance and Other Contexts* (Westport, Conn.: Greenwood Press, 1996) for a discussion of how Africanist art-making processes have been adopted by Europeans, Asians, and white Americans.

26. Prominent among cultural critics working with articulations of African diaspora culture are Paul Gilroy (*Small Acts: Thoughts on the Politics of Black Cultures* [London: Serpent's Tail, 1993]); Stuart Hall (*Stuart Hall: Critical Dialogues in Cultural Studies,* ed. David Morley and Kuan-Hsing Chen [London: Routledge, 1996]); and Kobena Mercer (*Welcome to the Jungle: New Positions in Black Cultural Studies* [New York: Routledge, 1994]).

27. See Robert Farris Thompson, *Flash of the Spirit: African and Afro-American Art and Philosophy* (New York: First Vintage Books Edition, 1983) for a further explication of Africanist aesthetic commonalities in diaspora.

28. The approach allows us to see affinities in, for example, music video dance performed by diverse groups of dancers, as well as in concert dances performed on a proscenium stage. For example, white choreographers, including Twyla Tharp and George Balanchine, have been clearly and profoundly influenced by the Africanisms outlined above. See Sally Banes, "Balanchine and Black Dance," in *Choreography and Dance* 3, part 3 (Reading, England: Harwood Academic Publishers, 1993), 59–77; and Dixon Gottschild, " 'Stripping the Emperor': George Balanchine and the Americanization of Ballet" in *Digging the Africanist Presence in American Performance: Dance and Other Contexts* (Westport, Conn.: Greenwood Press, 1996).

29. Thorpe's poor offering features ridiculous statements throughout, such as this from the introduction: "Whereas the dances of the white races are so often concerned with conveying grace, dignity, pride or elegance. . . . The beauty of black dance lies in its total lack of inhibition." Edward Thorpe, *Black Dance* (Woodstock, N.Y.: The Overlook Press, 1990), 13. Adamczyk's helpful, but extremely hard-to-find reference book finally succumbs to the effort to be all-inclusive. Alice J. Adamczyk, *Black Dance: An Annotated Bibliography* (New York: Garland Press, 1989). Other volumes in this vein include the young adult book by James Haskins, *Black Dance in America: A History through Its People* (New York: Thomas Y. Cowell Junior Books, 1990) that recounts events in the lives of certain artists.

30. Richard A. Long, *The Black Tradition in American Dance* (New York: Rizzoli International Publications, 1989).

31. See Paul Gilroy, *The Black Atlantic: Modernity and Double Consciousness* (Cambridge, Mass.: Harvard University Press, 1993) for an explication of contemporary usage of "black" by cultural theorists.

32. Frantz Fanon, writing of Negro consciousness, explains: "black consciousness is immanent in its own eyes. I am not a potentiality of something, I am wholly what I am. I do not have to look for the universal. . . . My Negro consciousness does not hold itself out as a lack. It *is*." *Black Skin, White Masks* (New York: Grove Press, 1967), 135 (original emphasis).

33. John O. Perpener III, "African American Dance and Sociological Positivism during the 1930s," *Studies in Dance History* 5, no. 1 (spring 1994): 23–30; and Malone, *Steppin' on the Blues*. As stated in the preface, Perpener organized the 1996 CORD conference, "African American Dance: Researching a Complex History," which provided the impetus for this volume.

34. Arthur Todd, "The Negro Folk Dance in America," *Dance Magazine* (January 1950): 14–15, 41; Arthur Todd, "Negro American Theatre Dance," *Dance Magazine* (November 1950): 20–21, 33–34; Arthur Todd, "American Negro Dance: A National Treasure," *Ballet Annual* 16 (May 1961): 92–103; Joe Nash, "Dancing Many Drums," *National Scene Magazine Supplement* 4, no. 8 (September–October 1976): 2–3, 8–11.

35. Lois Balcom, "What Chance Has the Negro Dancer?" *Dance Observer* (November 1944): 110–11; Lois Balcom, "The Negro Dances Himself," *Dance*

Observer (December 1944): 122–24. A steady stream of position pieces outlining the African American presence in classical ballet stretch from the 1930s to the late 1990s, including Arnold Lionel Haskell, "Further Studies in Ballet: Negro Dancing," *Dancing Times* (London) (January 1930): 455–57; "Negroes in Ballet," no author, *Dance and Dancers* (October 1957): 9; Harriet Jackson, "American Dancer, Negro," *Dance Magazine* (September 1966): 35–42; Don McDonagh, "Negroes in Ballet," *New Republic* 159 (November 1968): 41–44; Clive Barnes, "Barnes on . . . the Position of the Black Classic Dancer in American Ballet," *Ballet News* 3, no. 9 (March 1982): 46; DeFrantz, "The Black Body in Question" *Village Voice*, 23 April 1996, 29–32.

36. Linda Small, "Black Dancer/Black Traveler," *Dance Magazine* (October 1979): 78–81; Julinda Lewis Williams, "Black Dance: A Diverse Unity," *Dance Scope* 14, no. 2 (1980): 54–63; Zita Allen, "The Great American 'Black Dance' Mystery," *Freedomways* 20, no. 4 (1980): 283–91.

37. John O. Perpener III's excellent Ph.D. dissertation, that details the lives and careers of several key figures in concert dance history, including Hemsley Winfield, Edna Guy, Raymond Sawyer, Ollie Burgoyne, Charles Williams, and Asadata Dafora, belies this trend by grouping a series of sustained biographical essays around a theme of historical era. John O. Perpener III, "The Seminal Years of Black Concert Dance" (Ph.D. dissertation, New York University, 1992).

38. Dixon Gottschild's article "Between Two Eras: 'Norton and Margot' in the Afro-American Entertainment World" originally appeared in *Dance Research Journal* 15, no. 2 (spring 1983): 11–20, as written by Brenda Dixon-Stowell.

39. Valis Hill's article originally appeared in *Dance Research Journal* 26, no. 2 (fall 1994): 1–10.

40. See Naima Prevots, *Dance for Export: Cultural Diplomacy and the Cold War* (Hanover: Wesleyan University Press, 1998) for further details of the Eisenhower administration and its sponsorship of dance during this era.

41. For an extended treatment of African Americans in ballet, see Thomas DeFrantz, "Ballet," in *Encyclopedia of African American Culture and History* (New York: Macmillan Library Reference, 1995). See also Thomas DeFrantz, "Ballet in Black: Louis Johnson and African American Humor," in *New Writings in Dance,* ed. Anne Flynn and Lisa Doolittle (Banff, Alberta, Canada: Banff Centre Press, 2001), 178–95.

42. Zita Allen, "Blacks in Ballet," *Dance Magazine* (July 1976): 65–70.

43. Kariamu Welsh Asante, "Commonalities in African Dance: An Aesthetic Foundation," in *African Culture: The Rhythms of Unity,* ed. Molefi Kete Asante and Kariamu Welsh Asante (Philadelphia: Greenwood Press, 1985; reprint ed. Trenton, N.J.: Africa World Press, 1990), 71–82; Katrina Hazzard-Gordon, *Jookin': The Rise of Social Dance Formations in African American Culture* (Philadelphia: Temple University Press, 1990); Jacqui Malone, *Steppin' on the Blues;* Dixon Gottschild, *Digging the Africanist Presence.*

44. Stuckey's essay originally appeared in *Choreographing History,* ed. Susan Foster (Bloomington: Indiana University Press, 1995), 54–66.

45. Philosopher Gerald Myers, cultural historian C. Eric Lincoln, and dance archivist Joe Nash participated in this series of symposia.

46. See especially Marian Hannah Winter, "Juba and American Minstrelsy"

(1947), reprint in *Inside the Minstrel Mask,* ed. Annemarie Bean, James V. Hatch, Brooks McNamara (Hanover: Wesleyan University Press, 1996); and David Krasner, *Resistance, Parody, and Double Consciousness in African American Theatre, 1895–1910* (New York: St. Martin's Press, 1997) for overviews of this area.

47. Charles Dickens offers an early example of this tendency in his often-quoted description of Master Juba. Charles Dickens, *American Notes* [1842], introduction by Christopher Lasch (Glouster, Mass.: Peter Smith, 1968), 110–12.

48. Ann Cooper Albright, *Choreographing Difference: The Body and Identity in Contemporary Dance* (Hanover: Wesleyan University Press, 1997); Sally Banes, "Balanchine and Black Dance," in *Choreography and Dance* 3, part 3 (Reading, England: Harwood Academic Publishers, 1993), 59–77; Ramsay Burt, *Alien Bodies: Representations of Modernity, "Race," and Nation in Early Modern Dance* (New York: Routledge, 1998); Susan Manning, "Black Voices, White Bodies: The Performance of Race and Gender in How Long Brethren," *American Quarterly* 50, no. 1 (March 1998): 24–46.

49. Of African American concert dance artists, only Alvin Ailey, Katherine Dunham, Judith Jamison, and Bill T. Jones have received sustained biographical inquiry. To my knowledge, Beverly Anne Hillsman Barber's unpublished Ph.D. dissertation is the sole extant monograph devoted to Primus. Beverly Anne Hillsman Barber, "Pearl Primus, in Search of Her Roots: 1943–1970" (Ph.D. dissertation, Florida State University, 1984).

50. This listing, of course, is in no way exhaustive.

51. See fig. on pp. 24–25 ("Booty Control") for an attempt at criticism that acknowledges cultural underpinnings of work by Jawole Willa Jo Zollar and the Urban Bush Women.

52. Allen, "The Great American 'Black Dance' Mystery," 287.

53. Banes and Szwed's article originally appeared in *Performance Matters,* no. 27 (winter 1995–96): 59–79.

54. Stearns and Stearns, *Jazz Dance* (1994), 395–419. The listing includes brief annotations.

55. Mura Dehn, *The Spirit Moves,* produced in New York; directed, edited, and narrated by Mura Dehn; camera by Herbert Matter (1950). *Dance Black America,* filmed in performance by Chris Hegedus and D. A. Pennebaker at the Brooklyn Academy of Music (21–24 April 1983); produced by the State University of New York and Pennebaker Associates. Several African American companies and artists have created film records of their work or been the subject of documentaries, including the Alvin Ailey American Dance Theater, the Dance Theatre of Harlem, Ulysses Dove, the Katherine Dunham Dancers and Drummers, Garth Fagan Dance, and Bill T. Jones/Arnie Zane Company. The American Dance Festival has produced *Free to Dance,* a three-part documentary of African Americans in concert dance, scheduled for completion in 2001. The films are available commercially and may be viewed at the Dance Collection, the New York Public Library of the Performing Arts.

56. Donald McKayle, "The Negro Dances in Our Time," in *The Dance Has Many Faces,* ed. Walter Sorell, 2d ed. (New York: Columbia University Press, 1966), 187–92; Ric Estrada, "3 Leading Negro Artists and How They Feel

about Dance in the Community: Eleo Pomare, Pearl Primus and Arthur Mitchell," *Dance Magazine* (November 1968): 45. The *Dance Scope* publication also features interviews with and articles from Rod Rodgers, Gus Solomons Jr., Clyde Morgan, William Moore, and Ellis Haizlip (*Dance Scope* [spring 1967]).

57. Gerald E. Myers, ed., *The Black Tradition in American Modern Dance* (Durham, N.C.: American Dance Festival, 1988); Julinda Lewis-Ferguson, ed., and Halifu Osumare, comp., *Black Choreographers Moving: A National Dialogue* (Berkeley: Expansion Arts Services, 1991); *African American Genius in Modern Dance* (Durham, N.C.: American Dance Festival 1993).

58. For an overview of the historical sites of dance festivals, see Emery, *Black Dance in the United States;* and Roger D. Abrahams, *Singing the Master: The Emergence of African American Culture in the Plantation South* (New York: Penguin Books, 1992).

59. See Perpener, "The Seminal Years of Black Concert Dance."

60. The First National Congress on Blacks in Dance was held 26 June–1 July 1973 at Indiana University, Bloomington, Indiana.

61. For example, at the 1997 conference, held in Dallas, Texas, and hosted by Dallas Black Dance Theatre, master classes were taught by Chuck Davis and Ronald K. Brown; Donald McKayle offered a keynote speech about the role of education in a professional dancer's life; and the artistic directors of founding regional companies honored their tireless associate directors with awards: Darryl B. Sneed of Dallas Black Dance Theatre, Kim Y. Bears of Philadanco, Kevin Ward of Dayton Contemporary Dance Company, Tamika Washington of Lula Washington Dance Theater (formerly Los Angeles Contemporary Dance Theater), and Marceline Freeman of Cleo Parker Robinson Dance Ensemble. Panels included "How Are National Issues of Education, Dance Licensing and Training Impacting the History and Legacy of Black Dance and Dancers?" where moderator Walter Nicks wondered that esteemed black dance teachers without advanced degrees are too often passed over by colleges hiring faculty; "Alternative Careers in Dance," in which former Ailey company dancers Sarita Allen and Christopher Huggins explored possibilities such as criticism, coaching, and producing dance events for dancers making the transition from performing; and "Black Dance, Blacks in Dance, Dance Black: What Does It All Mean?" where choreographer Kevin Jeff reflected on the empowering spiritual connections that artists make to connect people to their communities. Jeff's comment deserves quotation: "Black dance facilitates growth, healing, and the economy of the people—that's what makes it relevant. We talk about what art can do from an aesthetic level, but it's the spiritual level which has made a difference in my life."

62. Closely linked to the formation of the IABD, the periodical *Talking Drums!: The Journal of Black Dance* (published by the Los Angeles–based International Center for Dance Orthopaedics and Dance Therapy) has served as the program for IABD conferences.

Part 1
Theory

1
Christian Conversion and the Challenge of Dance

P. Sterling Stuckey

> No thanks to the slaveholder nor to slavery that the vi-
> vacious captive sometimes dances in his chains; his very
> mind in such circumstances stands before God as an ac-
> cusing angel.
>
> *Frederick Douglass, "Speech on American Slavery," 1850*

Highly prized for the labor extorted from it, the African body
was also the object of exploitation for sexual reasons related to
its labor value. Sexual abuse of Africans began during the Atlantic voyage, the passage of slave ships from Africa to the Americas; so from the start of the slave trade, whites engaged in forced
miscegenation with blacks. A repulsive yet desirable object to
many whites, the black body posed problems of a psychological
nature for them. This was unavoidable for those who associated
blackness with din and lasciviousness and evil as did many white
Americans. In this regard, their observations on slave dance reveal enough of their own anxieties and longings to form a chapter
of the psychic history of white Americans. Reference to their psy-
che points up how fraught with irony the theme of the body and
dance is when the black body is the object of inquiry.

The gun and whip, prominent features of the apparatus of control in rounding up Africans, were used during the Atlantic voyage. At times during this voyage, there was the insistence that
Africans dance to assure whites that they would remain lively
enough to be delivered to the auction block in North America. In
fact, the total being of African men, women, and children was the

"Slaves Compelled to Dance during the Voyage to Keep Them Fit and Healthy and so Fetch a Higher Price," ca. 1830 (Drawing by Ruhiere; reproduced with permission of the Mary Evans Picture Library)

object of enslavement, and it was not uncommon for the branding iron to be used to identify them. But this was not the only brand they wore, for uncounted thousands wore that of the whip. In either case, to dance with such scars on one's body meant that, no matter how true to traditional dance forms a particular African dance was, a new history of dance had begun.

Like the sky above and the beat of anguished hearts, the moves of dancers were no mere social construct; their melancholy rhythms were as elemental as the flow of ocean currents, as real as the agony of those in the fetid holds of the death vessels. All who survived that passage would dance with such memories in mind. It is the greatest irony, therefore, that from the start in America dance by blacks was considered a measure of their frivolity.

The failure of whites to understand African spiritual and artistic values made it easier for slaves to use dance to exploit crevices in the system of slavery. Attempts to wipe out African culture did not succeed largely because the master's ignorance lasted throughout slavery. Slaveholders never understood that a form of spirituality almost indistinguishable from art was central to the cultures from which blacks came.[1] Distinguishing between the two for the African was like distinguishing between the sacred and the secular, and that distinction was not often made. African religion, therefore, could satisfy a whole range of human needs that for Europeans were splintered into secular compartments. This quality of culture helps explain why, for the descendants of Africa in America, the sacred so easily satisfied the deepest "secular" needs, and the two long remained the same when that which was sacred was labeled secular by outsiders. The sacred for slaves, as for Africans, was not demarcated by time: Threads of spirituality—of art itself—were woven into the fabric of everyday life. In fact, dance was the principal means by which slaves, using its symbolism to evoke their spiritual view of the world, extended sacred observance through the week. In an environment hostile to African religion, that denied that the African had a real religion, slaves could rise in dance and, in a flash, give symbolic expression to their religious vision.

Dance was the most difficult of all art forms to erase from the slave's memory, in part because it could be practiced in the silence of aloneness where motor habits could be initiated with enough speed to seem autonomous. In that lightning-fast process, the body very nearly was memory and helped the mind recall the form of dance to come. For in dance, such is the speed with which the mind can work, and the body respond to it, that the time between thought and action all but disappears. In a sense, then, the body is mind, and is capable of inscribing in space the language of the human spirit. When the tempo slows, of course, the body configures what the mind more easily recalls.

Yet at times, dance can begin so spontaneously that the thought somehow seems to follow the deed, and self-doubt, especially under those circumstances, can be made to yield ground. When that occurs, the mind is taken for a ride even before it is aware of wings beneath it. That reality, as much as any other, raises questions about the alleged mind–body dichotomy. In any case, threats and ridicule, even when backed by brute force, were not always a match for dance, which at times swept along participants even happily.

In a culture in which dance is highly valued, its basic ingredients are not likely to be forgotten, at least as long as one maintains lucidity. In this regard, age is vastly more important when one is younger than later, for the dancer who begins early remains a dancer, and people generally dance more readily than they sing. When that culture is also a highly musical one, then dance and music propel each other, and seldom is there one without the other, or joy without both in some form. Such values have their own momentum and can travel across borders with the victims of the most horrid forms of oppression.

In discussions of the movement of theory across borders, not enough attention is given to art. A certain elitism prevails, with the masses the object at which theory, fashioned by intellectuals, is sometimes targeted. In other words, the values of the masses are not founding stones of the house of theory, as in the work of an intellectual like Paul Robeson, who was interested in the movement of theory, especially as affected by sensibility, across borders.[2] It is therefore essential to distinguish between forms of ideology and the limitations of those forms, between theory based mainly on abstract reflection and theory derived from the concrete experiences and aspirations of humanity.

The Ring Shout entered as an ideology embedded in artistic experience, a form of dance ceremony in which a religious vision of profound significance was projected even as it underwent transformation in the face of the pressing challenge of slavery.[3] The more subtle and disguised the ideology of a greatly outnumbered and enslaved people, the better their chances of realizing crucial cultural and political goals. In this regard, the ideology of Africans in North America could hardly have been more effectively disguised, since dance to most Europeans was empty of sacred content and to Africans sacred like prayer. A radically different aesthetic masked a multitude of cultural differences between whites and blacks.

Since dance is the artistic means by which rhythm takes observable form, rhythm was as often seen as expressed by the slave, its imprint thereby the more indelible. And since the rhythm of sacred dance was, for the African slave, often the rhythm of "secular" dance, slave dance was rich enough in emotional content and complexity to have substantial cognitive value. Small wonder that Robeson believed that rhythm can lead to its own form of consciousness. But it was hardly necessary for Africans to think of dance during the middle passage to bring its forms of expression with them. The forms most valued were best remembered and most tenaciously clung to because they also enjoyed pride of place in the subconscious.[4]

If dance in all its complexity could survive the psychic pain of the middle passage, new work places and arrangements in North America would prove no real barrier to the perpetuation of rhythm-consciousness. Though rooted in the African village, it was a consciousness consonant with the Age of Technology, in fact, that gave it, with mounting complexity of sound, its artistic beat. Yet dialectically, sacred rhythm was the strongest conceivable force, in African terms, against the mechanical movements of an emergent capitalist world. Even before slaves and their descendants heard the machines, the forced labor extracted from them that made slavery a profitable part of the economy led them, after work, to draw on dance as a main form of recreation and relief.

There is no indication that any other group of workers in modern history brought such reliance on dance, to say nothing of the purposes to which they put it, to their daily lives. Relying on dance as much as they did assured reliance on music, and the rhythms of both reached the cities in the late nineteenth century to provide the complex underpinnings of jazz. Moreover, African-style dance was done to the blues, often to the playing of musical instruments that were remarkably similar to those in Africa. In that development, dance was a means by which the past itself paid homage to a new creative form.[5]

But a deeply perplexing problem had to be solved before the blues—and jazz—could be created. There was the initial absence of a common spiritual vision to guide Africans in their new lives as slaves. African dance, in their desperate situation, was their greatest spiritual and political resource, enabling them to recall the traditional African community and to include all Africans in their conception of being African in America. They discovered, despite the presence of different ethnic groups—Ibos, Akans, Bakongo, and Ashantees, among them—that they shared an ancestral dance that was common to them in Africa. Just as they crossed actual boundaries in being brought to America, enough were able to make an imaginative retreat to the ancestral home to discover, in the Ring Shout, the ground of cultural oneness. This dance was known to most slaves, whose people had mainly come from sections of Africa in which, as the Circle Dance, it was associated with ancestral ceremonies. Since respect for elders, who were nearest to being ancestors, was native to black Africans, such ancestral concern was a precondition for their formation into a single people, a process in which Africans irrespective of age and gender participated.[6]

They needed, in other words, to fashion a form of dance in slavery that was consonant with the religious values of the majority of Africans, an especially daunting problem. Yet to begin with, circular dance was to suggest a certain wholeness that encouraged the spirit of community. With the rhythms directed at ancestral concerns, a powerful means of reinforcement was introduced as the dancers moved counterclockwise in the ring. In that way, symbol and substance were fused and essential oneness of spiritual outlook achieved. The complexity of the process, its grounding in profound human need, is demonstrated by the degree to which, in the Shout, requirements of the sacred were fulfilled in the most profane of settings, that of slavery.

It is difficult to conceive of more ironic circumstances than when the African danced the Shout and slaveholders, with overwhelming power at their command, looked on with contempt and loathing. Ironic above all because, through the Shout at its highest point of resonance, the ancestors and the gods exerted supreme power over the dancer. At such moments, dance was at war with the values of the master class. But the slave master could hardly have sensed such depth of protest. In any event, when slaves danced the Shout and sang spirituals, they were chastised by whites for doing so. Their determination to dance, despite possible punishment, in some measure restored the body's place in spiritual terms, and in that sense was an act of physical renewal as well.

Where there was exposure to Christianity, Christian elements in time became integral to the ceremony as it revolved in a counterclockwise direction, with slaves singing spirituals to rhythmic clapping of hands and stamping of feet. Moreover, as Thomas Wentworth Higginson and others have reported, slaves improvised while shouting and sometimes shouted alone, as some hummed or sang when alone.[7] A description of the more prevalent group shout, witnessed late in slavery, suggests something of its power, and why it was a source of concern to Christians.

> The true "Shout" lakes place on Sundays or on "Praise"-nights through the week, and either in the praise-house or some cabin in which a regular religious meeting has been held. Very likely more than half the plantation is gathered together. Let it be the evening and a light-wood fire burns before the door to the house and on the hearth. The benches are pushed back to the wall when the formal meeting is over, and old and young, men and women, sprucely-dressed young men, grotesquely half-clad field-hands—the women generally with gay handkerchief twisted about their heads and with short skirts—boys with tattered shirts and men's trousers, young girls barefooted, all stand up in the middle of the floor, and when the "sperichil" is struck up, begin first walking and by-and-by shuffling, one after the other, in a ring. The foot is hardly taken from the floor, and the progression is mainly due to a jerking, hitching motion, which agitates the entire shouter, and soon brings out streams of perspiration. Sometimes they dance silently, sometimes as they shuffle they sing the chorus of the spiritual and sometimes the song itself is also sung by the dancers. . . . Song and dance are alike extremely energetic, and often, when the shout lasts into the middle of the night, the monotonous thud, thud of the feet prevents sleep within a half mile of the praise house.[8]

Harold Courlander has written in *Negro Folk Music, U.S.A.* that an ecstatic breaking point often occurs when the dancer is seized

"Ring-Shout in the Cabin" (Photograph by Maxfield Parrish Jr.; reproduced with permission of Joanna Maxfield Parrish Gordon)

by possession, and that state was no doubt a main factor in some Christians opposing the Ring Shout, especially in the context of a scene such as the one just described. But in that case slaveholders, having fled before the advance of Union troops, were not present to oppose the dance. Efforts at opposition, however, surely occurred, and that opposition carried with it the assumption of African mental, cultural, and physical inferiority. Since racism allowed such assumptions among those who knew that Africans entered America already knowing how to cultivate crops such as rice, cotton, and tobacco, major sources of income for the country, it should not surprise us that slaveholders had no respect for the dance most revered by slaves.[9]

As they stood by, or hid in the shadows, and watched slave dance, all manner of guilt and longing in some whites caused them to associate the Shout with sex. Such a misconception was applied to slave dance generally and to black life as a whole as whites projected their desires onto blacks. And it is possible that the recoil of whites from sacred dance stemmed from having considered it, in some measure, profane, especially when pelvic movement was involved. Such an attitude was opposed to that of the African, who had little conception of sexual activity, in and of itself, as dirty. This needs to be taken into account to understand the African conception of art as it relates to the sacred, a subject about which no one has written more perceptively than Roland Hayes. "To native Africans," he writes, "sexual intercourse is creative and holy, allusions to it in their songs are respectful, not obscene." In a passage that takes in dance, he adds that the "bodily movement which accompanies the performance of the songs of love is not vulgar to African eyes. On the contrary, it is an artistic symbol of exalted experience."[10]

The bodily movement of the Ring Shout was considered anything but exalted by white Christians, who associated it with sexual activity and barbarism at a time when sacred dance was no longer a force in Western religious ceremonies. Yet the Shout had so strong a hold on slaves that slave conversions to Christianity were overwhelmingly in that context. In fact, opposition to the Shout was perhaps the principal means by which slaveholders attempted to break the mold of African culture in America.

Courlander argues that a compromise was struck between master and slave. In *Negro Folk Music, U.S.A.,* he writes that the "Shout is a fusion of two seemingly irreconcilable attitudes toward religious behavior." According to Courlander:

> In most of Africa, dance, like singing and drumming, is an integral part of supplication. . . . In the Euro-Christian tradition, however, dancing in church is generally regarded as a profane act. The Ring Shout in the United States provides a scheme which reconciles both principles. The circular movement, shuffling steps, and stamping conform to African traditions of supplication, while by definition this activity is not recognized as "Dance."[11]

Definition holds, we are told, that by no longer crossing their legs during the Shout, slaves were no longer dancing. But there are problems with Courlander's notion of reconciliation, one of which is that he never raises the question of whether the crossing of legs was ever a part of the Shout. For obvious reasons, this is a crucial consideration. If the crossing of legs was never a part of the Shout, then of what significance was the slave's refusal to cross his or her legs? Except perhaps as a means of perpetuating the illusion of compromise, of what significance was the expulsion of those who violated the alleged decree? Equally troubling is Courlander's failure to tell us when and where slaves first ceased crossing their legs during the Shout. Moreover, he fails even to refer to the logistics involved in the movement of the prohibition from one plantation to another in the rural South. Related to this matter is the degree to which the Shout was revered by slaves and on what occasions and where it was performed. To alter one's performance at a slave funeral or in a cemetery when slaves were alone, unless of one's own volition, would be preposterous in a people as subtle as we know them to have been.

A certain confusion is at the heart of Courlander's argument, for he admits that the Ring Shout "is dance (contrary to the premise of the participants)."[12] Is it being suggested that slaves did not know they were still dancing? If so, it is an argument that cannot be taken seriously. Given Courlander's conviction that some compromise was reached, he would have been more credible had he argued that some slaves tricked the master into believing that they were not dancing while knowing they were. But given the characteristics of the Shout, even had slaves initially crossed their legs when Shouting and later ceased doing so, the performance would conform to African traditions of dance supplication. This leaves the master in a position similar to that of Covey, the overseer, who, beaten by Frederick Douglass, proclaimed victory after being released from the grip of the young slave.[13]

Not only was the Ring Shout not static following its crossing of borders—for one thing, the mood of the dancers changed dramatically in the slave environment—there was no single Shout on which Christians could focus hatred. Now that meant the problem of opposing the Shout was compounded in ways whites could hardly understand. The more powerful yet more subtle

Shout in which the dancer leaps into the air, turning in a counterclockwise direction, merits mention as a means by which *individual* Ring Shouts were similar to, yet different from, the more
standard Ring Shout. Fredrika Bremer provides a fine description of this subtle form of inscribing in space, through dance,
one's religious values. She describes solo performances of groups
of Africans leaping and spinning in the air in New Orleans in the
1850s and calls the effect of the whole an "African Tornado,"[14]
which is richly suggestive since tornadoes, in this hemisphere,
move in a counterclockwise direction. Variants of this type of
Shout were found elsewhere in the South and even in the North
and should be kept in mind when considering Courlander's argument regarding reconciliation.

Slave resistance to efforts to oppose the Shout help one appreciate the resilience and determination of those who entered the ring
to dance. One instance of such resistance in the 1830s involved a
man who would later be eminent among his people, the Reverend
Daniel Payne of the African Methodist Episcopal Church. A fer-
vent opponent of the Shout, Payne observed it on many occasions
without once raising the issue of the crossing of legs, revealing
instead enormous hostility to the ritual as a whole. His hatred
of the Shout, in fact, was such that he even opposed the singing
of spirituals in his church in Baltimore. There was no doubt in
his mind that the Shout was an expression of heathenism as remote from Christianity as could be imagined. Indeed, he opposed
it with such vigor that one Sunday two black women rose from
their seats and, reaching the pulpit, clubbed him and his assistant
pastor. Payne's attempt to end the singing of spirituals and sacred
dance failed, for he fled the church.[15]

In the 1850s, the Shout was practiced in Georgia under the
very noses of slaveholders at massive camp meetings. Fredrika
Bremer reports that at a meeting near Macon one night, 3,000 to
4,000 blacks and whites were present as white and black preachers
addressed the throng, the blacks preaching to blacks, the whites
to whites, as flames rose behind them, illuminating the scene.
For the slaves, the religious service under the night sky was more
formal than those held later in tents in which they were housed.

Entering one, Bremer found a group of black women "Dancing the Holy Dance," or Ring Shout, and states: "This dancing,
however, having been forbidden by the preachers, ceased immediately on our entering the tent. *I saw merely a rocking movement*
of women who held each other by the hand in a circle, singing
the while."[16]

Since Bremer writes that such tents could be seen "all over" the
grounds—they housed perhaps as many as 2,000 slaves—it is rea-
sonable to assume that such holy dancing went unnoticed in most
of the tents. Thus, slaves active in Christian worship remained at
home with African religion on entering the tents for more private worship ceremonies. Often appearances, one can conclude,
concealed the deep complexities and ironies of slave worship experience at such camp meetings.[17]

The presence of the Ring Shout in the North during the antebellum period greatly complicates matters for Courlander's thesis,
for one must ask if Southern slaves somehow got word to free
blacks and slaves that they were not to cross their legs when
Shouting. It is not likely that slave runaways entered the North
to reveal the prohibition when the master was not there to give it
substance. What is more likely is that the Shout developed there
largely on its own with no prohibition about leg crossing. Let
us take the classic case of Philadelphia's Fifth Ward. W. E. B. Du
Bois, in *The Philadelphia Negro*, writes of a church in that ward that
was established in 1837 that, in Du Bois's words, represented "the
older and more demonstrative worship." He then quotes from an
article by the Reverend Charles Daniels that describes another
variant of the Ring Shout, one that involves worshipers leaping
into the air, as in the New Orleans church, but from a rotating
ring. This Shout, with its leaping twist, was vastly more difficult
for white Christians to understand. According to the Reverend
Daniels:

> It took an hour to work up the congregation to a fervor aimed
> at. When this was reached a remarkable scene presented itself. The
> whole congregation pressed forward to an open space before the
> pulpit, and formed a ring. The most excitable of their number
> entered the Ring, and with clapping of hands and contortions led

the devotions. Those forming the ring joined in the clapping of hands with wild and loud singing, frequently springing into the air and shouting loudly. As the devotion proceeded, most of the worshipers took off their coats and vests and hung them on pegs on the wall. This continued for hours, until all were completely exhausted, and some had fainted and been stowed away on benches or the pulpit platform. This was the order of things at the close of sixty years history.[18]

Du Bois adds, probably also recalling his earlier experiences in the backwoods of Tennessee, "The writer scarcely does justice to the weird witchery of those hymns sung thus rudely." And he notes (the year was 1899) that "there are dozens of such little missions in various parts of Philadelphia. They are the survivals of the methods of worship in Africa and the West Indies."[19]

Again with no reference to foot crossing, Daniel Payne describes a so-called bush meeting that occurred in 1878 in Philadelphia, more than a decade following the end of slavery, but during the time the Ring Shout was being done in that city's Fifth Ward:

After the sermon they formed a Ring, and with coats off sung, clapped their hands and stamped their feet in a most ridiculous and heathenish way. I requested the pastor to go and stop their dancing. At his request they stopped their dancing and clapping of hands, but remained singing and rocking their bodies to and fro. This they did for about fifteen minutes. I then went and taking their leader by the arm requested him to desist and to sit down and sing in a rational manner. I told him also that it was a heathenish way to worship and disgraceful to themselves, the race, and the christian name.[20]

As weak as the case is for crossing legs when Shouting, there appears to have been a slight foundation in reality for it. It is likely that there was some discussion of this matter with some slaves acting on the "prohibition," for there are references in some sources to slaves seeming not to dance in a ring in the presence of whites, as in the example from Bremer, which could have been related to the crossing of legs. Moreover, there is the suggestion in one spiritual, in Alan Lomax's view, of strictures against the crossing of legs when Shouting, though walking is referred to in the song:

Sister, better mind how you walk on the cross,
Yo foot might slip and yo soul be lost.

Lomax provides an interesting possible context for understanding why some slaves might have *gone along* with white warnings against leg crossing in the Shout. "Whereas a wide stance was usual in black African dance," he writes, "a narrow stance with foot crossing is typical of clogging or stepping or other forms of West European dancing. The newly converted slaves came to view foot crossing as a lure of Satan."[21]

That the crossing of legs thesis could have been accepted for so long is a measure, above all, of the failure to appreciate the power and complexity of African culture in slavery. Had the work of Marshall Stearns received the attention it has long deserved, generations of scholars could have avoided wasting time by believing the indefensible. "The Protestant religion discourages dancing and the playing of instruments," asserts Stearns. For those with that view, "dancing is defined as crossing the feet, and in this religious ceremony of West Africa [the Ring Shout] the dancers never cross feet anyway."[22]

With the Ring Shout as pivot, black dance radiated outward in America to become a formidable presence. It was a dance that seemed to generate change, possibly because, as with African art generally, the great constant is change, improvisation being its motor. In the Shout, the Negro spiritual and essentials of jazz dance evolved. The Ring Shout was the immediate context in which these forms developed during and after slavery, probably because it was more directly tied to the ancestral past, a source of creative inspiration for the African. The presence of the motions of jazz dance in the Shout—the movements are frozen in time in the photographs found in Lydia Parrish's *Slave Songs of the Georgia Sea Islands*—is startling not only because that dance is sacred but because it is so modern despite its emergence centuries ago.[23] The complexity of the rhythms to which it is danced, their function as a kind of metronome for our age, is the surest evidence of the Shout being attuned to modern needs.

A variant of the Shout with even closer ties to jazz dance is done on John's Island off the coast of South Carolina at Moving Star

"Margaret." This photograph originally appeared in Lydia Parrish's *Slave Songs of the Georgia Sea Islands* where the caption reads: "Margaret, on the Left, Demonstrates the Correct Position of Arms and Feet in Shouting." (Photograph by Rutherford; © The University of Georgia Press; reproduced with permission)

Hall, a place of worship that is attended by a mainly elderly congregation, though it is led by a relatively young preacher. So close is this sacred dance to hip jazz dance of the 1950s, 1960s, and the present that it is indistinguishable from it. Did it precede, and if so by how long, that precise style of dancing in dance halls? Or was this full-blown expression of jazz dance developed in the ring? In this latter regard, it should be noted that the Moving Star Hall worshipers reluctantly admit to Ring Shouting "when the spirit moves" them. In any case, the dancers could easily be dancing to jazz music as they move their elbows somewhat like pistons, co-ordinating them to the beat of the music, shuffling first one and then the other foot as the opposite arm, left or right, reaches a high point.[24]

The fact that elements basic to jazz dance were in the Ring Shout, awaiting the sounds of jazz music, is astonishing. And since those elements, especially the positioning, at times, of the elbows, respond to the music of the spirituals, the influence of that music on jazz reminds us of the roots of jazz and jazz dance in the sacred. It is small wonder that generations of jazz artists have borrowed—and continue to borrow—from the music of the church. Yet one of the best-kept secrets is the role of certain segments of the black church in rooting out sacred dance and opposing any connection with jazz and the blues. With Methodists in the lead, these segments took an extremely retrogressive, harmful line.

But they did not triumph, for black religion at its best is rooted in ground that recognizes little distinction between sacred art and "secular" forms flowering from it. The Shout was the initial source of such flowering. Its spiritual transport and frequent association with sorrow—with funerals and memories of the dancing ancestors, to say nothing of the pain of slavery—reflect extraordinary depth of human experience. Small wonder, therefore, that the blues quality of jazz, a sadness miraculously mingled with joy, also finds resonance in the Shout. Only Frederick Douglass and James Baldwin have adequately treated the problem of the oneness of joy and sadness in black music, and I have discussed this elsewhere.[25] But I want to suggest here that those seemingly opposite qualities—qualities of sacred blues—characterized the feelings and thoughts of those who danced the Shout.

This comes through powerfully in *The Fire Next Time,* whose charging rhythms, over a handful of pages, carry black music criticism to heights not achieved since Douglass. Though Douglass remains the master theorist of black music, having formulated basic principles for his time and ours, he did not link dance to music, a curious development indeed for him. But Baldwin does. In *The Fire Next Time,* the collapsing of categories, the movement from one determination to another, is the secret to his genius as dance takes its rightful place with music:

> There is no music like that music, no drama like the drama of the saints rejoicing, the sinners moaning, the tambourines racing, and all those voices coming together and crying holy unto the Lord. There is still, for me, no pathos quite like the pathos of those multi-colored, worn, somehow triumphant and transfigured faces, speak-

ing from the depths of a visible, tangible, continuing despair of the goodness of the Lord. I have never seen anything to equal the fire and excitement that sometimes, without warning, fills a church, causing the church, as Leadbelly and so many others have testified, to "rock." Nothing that has happened to me since equals the power and the glory that I sometimes felt when, in the middle of a sermon, I knew that I somehow, by some miracle, was carrying, as they said, the "word"—when the church and I were one. Their pain and their joy were mine, and mine were theirs—they surrendered their pain and joy to me, I surrendered mine to them—and their cries of "amen!" And "Hallelujah!" and "Yes Lord!" and "Praise His name!" and "Preach it, brother!" sustained and whipped on my solos until we all became equal, wringing wet, singing and dancing, in anguish and rejoicing, at the foot of the altar.[26]

Go Tell It on the Mountain contains some fine writing on dance. In this work, another solo Shout is revealed, as was increasingly the case when slaves and their descendants moved into churches. The Shout in the novel is done to the music of the piano and tambourine as the whole congregation rises to support the shouter as the dance begins. The rhythms are complex, and the high point of possession occurs. But there is something about the movement of the arms as the dance begins, about dance to percussive sound, and dance leading to possession that link the performance style to that of the Ring Shout. Indeed, Baldwin provides the best description on record of the solo Shout, of its power and place in communal consciousness and collective performance. The call and response that marked the spiritual and artistic interplay of the preacher and his congregation is paralleled, in subtle but powerful ways, by that of sacred dancers. His early years as a preacher in Harlem storefront churches enabled Baldwin to view religion at its center, and that together with his extraordinary command of both music and dance enabled him to fashion this stunning tableau:

On Sunday mornings the women all seemed patient, all the men seemed mighty. . . . [Elisha] sat at the piano, singing and playing; and then, like a great black cat in trouble . . . he stiffened and trembled, and cried out. *Jesus, Jesus, oh Lord, Jesus!* He struck on the piano one last, wild note, and threw up his hands, palms upward, stretched wide apart. The tambourines raced to fill the vacuum left by his silent piano. Then he was on his feet . . . the muscles leaping and swelling in his long, dark neck. It seemed that he could not breathe, that his body could not contain this passion, that he would be dispersed into the waiting air. His hands, rigid to the very fingertips, moved outward and back against his hips, his sightless eyes looked upward, and he began to dance.

Elisha's dance, in the center of a circle of dancers, soon took on a driving, juba-like quality as he kept time, much like a black Baptist preacher, for himself and for those responding to him:

> Then his hands closed into fists, and his head snapped downward, his sweat loosening the grease that slicked down his hair; and the rhythm of all the others quickened to match Elisha's rhythm; his thighs moved terribly against the cloth of his suit, his heels beat on the floor, and his fists moved beside his body as if he were beating his own drum. And so, for a while, in the center of the dancers, head down, fists beating, on, on, unbearably until it seemed the walls of the church would fall for very sound; and then, in a moment, with a cry, head up, arms high in the air, sweat pouring from his forehead, and all his body dancing as though it would never stop.[27]

Such was the environment that nourished generations of jazz and blues musicians and dancers. On the other hand, there is little doubt that the music and dance of the church have been influenced by black "secular" forms of music and dance, that there was ongoing reciprocity between the two from an early period following slavery. Such reciprocity, for all the opposition to it by some churchgoers, has been no less enriching spiritually than artistically. Paule Marshall treats this theme, and does so brilliantly:

> And suddenly there it was: that strangled scream, stolen from some blues singer, that he was noted for. Each Sunday he carefully husbanded it, unleashing it only when he felt it was time to move the sermon to higher ground. From all over the church the amens rushed forward to embrace it. The dust motes in the spring sun-

light slanting into the pews from the windows broke into a holy dance.[28]

NOTES

This essay was originally published in *Choreographing History,* ed. Susan Foster (Bloomington: Indiana University Press, 1995). Minor changes have been made for consistency. Reprinted with permission.

1. See Sterling Stuckey, *Slave Culture: Nationalist Theory and the Foundations of Black America* (New York: Oxford University Press, 1987), chap. 1.
2. See Paul Robeson, "I Want to Be African," in *Paul Robeson: Tributes* (New York: Paul Robeson Archives, 1976), 55–59. Also see Stuckey, *Slave Culture,* chap. 6.
3. This process of change is discussed at some length in Stuckey, *Slave Culture,* 25–43.
4. Robeson, "I Want to Be African," 58.
5. Alan Lomax, *The Land Where the Blues Began* (New York: Pantheon, 1993).
6. The role of the ancestors, long neglected by students of black culture, has been treated throughout Stuckey's *Slave Culture.* Ancestral concerns of blacks in the Americas, expressed through dance, are treated in groundbreaking ways by Paule Marshall in *Praise Song for the Widow* (New York: Dutton, 1984), 231–51.
7. Stuckey, *Slave Culture,* 25.
8. *New York Nation,* 30 May 1867.
9. Sterling Stuckey, "Ironic Tenacity: Frederick Douglass' Seizure of the Dialectic," in *Frederick Douglass: New Literary and Historical Essays,* ed. Eric Sundquist (New York: Cambridge University Press, 1991), 23–32.
10. Roland Hayes, *Angel Mo' and Her Son* (Boston: Little, Brown, 1942), 29.
11. Harold Courlander, *Negro Folk Music, U.S.A.* (New York: Columbia University Press, 1963), 195.
12. Ibid., 196.
13. Frederick Douglass, *My Bondage and My Freedom* (New York: Dover, 1969).
14. Fredrika Bremer, *America of the Fifties,* ed. Adolph B. Benson (New York: Oxford University Press, 1924), 276–78.
15. Daniel Payne, *Recollections of Seventy Years* (New York: Arno, 1968), 92–94.
16. Bremer, *America of the Fifties,* 119.
17. Ibid., 18–20.
18. W. E. B. Du Bois, *The Philadelphia Negro* (New York: Shocken, 1967), 221–22.
19. Ibid.
20. Payne, *Recollections,* 253–54.
21. Lomax, *Land Where the Blues Began,* 494. Laurence Levine quotes ex-

slaves on the Shout and the crossing of legs: "Hit ain't railly dancing 'less de feets is crossed"; "dancin' ain't sinful iffen de foots ain't crossed." Lawrence Levine, *Black Culture and Black Consciousness* (New York: Oxford University Press, 1977), 38.

22. Marshall Stearns, *The Story of Jazz* (London: Oxford University Press, 1970), 13.

23. Lydia Parrish, *Slave Songs of the Georgia Sea Islands* (Hatboro, Penn.: Folk-loric Associates, 1965), 144–45. Parrish remarks in the caption: "Margaret, on the Left, Demonstrates the Correct Position of the Arms and Feet in Shouting." If that is in fact their correct position, then there is remarkable correspondence of hands and arms in Shouting and in jazz dance.

24. Thanks to Bernice Johnson Reagon, I had the opportunity to attend services at Moving Star Hall in the spring of 1986.

25. Stuckey, "Ironic Tenacity," 33–35.

26. James Baldwin, *The Fire Next Time* (New York: Dial, 1963), 47–48.

27. James Baldwin, *Go Tell It on the Mountain* (New York: Dell, 1953), 15–16.

28. Marshall, *Praise Song*, 199.

2

Dance and Identity Politics in American Negro Vaudeville: The Whitman Sisters, 1900–1935

Nadine A. George

At the dawn of the twentieth century, professional African American dancers were employed primarily in vaudeville, an idiom that combined the theatrical traditions of variety, minstrelsy, and traveling road shows and served as a proving ground for young talent. With a few notable exceptions, these performers were prohibited from touring on white vaudeville circuits. Therefore, black vaudeville circuits like the Theatre Owners Booking Association (TOBA) developed and promoted black talent and catered to black audiences. As early African American performers honed their craft, they helped pave the way for others by battling institutionalized racism and restrictions placed on black artistic expression. Barred from portraying serious dramatic roles, African American performers took the only genres available to them—comedy and musicals—and excelled.

Black female performers of this era faced special challenges reflecting national beliefs about the place of black women in the larger social framework. In this chapter, I examine the black vaudeville troupe known as the Whitman Sisters, which not only starred but was also operated in its entirety by four remarkable female siblings—Mabel, Essie, Alberta, and Alice. After discussing their contributions to the American stage, I argue that by undermining the race and gender categories of their day, while insisting upon high-class status and challenging the assumptions of audiences, producers, and theater owners, the Whitman Sisters made the vaudeville stage of their time into an unexpected site of resistance to the mores of a world molded by segregation.

A DAY IN THE LIFE

No matter the weather, it was standing room only when the Whitman Sisters came to town.[1] Whether they appeared at a local theater house or the black church, huge crowds packed the hall to the suffocation point and included some of the most distinguished people in town. Many were turned away at the door. Others waited outside to catch a glimpse of the show or hear some of the songs. Anyone who was anyone went to see the Whitman Sisters.

Several hours before the audience arrived, Mabel Whitman finalized details with the manager of the theater and argued with him as he tried to pay the company less than the agreed-upon salary. Mabel usually threatened to pull the show at the last minute, and when the manager called her bluff, he found that she was not bluffing. He gave in and went back to the original price, but this time Mabel demanded full payment in advance to ensure that he did not cheat them. She had won. She then went to oversee the final rehearsal. Mabel would yell at the dancers, "Get those feet *up* there. What the hell do you think you're doing? Get those feet moving!"[2] Some twenty-five performers scrambled to get into costumes and makeup. Dancers stretched and singers vocalized. Essie fixed the stitching on costumes. Mabel decided which of eight different programs the company would perform that night, informed the cast of the order, and gave notes to iron out some rough spots in the numbers. She then, perhaps, told one of the "picks"—short for "pickaninnies," as talented black child dancers were called—that his act would be cut in half because it still needed work. The little boy probably cried but did not consider leaving the show and going home because everyone knew that "when you joined the Whitman Sisters, you went with them, you worked with them, and you just learned—that was all. You just learned to perform."[3] This was the best show business education around. For a "pick" with the Whitmans, "You sang one week, danced the next, sold peanuts the next, and if you got caught breaking any of the rules they shipped you home in a hurry."[4]

The eight-member jazz band, led by Bennie Moten and featuring the young Bill (later Count) Basie, played an overture, either a classical piece or a new piece written for the show by Alberta Whitman or the band leader, offering a taste of the music they would play between each act. Mabel was the first to walk on stage, and when the applause died down she would address the audience. She spoke of the sisters' childhood, about how they had taken part in concerts and church work since their father was a minister of the gospel. She went on to speak about their education and, briefly, how they came by their success. When she finished her oration, the band began playing an upbeat popular number to warm the audience up, then switched to a sentimental sorrow song, the likes of which were undoubtedly well known to everyone.

The curtain rose to reveal a "before de wah" plantation act, reminiscent of minstrel shows, with Mammy in blackface peeling potatoes and the kids all in blackface, singing and dancing around her, in the quaint setting of a Southern dooryard at dusk. The backdrop was probably a painted scene with painted flats on either side that could easily be switched between the acts. Simple lighting illuminated the stage, although a special effect may have been used to achieve an evening atmosphere. The melancholy songs Mammy sang were melodramatic and brought tears to the eyes of many. Upon Willie Robinson's return to the house ("Little Georgia Blossom") with a rooster for supper, Mabel praised the Lord by singing psalms.

Next came the specialty numbers, solo singers and dancers. Willie Toosweet and "Sparkplug" George did a comedy act punctuated by Sparkplug's famous foghorn laugh that sparked one critic to remark, "When he's all washed up as a comedian, he should visit the tug-boat lines along the Hudson River and get a job, laughing in a fog."[5] The young Ethel Waters would enter and do her famous coon shouting.

Child dancer "Pops" Whitman or Willie Robinson sang popular songs like "Is Everybody Happy?" and nimbly danced breakdowns. Robinson, who was "as big as a couple of bunches of toothpicks," had a sense of humor that would "make a cow smile."[6] Essie Whitman's drunk act presented the audience with the character of the "The Beggar" and delighted all with her comic banter.

And then came the dancers! They had the stage to themselves and did not have to do the usual singing or comedy; they were specialty acts. They probably began with a cakewalk and then moved into a Tiller-style precision number—an intricate combination of high kicks. As company dancer Catherine Basie recalled, they would "kick to the left, kick to the right, kick straight up, and so on, to the tune of 'Stardust.'"[7] Then three of the girls, Alice Whitman, Jeni LeGon, and Basie herself, did a shake dance to "Diga Diga Doo." This was followed by a Snakehips dance that rivaled the original "Snake Hips" Tucker himself. They wore shimmery orange blouses with big sleeves, green satin pants, and sashes around their waists, so when they would shake and snake, it ALL shook. This number was always a show stopper.

Next came a comedy skit, probably by a newcomer who would not complain about having to follow such a great act. Then the three-foot-tall Princess Wee Wee, billed as the tiniest singing comedienne, paired up with the six-foot-tall Willie Bryant to sing, dance, and tell jokes in a act that brought audiences to their knees. The entertainment world was still enthralled with the bizarre pseudoscientific exhibits of shows like Barnum's circuses, which included Jo-Jo the Dogface Boy, Zip the Pin-Headed Man, Millie and Christina the Siamese Twins, and numerous African American fat ladies. Capitalizing on this trend, the Whitman Sisters hired the yard-high Princess Wee Wee. The top of her head just reached Bryant's waist. "She'd sing in a cute, high-pitched voice," Bryant remembered, "and then she'd dance around between my legs."[8] The sisters had discovered the talented midget and adopted her, and she became one of the chief attractions of the Whitman Sisters' show.

Mabel might then perform with her "picks," the Dixie Boys. She'd sing a medley of old favorites, then turn the stage over to the boys, who wowed the audiences with their energy, belting out songs, clapping out a Charleston, tapping like there was no tomorrow, turning flips, running up walls, and generally defying gravity and most other laws of physics. They probably also sang "coon songs," entertaining vestiges of minstrelsy that perpetuated black stereotypes—eating fried chicken, "fancy dressing," rowdiness, and the like.

Butterbeans and Susie (Jodie and Susie Edwards) might perform next. The hen-pecked husband and nagging wife team perfected their act on tour with the Whitman Sisters, with its low jokes, dancing, heckling, and insults. Butterbeans tried to stand up to his domineering wife, but his slight stature and less-than-imposing physicality only increased the hilarity of the situation. Susie sang the blues and cakewalked, and Butterbeans performed the "Itch," also known as the "Heebie Jeebies," in which he scratched himself in syncopation.

A handsome, debonair gentleman, the epitome of class and style, then strutted on the stage. Baby-doll Alice Whitman shuffled on after him, cute as a button; they danced together, with a chorus line as back-up. Sometime during this act, spectators realized that the man was actually a woman, none other than Alberta Whitman, the famous male impersonator. Willie Bryant then entered, and the three danced à la Williams, Walker, and Walker. Alice then began to sing, and as the stage cleared, she broke into a tap routine full of wings, pull backs, and timesteps that put other tappers to shame. Alice was billed as "The Queen of Taps" and well deserved the title. Willie Bryant called her "the best girl tap-dancer in the country—bar none."[9] The star of the show, Alice did Ballin' the Jack, Walkin' the Dog, the Sand, and the Shimmy. "In Ballin' the Jack I'd stop in the middle of the song, squeal, and make my kneecaps quiver—I used to have dimples on them. . . ."[10]

Alice typified the spirit of improvisation and enjoyment in early African American dance forms. Dancer Bill Bailey recalled:

When Alice came on stage, she walked out to the center, tossed *off* a tricky little step, and inquired of the bandleader in the pit: "How's this, Fess?"

"What is it?" asked the bandleader.

Alice replied, "I don't know what you call it but it sure feels good."....

"I'd make my exit with the Shim-Sham-Shimmy, mostly from the waist down—along with more squeals—wearing a shawl and a little flimsy thing around my middle with a fringe and a bow on the back. If I ever lost that bow, they used to say, I'd sure catch cold. . . . I could swing a mean . . . (wink) around."[11]

Alice then had to vamp as Essie took a long time backstage getting her appearance just right. After a dozen encores for Alice, Essie finally reappeared, this time not as a character but as a serious singer who amazed audiences with her low contralto rendition of "Some of These Days" that made Sophie Tucker sound like a soprano.

After a short break, four white women with blonde hair in Gibson Girl style paraded around the stage and sang a few songs. Spectators may or may not have recognized them as the famed Whitman sisters. A blues singer or comedy act followed. Finally Alberta, also known as Bert, would begin the finale with a strut and a sample of flash dancing, throwing her legs every which way. The finale was a huge production number, with every member of the company taking a turn and leaving the audience with a memory of the best parts of their acts. The entire company did the cakewalk and ended in a spectacular kick line that fed off the audiences' applause and response. The electricity in the air intensified as the curtain fell on the spirited singing and dancing. As an encore, "Pops" came out again to close the show.

If this was the last performance of the company's run—usually the second Thursday night in one town—the company would then pack up and prepare to move to the next town. The cast came to the stage and Mabel would give her lecture or, as some called it, her sermon. She told all the children that they had to finish their schoolwork for their tutor, her husband Dave Payton, or they would not be allowed to perform in the next show. She gave notes on the night's performance and admonished the cast, putting "the fear of hell-fire and brimstone into her proteges. . . . May had a stentorian voice and a powerful frown."[12] She ended the session with an ultimatum: "Now when we get to Cuthbert, the married couples will live together and the unmarried couples will not. It's a mortal sin, and I don't want to catch any of you young girls staying with any boys. Is that clear?"[13] The company then piled into their railroad cars and headed to the next town, which was eagerly awaiting their arrival.

A FAMILY AFFAIR

Little did the Reverend Albery Allson Whitman realize when he gave singing and dancing lessons to his four daughters that they would go on to form one of the most successful Negro vaudeville troupes. He taught Mabel (ca. 1880–1942), Essie (1882–1963), Alberta (ca. 1888–1964), and Alice (ca. 1900–1969) the "double shuffle" and religious songs with the idea that the girls would accompany him on evangelical tours and at church benefits. Perhaps he witnessed the Fisk Jubilee Singers give one of their first concerts at Wilberforce University when he was studying there in 1871 and was inspired to combine versions of sacred music with his preaching. The spirituals of the Fisk University students in the 1870s were the first undeniably black music idiom to reach the American concert stage, and these sorrow songs of bondage tugged at sentimental Victorian heartstrings throughout the United States and Europe.[14]

The sisters demonstrated remarkable musical abilities early on. George Walker, later of the famous dance team Williams and Walker, wanted to take the sisters to New York to promote their professional careers, but Reverend Whitman objected. The sisters continued their education at the New England Conservatory of Music in Boston and also at Morris Brown College in Atlanta, where their father served as dean. But the older sisters had ideas beyond the evangelical circuit. In 1899, at the ages of nineteen and seventeen respectively, Mabel and Essie Whitman created a repertory of jubilee songs, formed an act, and hired a hall. The sisters may have taken a cue from the Hyer Sisters, who started staging plays and touring combination acts (often with racial themes similar to the afterpieces of minstrel acts) in 1876.[15] After an initial success, the two Whitman sisters made the

The Whitman Sisters, *left to right:* Alberta, Alice, Mabel, and Essie (Reproduced with permission of Ernestine G. Lucas)

transition to popular songs. Mabel was noted to have a beautiful voice, but it was Essie's contralto that significantly impressed critics.

Initially billed as the Danzette Sisters, Mabel and Essie toured from Missouri to Florida. They made their professional debut as "filler" in an open spot on the bill at the Orpheum Theater in Kansas City, Missouri. Mabel later recalled that they were "an instantaneous hit."[16] In 1899, one Mr. Lehman, manager of the Orpheum, obtained permission from Reverend Whitman to sign the sisters to tour the Orpheum and Kohl & Castle circuits, making them one of the few black vaudevillian groups to appear on predominately white circuits. Caddie Whitman, the girls' mother, chaperoned the sisters, and after a successful tour abroad allowed the third sister, Alberta, to join the act.

Although he was a poet of considerable renown,[17] Reverend Whitman disliked the idea of his daughters performing anything but religious songs. His disdain was not surprising at a time when upstanding African American families carefully cultivated an air of respectability. When his daughters insisted on a secular repertory, he allegedly disowned them.[18] In 1901, at the age of fifty,

Reverend Whitman died in Anniston, Alabama, of pneumonia quickened by alcoholism. He did not live to see his daughters expand their company to include over twenty members and adopt a full vaudeville repertory.

The year after their father's death, the Whitman Sisters Novelty Company opened at the Grand Opera House in Augusta, Georgia, and received their first newspaper review:

> These three bright, pretty mulatto girls are the daughters of the pastor of the A. M. E. Church of Atlanta, Ga. They have wonderful voices, that of Essie being the lowest contralto on record. The sisters play banjos and sing coon songs with a smack of the original flavor. Their costuming is elegant; their manner is graceful and their appearance striking in a degree as they are unusually handsome.[19]

While in New Orleans in the summer of 1904, the sisters changed the name of the company to the Whitman Sisters' New Orleans Troubadours and began taking on other acts. Among their first protégés was the young Willie (later Bill "Bojangles") Robinson. In 1909 Caddie Whitman died, and the family's youngest daughter, Alice, who had been caring for their ailing mother, joined the troupe.

Mabel took some of the younger dancing acts from the Troubadours and opened her own "pick" show called Mabel Whitman and the Dixie Boys. Mabel took her cue from the practice of popular white female performers like Sophie Tucker, Eva Tanguay, and Nora Bayes, who surrounded themselves with "picks" on the road. They were considered insurance, because no matter how the solo singer fared, the kids would almost always succeed. Mabel's splinter company toured the United States, Europe, and Australia, and Mabel sent money back to her sisters.

Because there is no gap in press coverage of the Whitman Sisters' New Orleans Troubadours, it may be assumed that the company continued to perform while Mabel was touring with the Dixie Boys. After the tour ended, the four women reorganized the company as the Whitman Sisters; by 1910 they had earned the title "The Royalty of Negro Vaudeville." For the next thirty years the Whitman Sisters entertained countless black and white audiences in theaters and churches while simultaneously becoming the greatest incubator of black talent in vaudeville.

The Whitman Sisters' repertory drew on many African American dances and performance traditions. Alice Whitman won several cakewalk contests, and the Whitman Sisters are credited with introducing the dance to many audiences. Alberta Whitman did one of the first popular flash acts using leaps, somersaults, and splits. The company's repertory also included Ballin' the Jack, a serpentine, shuffling dance that had its roots in the Ring Shout,[20] as well as a version of Snakehips, the hip-gyration dance popularized by Earl Tucker. The Whitman Sisters' version, wrote one reviewer, was "a near show-stopper. Cute and vivacious, they imitate the gyrations of Mister Earl Tucker and I don't mean maybe."[21] Other dances popularized by the Whitman Sisters were Walkin' the Dog, the Sand, and the Shimmy.

The group was probably best known for its tap dancing. The Whitman Sisters employed many famous "pick" dancers, including Aaron Palmer, Samuel Reed, Julius Foxworth, and Tommy Hawkins. Throughout the 1910s and 1920s, the acrobatic flash dancing of Albert "Pops" Whitman (son of Alice Whitman and Aaron Palmer) and Willie Robinson anticipated the Nicholas Brothers and the Berry Brothers by at least ten years. Dancing the Charleston in a miniature tuxedo at the age of four, "Pops" developed into one of the first great acrobatic tap dancers, a master of cartwheels, spins, flips, and splits. The group's star tapper, however, was Alice Whitman, billed as the Queen of Taps and "the best girl tap dancer in the country." Jeni LeGon, later a Hollywood tap star often paired with Bill "Bojangles" Robinson, remembered Alice as "the best there was. She was tops. She was better than Ann Miller and Eleanor Powell and me and anybody else you wanted to put her to. She could do all the ballet-style stuff like Eleanor. And then she could hoof! But she never went out on her own, you know, she stayed with the sisters."[22] Alice became one of the first nationally acclaimed black women tap dancers.

The Whitman Sisters' careers lasted over forty years, ending just before the United States entered World War II. The company's longevity was largely due to the efforts of Mabel Whitman, who stopped performing to manage the company.[23] In 1904, Mabel was probably the only black woman managing her own company and booking it at the best Southern venues. She had a distinct advantage over white theater managers when it came to securing child acts. By playing the role of company matriarch, she was able to assure black parents that their talented children would be protected, a promise that competing male managers could not offer. Catherine Basie, Count Basie's wife, recalled: "Any mother could tell you that if your daughter was with The Whitman Sisters, she was safe."[24] This perception allowed the Whitman Sisters to develop some of the best child acts in vaudeville.

Mabel also championed desegregation in the theater and the rights of black patrons and performers. In 1904, after only four years on the professional stage, she insisted that black patrons be allowed to sit in the dress circle and parquet sections of Birmingham's Jefferson Theater. She achieved her goal, and for the first time in the history of this civic theater segregation codes were successfully challenged.[25] On another occasion the management of the Regal Theater in Chicago tried to take advantage of Mabel and pay the company less than it had agreed. So "May walked across the street to the Metropolitan Theater, which lacked a stage, had a new stage built, opened with a different show, and ruined the Regal's business for two weeks."[26] Mabel gained respect and a reputation for being a shrewd manager who would not be exploited because of her race or gender.

In an interview in the *Baltimore Afro-American,* Mabel discussed the problems facing company managers like herself:

> The trouble with this game is a set of unscrupulous owners and managers who seemingly have syndicated themselves together to stifle the progress along the lines of art and entertainment. They feel that any kind of show is good enough for a colored audience and their only desire is to have a comedian and a few half-naked girls on hand to keep the doors open. . . .When the crowd gets fed up on that sort of diet, they try to work a good show and try to get it for the same money they pay an amateur company which was made up overnight. This is what a certain owner told

me—and I'll name him when and if necessary—"I have been losing
money all year and I have to get out of the red on your engagement here. Therefore I won't pay you what you want. You have a
family company. You don't need money because you all work and
live together. Come in at my price or stay out."

Well I stayed out . . .

And now do you know what is the matter with show business?[27]

HOW DO YOU TELL A BLACK WOMAN?

Theatergoers who walked into a Whitman Sisters show expected to be entertained by four black women singing and dancing with a company of performers. What happened when they
were presented instead with four white women in full Gibson Girl
dress and high blonde pompadours? Or later, when a boy/girl
team danced, only to realize halfway through that the man was a
woman? Many probably double-checked their programs. Others,
who were not "fooled," happily suspended their disbelief. Whatever their reaction, their expectations had been definitely challenged.

Masters of the politics of performance and representation (not
that these were terms they would ever use), the Whitman Sisters
formulated several personas in order to shock, confront, and challenge their public into recognizing the shakiness of rigid construc-
tions of race and gender. As Judith Butler argues, identity is not
fixed; rather, it is something made manifest through power relations. It is also performative, meaning that it is created through
a "regularized and constrained repetition of norms. . . . Performance is not a singular act or event, but a ritualized production, a
ritual reiterated under and through constraint, under and through
the force of prohibition and taboo, with the threat of ostracism
and even death controlling and compelling the shape of the production, but not . . . determining it fully in advance."[28]

Performers like the Whitman Sisters took control of their identity and experimented with presenting a shifting, fluid self. If
we understand the stage to be a public space, traditionally the
realm of the male and politically separated from private space (traditionally understood as the female domain), then black female

performers like the Whitman Sisters, who transgressed the traditional boundaries of race and gender, challenged the expectations of who or what was entitled to occupy these different spheres. On stage, performers were able to safely try on different identities and experiment with, rework, and counter normative representations.

Reinventing the self and manipulating racial images were not new to African American performers but part of a tradition of "signifying." According to Butler, "there is power and agency in repeating restrictive hegemonic terms/norms in directions that reverse, displace, critique their originating aims."[29] When a symbolic gesture is revised or parodied, new meanings are created echoing the past and foreshadowing the future. As Henry Louis Gates writes: "The signifying monkey serves as the figure-of-figures as the trope in which are encoded several other peculiarly black rhetorical tropes."[30] In theater, for example, black minstrels made small but significant changes when they took over forms created by their white counterparts. While maintaining a claim to authenticity, they altered certain themes to criticize the image of an idealized South, replete with contented slaves and benevolent masters. For example, in the hands of white minstrels, "Old Darky" was a sentimental, nostalgic character who loved his white master and mistress and wouldn't take his freedom if it was handed to him. Black minstrels kept the sentimentality of "Old Darky," but now he longed for his wife and the children sold away from him by a much crueler master and mistress. Black minstrels were thus able to incorporate social protest into their "acts," while developing masks that satisfied white expectations. In dance, the cakewalk developed as a pastiche of the dances that slaves had witnessed their white masters performing in the big house. Certain derisive meanings were encoded in the dance, but it was read differently by whites who viewed the cakewalk as an amusing attempt at sophistication on the parts of their slaves rather than as a mockery of the manners of their masters. In both examples, we see the signifying monkey at work: the master trickster, altering the production of meaning.

The Whitman Sisters also produced plantation acts that entertained while criticizing certain perceived social norms. One popular act of theirs presented the familiar scene of a Southern cottage at eventide with Mammy peeling potatoes and the children happily singing and dancing. However, the sisters then turned to religious songs, which added humanity and depth to characters and expanded the images beyond stereotypes. Although negative images served to create and sustain ideological justification for the perpetuation of race and gender oppression, performers like the Whitman Sisters presented an implicit critique of these models, challenging expectations not only in the theater, but outside it as well.

The Whitman Sisters also negotiated the complicated issues of race and colorism in their repertory by choosing to perform sometimes as a black act, sometimes as a white act (since they were fair-complexioned enough to pass for white), and sometimes as a blackface act. They used their complexion to their advantage by dying their hair blonde and wearing it in a fashionably high pompadour. By presenting themselves as white, the sisters turned definitions of race and color upside down. It is also possible that the Whitman Sisters passed for white off-stage in order to get better service and accommodations for themselves and the rest of their troupe.

In donning blackface, the Whitman Sisters challenged audiences to deal with their own racialized expectations. On occasion, the Whitman Sisters performed in wigs and blackface and then, as a finale, removed them, returning to the stage with their blond hair down. This caught audiences off-guard, to say the least. Essie wrote: "The audience was always puzzled and someone was sure to ask, 'What are those white women doing up there?' Then they would recognize us as the performers and laugh in amazement."[31] Like other light-skinned African Americans, in order to be read as "black," the Whitman Sisters had to don a black mask.

By blacking up and freely switching white-, light-, and dark-skinned personas, the Whitmans gave their audiences access to a range of responses through which they could safely and humorously work out anxieties about race and gender. The laughter at the realization was a relief of tension and a return to certainty.

Audiences clearly experienced a degree of identification with the performers. This relationship was destabilized when the Whitman Sisters altered their appearance and played on expectations of the black female body. In varying degrees, they disrupted the "gazes" of various spectators. If nothing else, the Whitman Sisters succeeded in undermining the notion of a fixed sexual and racial identity.

Anthony Slide in the *Encyclopedia of Vaudeville* claims that the Whitman Sisters used blackface makeup in part because they were fair-skinned enough to pass for white and that such deception actually hurt their work when they appeared with black male performers. He argues that audiences were unwilling to accept the notion of blacks and whites sharing a stage, especially romantically. He quotes a 1902 critic who urged all fair-skinned black women to wear blackface makeup on stage since "black men making love to white girls look cheap."[32] Interracial erotic desire was clearly taboo, and enacting scenes of white and black bodies commingling was dangerous. Yet audience reaction also suggests that the hint at miscegenation was titillating. The safe haven of the theater allowed interracial romance, elsewhere forbidden, to be represented, however tentatively and indirectly.

In "passing," the Whitman Sisters evoked the practice of many light-skinned African Americans to live, usually for reasons of social or economic opportunity, as white Americans. As Elaine Ginsberg argues, "the possibility of passing challenges a number of problematic and even antithetical assumptions about identities, the first of which is that some identity categories are inherent and unalterable essences: presumably one cannot pass for something one *is not* unless there is some other, pre-passing, identity that one *is*."[33] Passing also challenges the idea that identity can be read on the body.

The Whitman Sisters performed as a white act in their early days. It is unclear the extent to which managers and audiences knew the "truth." At what point they decided to play black houses and fight for desegregation is also unclear; perhaps it was when they began taking on other acts with performers who were darker than they. Later, however, the Whitman Sisters were able to use their color to shuttle between racial identities, while retaining their popularity with both white and black audiences.

Chorus lines at the turn of the century glorified the light-skinned black woman. Shows such as *The Creole Burlesque Show* (1890), *The Smart Set* (1900–1920), and *Keep Shufflin'* (1928) employed beautiful light-skinned black women as dancers, casting that helped foster and preserve a fair-skinned beauty standard while excluding dark-skinned women. The Whitman Sisters, in contrast to shows of this type, rejected the light-skinned standard, even though they themselves were extremely fair-skinned, and made it a point to include black women of different shades in their chorus lines. As Jeni LeGon remembered: "The Whitman Sisters had fixed the line so we had all the colors that our race is known for. All the pretty shading—from the darkest darkest, to the palest of pale. Each one was a distinct looking kid. It was a rainbow of beautiful girls."[34] In their approach to color and beauty, the Whitman Sisters were well ahead of their times.

The Whitman Sisters also negotiated gender issues in their choice of so-called "specialty" acts. As a comedian, Essie specialized in drunk acts—traditionally a male line of business—amazing audiences with her low contralto voice and masculine singing. Alice, "The Queen of Taps," also performed in a traditionally male specialty and was often the only female tap dancer performing with "picks." Explains Jeni LeGon: "There weren't too many girl tap acts around. . . . You had to tap to be in the chorus line and there were excellent girl tap dancers all over the place. I just don't know why there weren't many soloists. Most of them danced in the chorus or did soubrette out in front of the chorus. But not too many of them went in for doing solo."[35]

Alberta practiced "gender passing" by cross-dressing and adopting the stage name Bert. She became known as the best male impersonator of her time, showing up colleagues such as Vesta Tilly, the famous gender-bender of the English music halls. Essie tells of a day when Tilly was supposed to follow Bert on a bill, "but when she saw Sister's act, she ran out of the theater and wouldn't come back. Sister Bert was the best in the business."[36] By

Alberta and Alice Whitman backstage, ca. 1928 (Reproduced with
permission of Ernestine G. Lucas)

manipulating dress, voice, walk, name, and mannerisms, Bert was able to alter the signs of identity, and thus use the ambivalence of drag to question the limits of sexual differentiation.

CLASS AND STATUS

"Mae Whitman, who has successfully guided the Whitman Sister's musical comedy productions for many, many years, has brought to New York and Harlem in particular, another novel singing, comedy dancing vehicle that lives up to the Whitman trade mark that stands for *high class* entertainment."[37] The reputation of the Whitman Sisters rested on their reputation as "high-class" performers. The importance of this status should not be understated. Not only did high-class troupes command higher salaries, they also commanded the respect of audiences and critics. To reach high-class status, performers had to prove their respectability by exuding sophistication, elegance, and morality. At a time when eugenics and Victorian notions of social Darwinism were used to demean African Americans, African Americans themselves sought bourgeois signs of status—sexual codes, moral codes, material goods, religion, and etiquette. Respectability became a tool through which African Americans could create an interracial and intraracial class structure. Respectability became an attack on racism at the same time that it served to distinguish one class of African Americans from another.

The Whitman sisters were high-class entertainers and were respectable. They created a family atmosphere within their company while enforcing a strict moral code. They arranged their programs so as not to offend the more conservative members of their audiences, and they toured respectable black churches where they were invariably well received. "Every church of any prominence (was) opened to these artists."[38] In an address at the Metropolitan Church in Washington, D.C., Mabel spoke of the strict moral and religious upbringing they had received from their minister father and how they had struggled to maintain both their reputation and their honor.[39]

Maintaining high-class status while performing race was a complex negotiation. A vocabulary of "yours" and "ours" developed in early-twentieth-century African American communities, where high achievers were placed on pedestals as representatives of the race and its potential. The key to the Whitman Sisters' success lay in their ability to appeal to both white *and* black audiences. By 1918 they had successfully toured most of the major white vaudeville circuits in the South, East, and Northeast, including Poli and Fox, the Orpheum, Greenwald, Kohl & Castle, Keith & Proctor, and Pantages. Playing to white audiences increased their popularity and revenue; indeed, it would have been financially impossible for them to ignore white audiences. However, the Whitman Sisters also maintained loyalty to their black audiences and TOBA. As an unidentified critic wrote in the *Chicago Defender:* "Both as to ability and personality these young ladies are thoroughly qualified to attach themselves in a line of activity which would take them entirely away from 'our people' but, despite the efforts made by many managers to effect this result, we still are proud to say that we have them with us."[40]

The Whitman Sisters assessed race and gender issues and challenged their audiences' expectations while promoting themselves as high-class entertainers. Their act helped sustain African American cultural forms, popularizing black social dance and enriching the nascent African American entertainment industry. They were instrumental in elevating black dancers to prominence on the vaudeville stage; indeed, they were "by far the greatest incubator of dancing talent for Negro shows on or off TOBA," giving rise to stars such as Bill Robinson, Ethel Waters, Pops and Louis, and Count Basie.[41] They helped secure a prominent place for African Americans on the national stage and well deserved their title as "The Royalty of Negro Vaudeville."

NOTES

For further information about the Whitman Sisters, please see Ernestine Garrett Lucas, *Wider Windows to the Past: African-American History from a Family Perspective* (Decorah, Iowa: E. G. Lucas, 1995); and Nadine George-Graves, *The Royalty of Negro Vaudeville: The Whitman Sisters and the Negotiation of Race, Gender and Class in African American Theatre 1900–1940* (New York: St. Martin's Press, 2000).

1. This reconstruction of a Whitman Sisters' show is pieced together from personal accounts by the sisters and others who performed with them.

2. Marshall Stearns and Jean Stearns, *Jazz Dance: The Story of American Vernacular Dance* (New York: Macmillan, 1968), 91.

3. Rusty E. Frank, *Tap! The Greatest Tap Dance Stars and Their Stories, 1900–1955* (New York: Da Capo Press, 1994), 122.

4. Stearns and Stearns, *Jazz Dance*, 91.

5. Bennie Butler, "The Whitman Sisters and Moten's Band at Lafayette," *Inter-State Tattler*, 17 December 1931.

6. *Springfield News*, 8 October 1906.

7. Stearns and Stearns, *Jazz Dance*, 90.

8. Ibid., 89.

9. Ibid., 88.

10. Ibid.

11. Ibid., 88–89.

12. Ibid., 91.

13. Ibid.

14. Along with continuing a religious tradition, these songs crossed over to the entertainment industry and soon became a staple of minstrel shows, folk choruses, and black concert companies. See Langston Hughes and Milton Meltzer, *Black Magic: A Pictorial History of the African American in the Performing Arts* (New York: Da Capo Press, 1967), 126.

15. The Hyer Sisters' *Out of Bondage* (1877) was among the first musical shows to be fully produced by a black organization.

16. "The Whitmans," *Chicago Defender*, 26 January 1918, 4.

17. An orphan by the age of twelve, Reverend Whitman worked his way from slave to become "Poet Laureate of the Negro Race." He published seven volumes of poetry. For a critical analysis of Reverend Whitman's poetry, see Joan R. Sherman, *Invisible Poets: Afro-Americans of the Nineteenth Century* (Chicago: University of Illinois Press, 1974); and Joan R. Sherman, *African-American Poetry of the Century* (Chicago: University of Illinois Press, 1992).

18. See Clarence Muse and David Arlen, *Way Down South* (Hollywood: David Graham Fischer, 1932).

19. *Birmingham News*, 22 February 1902, 10.

20. In this dance, the head, shoulders, and feet stay still while the rest of the body undulates and the hips rotate. A description of the choreography is found in the lyrics to the popular song "Ballin' the Jack"; see Stearns and Stearns, *Jazz Dance*, 99.

21. Butler, "The Whitman Sisters and Moten's Band at Lafayette."

22. Quoted in Frank, *Tap!* 122.

23. The sisters took on all of the production responsibilities themselves rather than hire outside the family. Mabel took care of all of the bookings and business; Essie designed and made costumes; and Alberta was financial secretary and composed the music for the show.

24. Quoted in Stearns and Stearns, *Jazz Dance*, 90.

25. Henry Sampson, *The Ghost Walks: A Chronological History of Blacks in Show Business, 1865–1910* (Metuchen, N.J.: Scarecrow Press, 1988), 321.

26. Stearns and Stearns, *Jazz Dance*, 87.

27. *Baltimore Afro-American,* 19 January 1929, 8.

28. Judith Butler, *Bodies That Matter: On the Discursive Limits of Sex* (New York: Routledge, 1993), 95.

29. Butler, *Bodies That Matter,* 123.

30. Henry Louis Gates Jr., *The Signifying Monkey: A Theory of African American Literary Criticism* (New York: Oxford University Press, 1988), xxi.

31. Stearns and Stearns, *Jazz Dance*, 86.

32. Anthony Slide, *The Encyclopedia of Vaudeville* (Westport, Conn.: Greenwood Press, 1994), 50.

33. Elaine Ginsberg, *Passing and the Fictions of Identity* (Durham, N.C.: Duke University Press, 1996), 4.

34. Frank, *Tap!* 122.

35. Ibid., 126–27.

36. Stearns and Stearns, *Jazz Dance*, 88.

37. Butler, "The Whitman Sisters and Moten's Band at Lafayette."

38. "Hear What the Press Has to Say," *Bee,* 23 May 1908.

39. "At the Metropolitan," *Bee,* 30 May 1908.

40. "The Whitmans," *Chicago Defender,* 26 January 1918, 4.

41. Stearns and Stearns, *Jazz Dance*, 85.

3
Awkward Moves:
Dance Lessons from the 1940s

Marya Annette McQuirter

Social dance became critical to African Americans as they adapted to the numerous changes of the 1940s. In that decade, African Americans experienced major social transformations, including one of the largest migrations of the century from the rural and urban South to northern, western, and midwestern urban centers. This migration was precipitated by a desire for better education, employment, and a relief from segregation and discrimination. Also important, but often ignored as a major factor in this movement, was the desire for more access to leisure and culture. Indeed, greater access to government jobs and increased income allowed for fuller participation in the ever-expanding leisure and consumer culture. Within this culture of consumption—shopping at chain stores, listening to the radio, purchasing records, and going to the movies—African Americans from a range of geographical spaces attempted to create new urban identities. Social dance figured as one of the central arenas in which the process of identity formation became manifest. This was a process both awkward and exciting, and in this chapter I shall focus on the notion of awkwardness.

Awkwardness is generally seen as anathema to the discourse on black dance. Too often, both dancers and analyses of dance as a vital and pleasurable social practice hide moments of awkwardness. But awkwardness is felt in many instances: by those who cannot dance, by dance partners who do not move well together, in those first moments when two strangers attempt to dance together, when a band attempts to swing the crowd and fails, when one first tries to learn a new dance, and when saying no (or being told no) when asked to (or being asked to) dance. Recognition and exploration of the concept of *awkwardness* is central to understanding the formation of a dancing public in the 1940s.

DANCE LESSON 1: LOCU-MOTIONS

[I would go] up to the Savoy Ballroom very often to hear Count Basie . . . downtown to hear Don Shirley, and back up to Manhattan Casino to hear Charlie Parker and get "twisted around" trying to dance to those "off beat riffs," and down to the Apollo to hear Dizzy Gillespie take flight.

Paul Robeson, Paul Robeson, *ca. 1960*

Researchers of jazz music and dance posit that prior to the 1940s, when "swing" was in full effect, citizens across the United States danced incessantly to big band sounds. But by the end of World War II—because of a tax levied on large dance halls,[1] the growth of small clubs that had little or no dance floors, and the advent of "bebop"—dancing was obliterated. To these researchers, social dancing virtually ended in the 1940s, and a vibrant dancing public was transformed into a sedentary listening public because of that blasted bebop.[2]

I find this narrative problematic for several reasons. First, it is based primarily on the dancing scene in New York and a lessening of opportunities for professional dancers, particularly tappers, who performed with musicians.[3] Second, it is written as if prior to the 1940s, "dancers" and "listeners" were not sharing and battling for the dance floor. This assumes that the body that "dances" does not also "listen." Finally, it allows little acknowledgment of a consistent ebb and flow of citizens' fascinations with a range of dance styles.

Did bebop portend the end of social dancing in the 1940s? A perusal through *Down Beat,* a popular jazz music magazine, belies this assertion. Articles about dance clubs opening up throughout the country and the various dances performed in them counter this common claim. In 1945, an article in *Down Beat* proclaimed,

"Terp Lovers Get Own Ballroom": "Two combination ballrooms and dancing schools have opened and promise a new fad for the area. Both spots teach the wall-huggers how to terp and then send them into their own dance halls to practice what they teach." In 1947, *Down Beat* reported, "New Dancery for Chi South Side": "Newest ballroom here, the Parkway Arena, is on the old White City Amusement Park Grounds, where the old ballroom has operated sporadically the last few years. Tony Pastor was the first attraction . . . with the International Sweethearts of Rhythm, Lois Russell and Dizzy Gillespie, following."[4]

Further evidence for the continued existence of social dancing in the 1940s comes from a more accurate understanding of bebop. As the decade was ending, bebop became a popular music form that spawned its own dances. The fact that it took some dancers time to adjust to the new rhythms of bebop should not translate into an erasure of social dance in the 1940s. Just as it took some musicians and critics time to adjust to the "new" sounds of bebop, many dancers also needed to create, learn, and adapt new dances to bebop.

Sarah Vaughan remembers that the few who understood the music "would be in a corner, jitterbugging forever, while the rest just stood staring at us. . . . We were just trying to play some music for the people, that we knew was together. We were trying to educate them. And it took a while!"[5]

Eventually, however, jitterbugs and others created and adapted new dance styles to go with bebop. A 1949 article in *Our World* magazine both reinforced bebop as a dancing music and offered lessons to curious and determined dancers:

> Let's get off on a limb. Bebop is music despite the terrific lambasting it has been taking. You may not believe it and we don't blame you. Almost every newspaper and magazine in the country has been taking pot shots at the "new listen." Out of the music of bebop have developed two dance phases—the Applejack and the Bop, which, unlike the Applejack, is done by a couple.[6]

In six photographs, a male demonstrates the parts of the Applejack: the Corkscrew Crawl; the Half Nelson, which is a pose;

Out of the music of bebop have developed two dance phases—the APPLEJACK

THE APPLEJACK STEP IS CUTE

THIS IS THE CORKSCREW CRAWL

THE HALF NELSON IS A POSE

THE CORKSCREW IS AN UPRIGHT

STEP COMBINING THE POSE

AND THE FAMOUS SWING KICK.

AND the BEBOP—which, unlike the Applejack, is done by a couple.

THE FREEZE EXPLAINS ITSELF

AND SO DOES THE SUBWAY

THE DIP IS AN EXAGGERATION

OF THE SLIDE, WHICH CAN BE

THE BEGINNING OF THE STEP

WHICH IDENTIFIES THE BEBOP.

"Bebop: Music or Madness?" *Our World* (January 1949): 34

and the Corkscrew, an upright step combining the pose and the famous swing kick. In the same number of photographs, a couple demonstrates the Freeze; the Subway, in which the female partner goes underneath the male partner's arm; and the Dip, "which is an exaggeration of the Slide, which can be the beginning of the step, which identifies the Bop." The article ends optimistically for dancers: "Bebop seems to have taken root in dress, in talk, and as a new music form. In fact look across the page, pops. And dig the new dances the cats are cooking. That should squash the dead-pans who say Bebop isn't danceable."[7]

Ira Gitler, in his study of jazz, reinforces the popularity of bebop and the fact that blacks did dance to bebop:

> whether it was a record store in Harlem, a shoeshine stand in St. Louis, a rib joint in Chicago, or someone's apartment in Brooklyn, I heard bebop coming out of loudspeakers, juke boxes, and an assortment of phonographs from consoles to portables. It was said that black people didn't dance to bebop and, for the most part, this was true, but black people figured out a way to make those fast tempos by cutting the time in half whether they were doing a new dance called "The Apple Jack" or the older Lindy Hop.[8]

Gitler's comments also hint at the supposed dichotomy of dancers and listeners. As noted above, numerous scholars assert that the advent of bebop turned a nation of "dancers" into a nation of "listeners." But this dichotomous vivisection of the mover from the listener is problematic. As Paul Robeson vividly suggests in the above epigraph, the body that "listens" also "dances." Second, the change in the consumptive relationship between the public and musicians has roots dating back at least to the 1930s. According to historian David Stowe,

> Swing enthusiasts helped transform swing from a functional music for dancing to an art music performed for attentive spectators. This change in the performance practices surrounding jazz is generally thought to have occurred later, with the rise of bebop during the mid-1940s, but even the early days of swing gave evidence that the cultural status of jazz was beginning to change, at least among its adherents, from dance music in the direction of "art" music.[9]

Thus, the change that most scholars attribute to the 1940s actually began in the early stages of swing. A 1935 article by William Dutton in *American Magazine* confirms this thesis. Dutton claimed that the new music was "designed less for dancing than for home consumption via the radio, while reading a newspaper."[10]

Many factors contributed to this shift in perception about the uses of popular music. Dutton alludes to one of the most important factors, technological changes in the music industry, as well as the availability of consumable goods to a wider range of the U.S. population. As radios, phonographs, and jukeboxes became more readily available, audience members enjoyed greater flexibility in access to new music. Two events, in particular, were instrumental in this development. First, Decca, a recording company, reduced its price of popular records to thirty-five cents in the early 1930s. (Prior to that records cost at least seventy-five cents.) Second, by the end of the 1930s, there were 300,000 jukeboxes located in restaurants, bars, cafes, and other establishments throughout the country. For five cents, women, men, and children could hear the latest records. These new technological developments had a great affect on the relationship between musicians and audiences, offering greater access to music than ever before.[11]

The invention and circulation of social dances is, in and of itself, a fascinating process that can never be completely documented. Still, despite extensive regional differences in their performance, one can attempt to map the waxing and waning popularity of certain dances. There can be no doubt that after the wane of the Lindy and the jitterbug nationally, other swing-era dances were soon to follow.[12]

Reporter Ed Wallace offers this explanation: "The rumba broke up the crowd of doleful listeners who had begun to accumulate like barnacles around the bandstand: it got people back on the dance floor. The rumba came along just as dancers were becoming listeners. Then, when the kick of the rumba was beginning to wane, along came the mambo and eeuugghh! we're gone again."[13] Once new dances surfaced, their predecessors were hardly missed. As one enthusiast noted about the mambo, "It's more graceful than jitterbugging but it's less inhibited. It can be adapted to any style. It's greater than the Charleston, greater than swing."[14]

If I have effectively dispelled the claim that social dancing ended in the 1940s, thereby exonerating bebop as being guilty of its demise, then what can be said about social dancing in this period?

Among the many valuable lessons to be learned are the role of dance in the construction of individual and group identity and the struggle over this construction in discursive and performative spaces. I begin with a discussion of how black folks learn to dance. I maintain that if we begin a discussion of black dance practices anywhere else, we render the dance arena as an automatic, already-constituted cultural space. Elucidating the steps taken to learn to dance, which feed directly into a consideration of the performative dimensions of "blackness" and community, forces us to rethink assumptions about black social dance and black urban communities.

DANCE LESSON 2: ERASING AWKWARDNESS— LEARNING TO DANCE

> Like hundreds of thousands of country-bred Negroes who had come to the Northern black ghetto before me, and have come since, I'd also acquired all of the other fashionable ghetto adornments—the zoot suits and conk . . . liquor, cigarettes, then reefers—all to erase my embarrassing background. But I still harbored one secret humiliation: I couldn't dance.
>
> *Malcolm X,* The Autobiography of Malcolm X, *1964*

> The hip code sometimes appeared compensatory rather than avant, insecure rather than assured, but it expressed real defiance.
>
> *Eric Lott,* Callaloo, *1988*

Malcolm X serves as a powerful icon in the black historical imagination; invariably, scholars writing about the 1940s use his autobiography to represent the normative experience of black life in this decade. His continuous transformations—from country bumpkin to hipster to underground economist to prisoner to Muslim to progressive—offer a Horatio Alger–like epic with a radical and racialized trajectory. In particular, his love of dance and his descriptions of the ballrooms in Boston and New York have been used to illumine night life in the 1940s. Writ large, his story serves as the metanarrative for this historical moment. It is because of its powerful import that I seek to intervene in the typical reading of Malcolm X's dramatic transformation from awkward to graceful.

Malcolm Little left Lansing, Michigan, in 1941, at the age of fifteen, to live with his sister Ella in Boston. Little was part of a throng of migrants who left the rural and urban cities and towns for northern, midwestern, and western cities. This migration circulated not only people but also cultural ideas, beliefs, information, and dance styles. Little missed the dance craze as it swept across the country. Either the Lindy and the jitterbug had not reached Lansing before he left, or he had not learned them. Once in Boston, his dance incompetence caused him great anxiety, along with other indicators of his "country roots," his hairstyle and his clothes. While he was easily able to acquire the accouterments of the conk hairdo and the fashionable zoot suits, learning to dance proved much more difficult.

Malcolm Little was not alone; scores of migrants left their hometowns unable to dance. Among them was Manolia Young, a native of Camden, South Carolina, who migrated to Washington, D.C., in 1939.[15] She had not learned to dance because her parents saw a contradiction between religion and social dancing and because she had little access to popular music: "We did not have a radio in our house when I was growing up. We had a piano which my mother played as we sang religious songs. My Aunt Mary, who lived nearby, had a phonograph. But I don't remember listening to much popular music." Once in Washington, D.C., Young frequented dances at the YWCA, the YMCA, and various USO clubs during the early 1940s. She contends that half of the women and men did not know how to dance. It was not until they reached urban centers like Washington, D.C., that they began to experience nightlife or public social dancing.

Even those who had been born in urban centers were not necessarily dancing dervishes; many of them also experienced a sense of anxiety and awkwardness in the dance arena. Warren Wall, a native Washingtonian, shared his dance history with sociologist E. Franklin Frazier for a study Frazier conducted on black youth in Washington, D.C., and Louisville, Kentucky.[16] Wall, "a tall lithe, well-built, dark brown boy of sixteen," recounted:

> I manage to get to a dance or so a month. I like dances and I like
> to rug-cut. I like the other dances, too, but the average girl can't
> even two-step but they can all clown and be jitterbugs. So I do,
> too. I never go to house-hops; first, because I don't get invitations,
> and second, because I don't like them anyway. My father never says
> anything about these house parties but I don't think he'd like it if
> we went to them.[17]

Frazier noted that Warren also admitted to being "sometimes embarrassed around girls because of his shabby clothes."[18]

Like Manolia Young, the "girls" at Warren's school and in his
neighborhood did not know how to two-step. Although Warren
could two-step and jitterbug, other factors affected his ability to
dance. He did not get invited to dances; he disliked house-hops
because of the drinking and smoking that took place there; and
his "shabby clothes" prohibited him from feeling confident about
his moves on and off the dance floor. For Warren, the dance arena
was a site of anxiety and awkwardness because of accouterments
he was unable to acquire.

How did Warren Wall, Manolia Young, Malcolm Little, and
countless others learn to dance? Little narrates his dance lessons
this way:

> I was up in the jostling crowd idea. My long-suppressed African
> instincts broke through, and loose. Having spent so much time in
> Mason's white environment, I had always believed that dancing in-
> volved a certain order or pattern of specific steps—as dancing is
> done by whites. But here along my own less inhibited people, I
> discovered it was simply letting your feet, hands and body sponta-
> neously act out whatever impulses were stirred by the music.[19]

There is, I have noticed, a curious omission in Malcolm's narrative of transformation. When he recounts how he acquired accouterments of urban cool, he acknowledges the assistance of others,
especially his friend Shorty. Shorty arranged for him to be fitted
for his first zoot suit at a neighborhood clothing store; Shorty
composed the list of ingredients needed for Malcolm's conk, then
administered the hair-straightening process; Shorty got Malcolm
a job as a shoeshine boy at the Roseland State Ballroom. Malcolm

spends considerable time outlining his indebtedness to Shorty, but he noticeably acknowledges no one for teaching him how to dance.

> I can't remember when it actually was that I actually learned how — that is to say, I can't recall the specific night or nights. But dancing was the chief action at those "pad parties," so I've no doubt about how and why my initiation into lindy-hopping came about. With alcohol or marijuana lightening my head, and that wild music wailing away on those portable record players, it didn't take long to loosen up the dancing instincts in my African heritage. All I remember is that during some party, around this time, when nearly everyone but me was up dancing, some girl grabbed me—they would often take the initiative and grab a partner for no girl at those parties would ever dream that anyone couldn't dance—and there I was out on the floor.[20]

Why is it that Malcolm X does not acknowledge anyone's assistance? Is it possible that he went from not knowing how to dance to becoming a jitterbug in one night? I posit that Malcolm's narration of his stepping "out" on the dance floor—signifying his now-complete and successful transformation to an urbanite—had more to do with his views of race and culture during the early 1960s, when his autobiography was written, than with his corporeal reality. Robin D. G. Kelley was among the first scholars to reexamine the prevailing representation of Malcolm X's youth with a critical eye. He argues that "Malcolm tells his story from the vantage point of the Civil Rights movement and a resurgent Pan-Africanism."[21] Although Kelley refers mainly to the purchasable commodities that Malcolm X shunned as "ghetto adornments," his critique can also be applied to Malcolm's retelling of his dance lessons. In refashioning his personal history for the pan-Africanists, Malcolm X did not deride the fascination and preoccupation with dance of his earlier alter ego, Malcolm Little. The innate superiority that blacks had over whites in dancing fit into Malcolm X's ideology of racial difference. However, this assertion of racial superiority in dance skirts the process of acculturation that African Americans underwent in the mid-twentieth century.

Like Malcolm X, historians of social dance also pass over this crucial step of acculturation. The yawning lack of discussion about the process of moving from awkwardness to ballroom accomplishment implies an innate dance ability in African Americans.[22] Thus, an explicit rendering of the actual steps involved in learning to dance is key to a fuller and more complex understanding of the role of dance in community and cultural formation.

We must look elsewhere for clues about how Malcolm Little and others learned to jitterbug, foxtrot, waltz, and two-step. According to Manolia Young, soldiers who did not know how to dance taught each other at camp. Her remembrance, however, stands in contrast to an article in a 1942 issue of the *Washington Post:*

> No dancing lessons are listed among free services to USO guests at the Negro Y.M.C.A. Unlike most of Washington's USO clubs, this busy establishment on Twelfth Street, near T, has never had to teach guests how to jitterbug or do the Lindy Hop. The 300 or so service men who dance here every Saturday night, with as many girls, represent all sections of the country and a wide range of professions and skills, but they have one badge in common: they all know their way around the dance floor.[23]

While the stereotypical tone of the *Post* reportage is obvious, a consideration of the acceptable ways to learn social dancing suggests that Young's contention and the article may not be so antinomic. Soldiers may have been unwilling to take lessons in a public forum. If the soldiers came from rural settings, and had not grown up dancing, they had to devise acceptable ways to learn dance protocol and moves.

Photographs of men at various army camps suggest that males did in fact teach each other to dance and practiced together. In archival images from the Civil Conservation Corps camps, agricultural work camps, and Fort Huachuca, in Arizona, men were captured dancing together, teaching each other moves, and watching each other. Clearly, these camps offered a scarcity of female partners. Still, from photographs that include one or more women among a group of men, it appears that men may have preferred partnering one another as they learned to dance. Historian Robert Jefferson corroborates this. During his extensive interviewing of black soldiers who served in the army during the

"Every Night Is Dance Night in the Big Recreation Tent of the Camp," Farm Security Administration Agricultural Workers' Camp, June 1942 (Photograph by Jonathan Collier; from the collections of the Library of Congress)

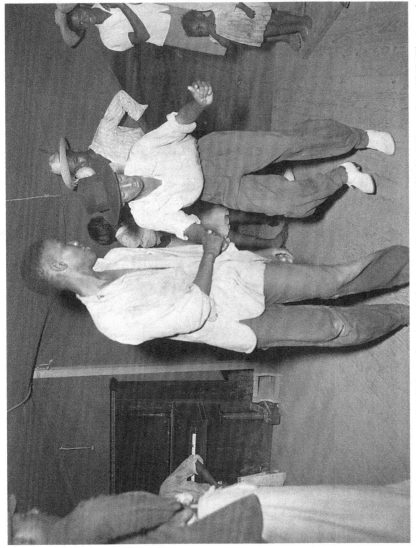

"Dancing in the Recreation Tent," Farm Security Administration Agricultural Workers' Camp, June 1942 (Photograph by Jonathan Collier; from the collections of the Library of Congress)

"Activities of Negroes, Beltsville, MD," Civilian Conservation Corps prints, 1937 (Photograph by Wilfred J. Mend; from the collections of the Library of Congress)

1930s and 1940s, he was repeatedly told that soldiers learned to dance at camp, and that they danced with fellow soldiers.[24] Learning from other men in the homosocial space of the army camps may have smoothed the awkward edges of dance apprenticeship. Learning in the "private" setting of the camp prepared them for the "public" setting of a USO club, a YMCA, a nightclub, or a house party.

The experiences of these men are not very different from those of women and men who learned to dance at an earlier age. As John W. Roberts documents in his interviews with Philadelphians who danced during the 1940s, many African Americans learned to dance at home: "My parents used to literally roll back the carpet and dance for us. I mean they'd show us. All my brothers learned how to dance initially from my father, who was a magnificent dancer, and my mother, who was a wonderful dancer."[25] For these young people and their families, dancing served as an acceptable way of expressing and creating a sense of self. As children danced with each other, parents, aunts, uncles, cousins, and grandparents, their lessons included not only how to dance but how to create a physical and psychic intimacy that was often more difficult in other settings. Same-sex partnering in the home— females dancing with females and males dancing with males— was not only quite common but was also a fundamental part of learning how to dance. These lessons were then displayed or performed in heterosexual, public settings where other dance movements could be observed and later refined in practice at home.[26]

Manolia Young and Malcolm Little were not privy to these private dance lessons during their childhood. Because of this, their feelings of awkwardness were magnified when they stepped into the numerous dance arenas that existed in urban centers. Still, as Warren Wall relates, knowing how to dance did not automatically erase the sense of awkwardness. Anxieties about appearance, gender, and class also surfaced in the dance arena, marking it as a critical space in which African Americans registered points of difference.

DANCE LESSON 3: SILK AND SATIN MEN AND WOMEN—NEGOTIATING COMMUNITY

It is being discussed at the bridge games, at the beauty parlors, at the club meetings, in fact everyone is talking about the season's most sensational affair: The Impersonators' Grand Ball which will be known as "Fairies on Parade."
Washington Afro-American, *1934*

Cultural historian David Nasaw argues that public amusements—moving pictures, amusement parks, and sports stadiums—helped to create a corporate body, or American public, that both transcended class and gender divisions and were the places in which these divisions were formed.[27] Social historians have also tilled some of this ground. Researching the "lives and labors" of the black working classes, they have explored the importance of dance to the formation of communities. Interested in the various tools used by those who had little access to conventional forms of power—wealth, voting, property—scholars search for other "weapons" of power that were used to gain sustenance and ensure prosperity. For these scholars, dance sites are spaces of heterotopia, or "safe spaces," where a black aesthetic is forged and where working-class black people recuperate from the slurs of racist bosses and the disdainful gaze of the middle class. Tera Hunter's work on social dance offers one of the most evocative and original analyses of the place of dance in black social history. Writing about black female domestics in turn-of-the-century Atlanta, she asserts that "controversies over dance during this period reveal the power of dancing as a cultural form and the way it embodied (literally and figuratively) racial, class, and sexual tensions in the urban South." Further, these workers "helped to inscribe social dancing as a distinctive, transgressive cultural form."[28]

How does dance, as a cultural form and embodiment of tensions, play out in the later decades of the twentieth century? In the 1930s and 1940s, there was more of a mixing of classes, genders, geographies, and sexualities within the dance spaces. The discursive and performative embodiments that Hunter elucidates expanded in the mid-twentieth century and took place on and off the dance floor. One of the best examples of this change is the extraordinary popularity of "pansies' balls," which were major social events of this era.[29] Popular in Washington, D.C., Harlem, and other cities throughout the country, these annual galas offered dancing and the spectacle of men dressed up as women in the finest silks and satins in competition for prizes. These affairs offer further evidence that class not was the only, or most prevalent, marker of identity; sexuality and gender also came into play.

The *Afro-American,* one of Washington's major black weeklies, announced the upcoming Impersonators' Grand Ball of 1934.[30] In an article and advertisement, the newspaper informed its readers that the ball would be held at the Masonic Temple, a popular venue for dances located on the infamous "You" Street.[31] Promotion of the ball was located on the same page as the advertisement for the Capital Colored Citizens' Birthday Ball for Franklin Roosevelt, also booked at the Masonic Temple and featuring the same house band, the Blue Birds. In some ways, this juxtaposition "normalized," or flattened out, differences between the two events. One important difference is that the Impersonators' Grand Ball included a larger cross-section of Washington's black population than did the Capital Colored Citizens' Birthday Ball. The Impersonators' Club did not practice the exclusivity that characterized most other black social clubs of the time.

The *Afro-American* article included a photograph of Alden Garrison, a member of the Impersonators' Club and the event coordinator. What made this event the "talk of the town" was its triple offering of dance, spectacle, and competition. Guests who were not interested in dancing "could reserve seats on the lounge," presumably with a clear view of the contestants. These included such notable female impersonators as Babe Williams of Baltimore; Haney Stewart of Philadelphia; and Jacky Jones, Gregory Rand, and Harry Boris of New York, who competed for prizes against Washington's leading drag queens: Kitty May, Sugar Martin, Babe Booker, and George (Lady Isabelle) Lewis.

Unfortunately, only scant information is available about Washington's grandest dance event. We can look to similar galas in Harlem to flesh out the story. According to George Chauncey, the Masquerade and Civic Ball, organized by the Hamilton Lodge No. 710 of the Grand United Order of Fellows, was unofficially known as the "Faggots Ball."[32] This affair, unlike the one in Washington, also had white guests and contestants, as well as lesbian male impersonators. Gay men, however, constituted the vast majority of the dancers.

An article in the *Amsterdam News,* one of New York's most popular weekly newspapers, shared with its readers that "four thousand citizens, numbering some of Harlem's best, elbowed and shoved each other aside and squirmed and stepped on one another's toes and snapped at each other to obtain a better eye-ful."[33] Three years later, in 1937, there were 8,000 guests and participants. The *Amsterdam News* gave extensive coverage to the ball, "regularly publishing photographs or drawings of the winning contestants, interviewing them and describing their costumes, and listing the dozens of society people in attendance." The events in Harlem also brought out a wide cross-section of guests. Chauncey reveals that they included "celebrities, avant-garde writers, society matrons, prostitutes, and whole families who sometimes brought their suppers" to the balls.[34]

As I suggested earlier, these events are an important, but neglected, part of the history of black social dance. They clearly demonstrate that the dance arena was one of the central sites in which tensions around a black public identity could be contested. Tensions around identity were often resolved in these spaces, if only momentarily. For example, black participants in the balls bonded across lines of sexuality and gender to protest the inordinate presence of whites at the balls. Female impersonators and newspaper editors decried the spate of white winners as well as the absence of African American judges in the gay dance arena.

The events surrounding the Impersonators' Grand Ball in Washington reveal how easily the traversing of difference could be fractured. A bold headline on the front page of the *Afro-American* stated, "D.C. Police Halt Pansies' Dance."[35] The accompanying article informed its readers that 1,500 guests had been detained at the door to the Impersonators' Grand Ball as police negotiated with its sponsors. Eventually, the dance continued, as the compromise between police and event organizers allowed impersonators to perform on stage but not to parade in the streets afterward. In other words, the dance arena was an acceptable place to display a range of black identities, but the street was not. This policing of the streets was carried out not only by the compromise between the police and organizers but also by "ruffians" who physically attacked fellow blacks who were refused entry into the Masonic Temple by police. (The use of the term "ruffians" by the *Afro-American* also indicates other boundaries that existed within black communities.) Although the dance did not proceed without controversy, it did enable a confrontation with issues of sexuality, gender, and performance in the public sphere. A mere three years later, female impersonators Billie McAllister and Louis Diggs (known as "Louis the Magnificent") were featured acts in nightclubs located on the same street as the Masonic Temple. According to an article in *Flash!* magazine, "Female impersonators enjoy complete freedom in the capital, and it is not strange to see groups attending night spots together."[36]

CONCLUSION

In this chapter I have ventured to widen our lens as we look back to understand the importance of dance for African Americans. The centrality of dance to our collective identity is undeniable. Yet, our understanding of how that aesthetic import was maneuvered on the dance floor has been less than clear. What lessons can be learned from the 1940s? Throughout this decade, dance served as a galvanizing point of reference for communities and individuals in transition. The dance space housed anxieties about dance ability, tensions within the community over gender and sexuality, and a constantly evolving performance of an urban black identity. The dance space provided a principal site where the numerous processes of urbanization were contested and registered. Dancing and dance spaces existed amid the awkward changes that accompanied these processes—social, economic, technological, geographic—that affected all African Americans in the 1940s. The dance arena, then, did not offer a retreat from this awkwardness, but it was where women and men worked out the complex and difficult moves required to navigate the new and different terrain of urban centers throughout the United States at mid-twentieth century.

NOTES

The research and writing of this chapter was greatly assisted by a fellowship from the National Museum of American History, Smithsonian Institution.

1. "That wartime emergency measure and drag to the entertainment business, the 20 percent amusement tax, may come to an end shortly, probably when

the war period is declared officially at an end. The 5 percent prewar tax may reappear, however. In April 1944, the 5 percent tax was raised to 30 percent in order to raise money for the cost of the war. Congress lowered it to 20 percent in July of that year, on complaint from the entertainment business. Though the advent of such a high tax nearly ruined many amusement enterprises, the public, earning boomtime money evidently felt it could afford to pay and soon became used to it. It's certain no one will complain if it disappears, however." "20% Tax May Go," *Metronome* (October 1945): 13.

2. Interview with Norma Miller, 1992, Smithsonian Institution Jazz Oral History Program, National Museum of American History. (Transcript available at the Smithsonian Institution.) Ernie Smith was the interviewer. Norma Miller, one of the original Savoy dancers, comments that bebop brought an end to jazz dance. Marshall Stearns, coauthor of *Jazz Dance,* also states that "when the swing era faded in the forties, a blackout of about ten years intervened—from 1945 to 1954—with little or no dancing. Big-band devotees—grey-haired in the 1960s—are still arguing about what caused it: the federal tax on dance floors; the new and 'undanceable' kind of jazz (bop); the recording bans of 1942, most of 1943, and again in 1948 which brought hitherto unknown composers and vocalists such as Johnnie Ray into prominence; and the consequent disappearance of ballrooms along with the expensive big bands that played them." Marshall Stearns and Jean Stearns, *Jazz Dance: The Story of American Vernacular Dance* (New York: Macmillan, 1968), 1. "In the beginning, jazz was dancing music. Dance remained integral to the jazz scene until the end of the swing era in the late 1940s." Robert P. Crease, "Divine Frivolity: Hollywood Representations of the Lindy Hop, 1937–1942," in *Representing Jazz,* ed. Krin Gabbard (Durham, N.C.: Duke University Press, 1995), 207.

3. Jacqui Malone, in *Steppin' on the Blues: The Visible Rhythm of African American Dance* (Urbana: University of Illinois Press, 1996), explores the relationship between jazz music and dance. Most studies of the "jazz era" focus on musical expression, neglecting dance as a crucial element in the development of jazz music. Malone corrects this imbalance. According to Malone, tappers were instrumental in the creation of bebop; they were also present at the jam sessions on Fifty-second Street. At the same time that she restores professional dancers to their rightful place in the history of bebop, she dislocates social dancers from it. "To an extent white America did stop dancing. African Americans, however, filled that *public dance void of the forties* by continuing to dance at rent parties, family gatherings, and any other occasion that offered even the slightest opportunity to 'get down'" (italics mine).

4. "Terp Lovers Get Own Ballroom," *Down Beat* (15 November 1945): 11. "New Dancery for Chi South Side," *Down Beat* (27 August 1947): 4. "New Dancery Planned for L.A.'s East Side," *Down Beat* (15 August 1945): 11. "Schooler Starts Morning Dances," *Down Beat* (1 October 1944): 12. "Splinterbugs' Nude Feet Thrill Miami," *Down Beat* (1 April 1940): 6. "Old Time Dancing Hollywood Whim," *Down Beat* (11 March 1946): 12. "Constructs Dancery," *Down Beat* (25 March 1946): 17. "New D.C. Dance Hall Opened," *Down Beat* (29 December 1947): 17. "D.C. Opens New Ellington

Nitery," *Down Beat* (29 December 1949): 16. "Cleveland Dancery Reopens after Year," *Down Beat* (15 July 1949): 3.

5. Scott DeVeaux, *The Birth of Bebop* (Berkeley: University of California Press, 1997), 348.

6. Dave Hepburn with Nard Griffin, "Bebop: Music or Madness," *Our World: A Picture Magazine for the Whole Family* (January 1949): 30–35. *Our World,* founded by John P. Davis in New York, began publication in April 1946, less than a year after John H. Johnson launched *Ebony* in November 1945. I am grateful to Eric Porter for the *Our World* citation. See Eric Porter, " 'Out of the Blue': Black Creative Musicians and the Challenge of Jazz, 1940–1955" (Ph.D. dissertation, University of Michigan, 1997), for a discussion of bebop's popularity in the late 1940s.

7. Dave Hepburn with Nard Griffin, "Bebop," 30–35.

8. Ira Gitler, *Swing to Bop: An Oral History of the Transition in Jazz in the 1940s* (New York: Oxford University Press, 1985), 4–5.

9. David W. Stowe, *Swing Changes: Big-Band Jazz in New Deal America* (Cambridge, Mass.: Harvard University Press, 1994), 22.

10. William S. Dutton, "We've Got Rhythm," *American Magazine* 119 (March 1935): 52–53, 126–28.

11. Stowe, *Swing Changes,* 112–20. For a discussion of the gender dynamics of listening to phonographs, see Keir Keightley, " 'Turn It Down!' She Shrieked: Gender, Domestic Space, and High Fidelity, 1948–1959," *Popular Music* 15, no. 2 (1996): 149–77.

12. The regional differences in performance were often great. For example, Washingtonians did not begin to Lindy until 1937: "D.C. has accepted swing music and the folks are fast developing the swing dance . . . oldsters as well as youngsters are gradually mastering the swinging steps in this newest dance called the Savoy, Lindy, Wampus or what-have-you. . . . 'Rugcutter' is the name they give these dance devotees, and their whirling capers will leave you dizzy" (*Flash!* [10 April 1937]: 12).

13. "Darwin & the Mambo," *Time* (6 September 1954): 34.

14. "Uncle Sambo, Mad for Mambo," *Life* 37, no. 25 (20 December 1954): 17–19. According to the article, "King of the mambo is its inventor, Perez Prado. Composer of scores of mambos, Prado created dance in 1943 in his native Cuba, made Mexico wildly mambo-minded and has been highly successful in U.S. tours."

15. Interview with Manolia Young, March 1995. Transcript in possession of author.

16. E. Franklin Frazier, *Negro Youth at the Crossways: Their Personality Development in the Middle States,* prepared for the American Youth Commission (Washington, D.C.: American Council on Education, 1940).

17. Frazier, *Negro Youth,* 220–21.

18. Ibid. Businesses and entrepreneurs recognized the importance of dress to dancers and party-goers and began to market "jitterbug pants." Newspaper advertisements for stores like Lew's Pants Stores, Inc., located at 211 West 125th Street in Harlem, featured pants and hats. The "jitterbug pants" were available

in eighteen different styles for boys and men. Girls and women could purchase "ladies' models" of the men's drapes for an extra $1.25. *Afro-American*, 29 January 1944, 19.

19. Malcolm X with the assistance of Alex Haley, *Autobiography of Malcolm X* (New York: Ballantine Books, 1965), 62.

20. Ibid., 59–60.

21. Robin D. G. Kelley, "The Riddle of the Zoot: Malcolm Little and Black Cultural Politics During World War II," in *Malcolm X: In Our Image*, ed. Joe Wood (New York: St. Martin's Press, 1992), 156–57.

22. Katrina Hazzard-Gordon offers an exception to this practice in her study of social dance formations, *Jookin': The Rise of Social Dance Formations in African-American Culture* (Philadelphia: Temple University Press, 1990).

23. Louise Proctor Engle, "Capital's USO Clubs Offer Varied Program," *Washington Post*, 4 October 1942, n.p.

24. Telephone conversation 26 February 1996 with Robert Jefferson, author of "Making the Men of the 93rd: African-American Servicemen in the Years of the Great Depression and the Second World War, 1935–1947" (Ph.D. dissertation, University of Michigan, 1995).

25. John W. Roberts, *From Hucklebuck to Hip-Hop: Social Dance in the African American Community in Philadelphia* (Philadelphia: ODUNDE, Inc., 1995), 25.

26. This symbiotic relationship between the "public" and the "private" should propel us to reevaluate the notion of distinct private and public spheres. The common historiographical assertion that the 1940s was a more "public" decade and that the 1950s represented a retreat into the home needs to be reexamined.

27. David Nasaw, *Going Out: The Rise and Fall of Public Amusements* (New York: Basic Books, 1993). Nasaw was referring to a white American public. See my study, "Claiming the City: Blacks and Leisure in Washington, D.C., 1927–1957" (Ph.D. dissertation, University of Michigan, 1999), in which I chronicle the development of a black American public created through participation in leisure.

28. Tera W. Hunter, *To 'Joy My Freedom: Southern Black Women's Lives after the Civil War* (Cambridge, Mass.: Harvard University Press, 1997), 170–71, 183.

29. Shane White and Graham White, in *Stylin': African American Expressive Culture from Its Beginnings to the Zoot Suit* (Ithaca: Cornell University Press, 1998), argue that these pansies' balls were modeled after beauty contests that were also popular during this period. Part satire, the coordinators and participants sought to emulate and mimic the pretensions inherent in the display of female bodies at these beauty contests.

30. *Afro-American*, 27 January 1934, 4. Newspapers were another critical arena for the creation of a national black identity. The reading of newspapers helped to create a national community of geographically dispersed peoples.

31. "Washington's You Street," *Newspic* (April 1946): 5.

32. George Chauncey, *Gay New York: Gender, Urban Culture, and the Making of the Gay Male World, 1890–1940* (New York: Basic Books, 1994), 257–67.

33. Chauncey, *Gay New York,* 258.

34. Ibid.

35. "D.C. Police Halt Pansies' Dance," *Afro-American,* 10 February 1934, 1–2.

36. "Billie McAllister," *Flash!* (13 December 1937). Published in Washington, D.C., from 1937 to 1939, *Flash!* was one of the first news-picture magazines, predating *Ebony, Jet,* and *Our World.*

4

(Up)Staging the Primitive: Pearl Primus and "the Negro Problem" in American Dance

Richard C. Green

> I say the Negro is not our salvation because with all my feelings for what he instinctively offers, for his desirable indifference to our set of conventions about emotional decency, I am on the side of civilization.
>
> *Gilbert Seldes,* The Seven Lively Arts

In writing about the dancer/choreographer Pearl Primus and the role of the Negro in American concert dance, I seek to go beyond the notion that art merely "mirrors" reality and to explore some of the ways in which it possibly functions to realize racial identities and political constituencies.[1] What, I ask, could a dancing body like Primus's do to resolve an American racial dilemma? Moreover, how do revisionist historical and reconstruction projects recuperate this dancer and her work in order to identify a black tradition in American dance? In 1944, Gunnar Myrdal wrote that "the American Negro problem is a problem at the heart of the American."[2] His observation touches the "heart" of my investigation—the intersections of body politics and political bodies.

From the beginning of her career during World War II, Pearl Primus dealt explicitly with political issues in her dances. For her first professional appearance at the Ninety-second Street YM-YWHA on 14 February 1943, she presented four solos: *African Ceremonial, Hard Time Blues, Strange Fruit,* and *Rock Daniel.* For this critically acclaimed debut, Primus thematically focused on such issues as cultural heritage (*African Ceremonial*), racial prejudice and violence (*Strange Fruit*), and economic systems of op-

Pearl Primus with dancer Joe Nash and drummer Alphonse Cimber, *Dance of Strength,*
ca. 1946 (Photographer unknown; Photographs and Prints Division, Schomburg Center for Research in Black Culture, the New York Public Library–Astor, Lenox and Tilden
Foundations; reproduced with permission)

pression (*Hard Time Blues*). Two of the solos, *Strange Fruit* and
Hard Time Blues, can be situated historically within the American social-protest dance tradition that began in the 1930s.[3] However, by 1943, the year of Primus's debut, many white dancers had
moved on to other artistic and political concerns, while the Negro

dancer was still protesting against the occurrence of lynchings and other forms of physical violence. In 1943, for example, Negroes faced hostile white mobs in places like Beaumont, Texas, where on 16 June two Negroes were killed; Detroit, Michigan, where on 20 June thirty-four Negroes were killed and federal troops were called out; and Harlem, New York, where the clashes lasted for two days, from 1 August through 2 August, although no one was killed.

Gordon Heath, who narrated Primus's concert, remembered the Detroit riots and their effect on the city, its citizens, and the company: "Most memorable was our concert engagement in Detroit the day after a devastating race riot raged through the city. Tension was in the air like smoke but there was [*sic*] no incidents. We flew back to New York the next day—safe, but shaken."[4]

To placate the restless masses, the U.S. government encouraged artistic productions that portrayed the Negro favorably. Twentieth Century-Fox's film version of the musical *Stormy Weather* (1943), which featured Katherine Dunham and her company, Bill Robinson, the Nicholas Brothers, and the Lester Horton dancers, was one example of this cinematic effort to ameliorate "stormy" race relations. The fight against tyranny and oppression abroad during this period called attention to the blatantly racial discriminatory practices that Negroes encountered at home. The violence and atrocities of the Fascists and the Nazis, justified by ideologies of racial supremacy, struck a resonant chord for the Negro living in a nation that did not practice the democratic ideals it preached; in effect, the menace of Hitler and Aryanism "over there" bore a striking resemblance to the menace of white mob violence and Jim Crow laws and practices in America. Primus, attentive to the political issues of the wartime period, cleverly linked the concerns of race and democracy: "In America's bosom we have the roots of democracy, but the roots don't mean there are leaves. The tree could easily grow bare. We will never relax our war efforts abroad, but we must fight at home with equal fierceness. This is an all out war; we will not stop fighting until everyone is free from inequality."[5]

Primus developed her skill in political rhetoric and dance technique at the New Dance Group's school in New York City. As a scholarship student, Primus was greatly influenced in her formative years by its politicized approach to making art for "the people." Founded in 1932 as part of the Worker's Dance League, the New Dance Group was committed to working for change in factories (sometimes involving workers as performers as well as spectators) and on the streets. Members of the Group performed dance and movement sketches at demonstrations and rallies in an attempt to increase the political awareness of its preferred public—the workers. Their slogan, The Dance Is a Weapon in the Class Struggle, characterized their explicit concern in using dance as a tool for social reform. Judith Delman, writing in the *Dance Observer,* described the Group's goals as striving "to bring the dance to the working people and make it a medium of expression of their needs. . . . It was created as a fighting force for a better world."[6]

As a Negro youth living in New York of the 1930s, Primus's artistic craft and vision were also undoubtedly shaped and influenced by the legacy of the Negro or Harlem Renaissance. During the 1920s, such self-defined "New Negro" artists and intellectuals as Alain Locke, Langston Hughes, and W. E. B. Du Bois directed their energy to using art as a means of articulating a socio-historical identity and advancing the race. Locke, editor of the immensely influential *The New Negro Anthology* (1925), wrote about the "promise" of "recent art" by the Negro in America:

> The social promise of our recent art is as great as the artistic. It has brought with it, first of all, that wholesome, welcome virtue of finding beauty in oneself: the younger generation can no longer be twitted as "cultural nondescripts" or accused of "being out of love with their own nativity." They can have instinctive love and pride of race, and, spiritually compensating for the present lacks of America, ardent respect and love for Africa the motherland.[7]

Locke emphasizes the social and aesthetic function of art in the same breath: By expressing himself in the arts, the Negro could gain recognition (by whites and other Negroes as well) as a person with not only physical and expressive capabilities, but creative and intellectual ones as well. "The newer motive, then, in being racial," wrote Locke, "is to be so purely for the sake of art. Nowhere is this more apparent, or more justified than in the increasing tendency to evolve from the racial substances something technically distinctive, something that as an idiom of style may become a contribution to the general resources of art."[8]

Langston Hughes, like Du Bois, forcefully proclaims the "coming of age" of a New American Negro and the pivotal role that race would play in his struggle for social acceptance and political rights. In his 1926 landmark essay, "The Negro Artist and the Racial Mountain," Hughes observed that: "The vogue in things Negro, although it may do as much harm as good for the colored artist, has at least done this: It has brought him forcibly to the attention of his own people among whom for so long, unless the other race has noticed him beforehand, he was a prophet with little honor."[9]

Apart from Locke and Hughes, other figures in the political arena were attempting to solve the Negro's problems in American society. Marcus Garvey, Adam Clayton Powell, the Communist Party, and the Harlem Labor Party were among those striving to direct the anger, energy, and frustration of the Negro people during the period in which Primus was attending Hunter College High School in the 1930s. Better known for his "back to Africa" movement, Marcus Garvey spoke of raising the consciousness of Negroes through the Universal Negro Improvement Association, whose mission was to "arouse the sleeping conscience of Negroes everywhere to the point where we will, as one concerted body, act for our own preservation. By laying the foundation for such we will be able to work towards the glorious realization of an emancipated race and a constructed nation."[10]

Whereas Garvey often advocated a literal return to Africa to solve the Negro's problems with America, Pearl Primus returned there symbolically through her dances. Primus strongly believed, and attempted to demonstrate through dance, that despite the "middle passage" from Africa to Americas, the Negro in America had retained some of his African culture in movement (in addition to specific American Negro syncretic cultural formations).

Through this connection with Africa, she could claim that American Negroes do indeed possess a rich cultural heritage, even though dance critics like John Martin would write: "As for dance tradition, the American Negro as such has virtually none . . . and lived in cultural isolation."[11] Walter Terry, in a 1940 review entitled "The Negro Dances," wrote: "But while Africa possessed a rich store of native dances and ceremonies, the Africans in America were not content to perform the dances of their remote ancestors nor did they have a dance which was both Negro and American at the same time."[12]

Given the wealth of research and information now available on the subject of African cultural retentions, syncretisms, and creolization, these statements on the Negro's culture-less plight (and the attitudes they reflect) are quite revealing. In this context they seem to "expose" themselves as complicitous with other agendas and concerns that are often veiled — as behind an aesthetic curtain. It is against this perception of the American Negro as lacking in a dance tradition, espoused in this instance by two major American dance critics, that Primus's dances and career must be evaluated.[13]

BIRTH OF A NEGRO DANCER

Pearl Primus came, like many other "Americans" at the beginning of the twentieth century, to the shores of this country from elsewhere.[14] Born in Woodstock, Port of Spain, Trinidad, in 1919, Primus's maternal grandfather was Ashanti, and her mother, according to Margaret Lloyd's interview with Primus, "was such a beautiful social dancer that she was called the Queen. Her grandfather was one of the great voodoo drummers, so popular he was given the name 'Lassido,' a term of endearment."[15]

Primus's family moved to New York in 1921 when she was two years old. She lived on 69th Street and Broadway, in the building where her father was superintendent, and attended Public Schools 94 and 136 and Hunter College High School. Even while majoring in biology and pre-medicine at Hunter College, Primus found time to participate in sports and athletic events. But "when Pearl left Hunter," writes Lloyd, "where no issue was made of color, she was shocked at the racial prejudice that confronted her."[16] After graduating from Hunter College, she briefly attended New York University, planning to specialize in psychiatry. Dissatisfied because she found herself "too involved with the cases, too sympathetic," Primus decided to transfer to Columbia University for graduate work in anthropology.[17]

Primus had her first taste of theatrical performance in 1941 with a National Youth Administration group. After searching everywhere for work, she finally secured a job in the wardrobe department for the National Youth Administration. When one dancer decided to marry, Primus was summoned from her corner sewing costumes to replace her. Primus and her partner, Joe Nash, were placed in the rear because Primus had no formal dance training. Nevertheless, she caught people's attention in the social dance part of the program, "America Dances," and found herself featured in subsequent performances.

Later that year, after a successful work-scholarship audition, Primus began her studies at the New Dance Group's school.[18] Judith Delman, writing for the *Dance Observer*, singled out Primus (the only Negro student there at the time):

> The school maintained by the New Dance Group is not just another dance school and those of us who work with it intend that it shall never resolve itself merely to that. It was created as a fighting force for a better world. If it were limited to giving classes and lost its broader concepts, it would soon lose its cohesiveness and its very reason for being. It exists today as a place where people from all walks of life may come for whatever type of dancing appeals to them and for whatever reason; where talented young people may study regardless of their means; where new talent is sought, developed, encouraged through constructive criticism and opportunities to dance. *Pearl Primus is an outstanding example of the result of this type of activity.*[19]

At the New Dance Group she studied with such instructors as Sophie Maslow, Jane Dudley, Eve Gentry, and Mary McBurnie/La Belle Rosette; she also had the opportunity to develop her skills as a choreographer. McBurnie/La Belle Rosette, like Primus, came from Trinidad and joined the New Dance Group faculty when she moved to New York in 1938. Studying at the New

Dance Group often led to public recitals, and Primus performed in McBurnie's program *Antilliana* for a YMHA Coffee Concert program on 12 April 1942.[20]

Encouraged by her instructors, Primus decided to audition for the Ninety-second Street YM-YWHA showcase with her first two solos, *African Ceremonial* and *Hear de Lans a-Crying*. Jane Dudley, a well-known dancer/choreographer and teacher at the school, invited Primus home to fit her into a costume for her audition. Primus was delighted to receive this gift from someone she respected. In this way the school served as a creative space and supportive environment for Primus to develop as a dance artist, particularly since her family initially disapproved of her decision to pursue dance. Asked to leave the house, Primus secretly slept for a time at the school, her "artistic" home.[21]

Primus made her professional debut on the "Five Dancers" program (14 February 1943) with Nona Schurman, Iris Mabry, Julia Levien, and Gertrude Prokosch. After this successful engagement, she was able to get a job at the racially integrated Café Society Downtown in April 1943 by presenting favorable newspaper reviews by critics such as John Martin to the manager, Barney Josephson. Thus, Primus secured her reputation as a legitimate concert dancer on the same small stage where Billie Holliday debuted her famous version of Lewis Allan's poem about lynching titled "Strange Fruit."[22] By August of the same year, John Martin had bestowed his *New York Times* dance laurel award on Pearl Primus for "most distinguished newcomer of the season":

> At the moment she is dancing nightly at the Café Society Downtown, where the space at her disposal extends no farther in any direction than the reach of her arms, but when she appeared not so long ago at the great Negro Testimonial performance at the Madison Square Garden she filled that huge place with vital movement, much of it way up in the air, and drew spontaneously excited applause from the assembled crowd, most of whom had never so much as heard of her before.[23]

Martin went on to commend Primus as "the most gifted artist of her race (she is Negro) to appear in the field."[24] The "Negro Testimonial" program at Madison Square Garden, where Primus made such an impression on Martin and the audience, was the First Negro Freedom "For This We Fight" Rally organized by Harlem Congressman Adam Clayton Powell. The following year Primus returned to perform at the second rally organized by the Negro Labor Victory Committee on 26 June 1944.[25]

Edwin Denby, another influential dance critic, provided his readers with a description of Primus's talents that almost rivaled Martin's in enthusiasm:

> Another concert dancer, a discovery of last season, Miss Pearl Primus, is appearing at Café Society Downtown. She does serious dances, including some Josh White "blues" accompanied by Josh White in person; but her serious style is not inappropriate to this slightly earnest club. She is an unusual dancer and deserves her quick celebrity. *All her movement has a native Negro quality* — an unction and a spring — that is a great pleasure to watch. In schooling she is a straight "modern"; but the personal simplicity of her dances and her clear sense of drama and climax make her numbers easy for an audience to follow. For her best effect, she needs a great deal more room than she has on the floor of Café Society, but she couldn't find a more attentive nightclub public.[26]

Such high praise from major New York dance critics of the day gave Primus's artistic career a very strong start. Her almost immediate success almost certainly owed a great deal to the power of the press and critics like Martin and Denby, whose opinions helped establish unknown dancers.

During this period at the Café Society Downtown (which lasted approximately ten months), Primus appeared as a guest soloist on the "African Dance Festival" program held at Carnegie Hall, 13 December 1943. Asadata Dafora organized the event as the first arts project of the African Academy of Arts and Research. The Academy's purpose was to "foster goodwill between the United States and Africa through a mutual exchange of cultural, social and economic knowledge."[27] Two guests of honor, Eleanor Roosevelt and Mary McLeod Bethune, spoke during the intermission in support of the Academy and its artistic project.

Critic George W. Beiswanger wrote a review of the concert for the *Dance Observer* that compared the work of Dafora and Primus.

"In her two solo numbers, Pearl Primus, as was to be expected, completely took over the stage. The reviewer got a kick out of the fact that a genuine modern dancer, *the least 'racial' (whatever that means) in her style and range of abilities,* gave the audience what many of them would call its most 'Negro' numbers."[28]

Despite her "genuine" modern training, "race" still clings to Primus in performance; to the reviewer's delight, she just cannot escape from giving the audience numbers that are more Negro than those presented by an African. Beiswanger was referring not only to the themes of Primus's dances but also to "racial" characteristics and how they supposedly affect dance style and ability. Thus, the emphasis on race in relation to dance themes and styles haunted Primus's career from almost the beginning.

The critical reception of a concert she gave on 23 January 1944 reveals racialized expectations at work. Primus and Valerie Bettis, a white modern dancer, presented solo dances at the Ninety-second Street YM-YWHA. Denby, commenting favorably on Primus's technique and skill, wrote: "Miss Primus' subjects were African, Haitian, and North American, several of the last quite naturally concerned with race oppression. What she intends her gesture to mean is always completely clear. But her sense of movement is so powerful that besides telling a story, her dance has constantly the direct force of dancing. . . . In several numbers she attains a *fine Negro grandeur.*"[29]

While Bettis is acknowledged in Denby's review as a modern dance artist with no mention of her whiteness, Primus slips uncomfortably between the categories of Negro and modern dancer.[30] Denby's assumption that Primus's dances would "naturally" involve "race oppression" suggests how commonplace this topic had become. Because Primus occupies the position of a "real" Negro and not that of a white modern dancer, her dances about the Negro problems resonate in a specific racialized manner during the 1940s, if not today. The provocative phrase "fine Negro grandeur" suggests that the Negro's potential for artistic success was always delimited by the critic's racialized expectations, however complimentary those expectations might be. The clarity of gesture to which Denby refers springs from both

Primus's "sense of movement" and her "fine Negro grandeur" because he interprets the story she tells in movement as belonging to her in a way that differs for a white dancer like Bettis or Helen Tamiris.

I mention Tamiris, who specialized in the early part of her career in dances based on Negro spirituals, to emphasize some of the ways in which the act of speaking or standing in for "the people" (representing by re-presenting the Negro's problems, in the case of Tamiris) is complicated by notions of racial identification and authenticity. In 1928 Tamiris presented her first solo concert, which was entitled "Negro Spirituals." Throughout her career in the 1930s and 1940s, she staged dances for and about Negroes that were enthusiastically received by critics and audiences alike. Like Tamiris, Primus also presented "dance spirituals" in the 1940s. Did Primus, for some critics at least, doubly represent "the people" because of the nature of her material (e.g., Negro spirituals) and because she was an authentic Negro, as opposed to a white dancer imitating or interpreting a Negro character?[31]

After concert engagements that included performances at the Ninety-second Street YM-YWHA in April and at Hunter College in June 1944 with Randolph Scott (another well-known Negro dancer), Primus decided to spend the summer in the South. Visiting rural Negro communities in such states as Alabama, Georgia, and South Carolina was an eye-opening experience for Primus, the budding anthropologist and social-protest dancer. She was particularly interested in African cultural retentions in the music and movement she found in churches and fields.[32]

After her summer in the South, Primus finally made her Broadway debut on 4 October 1944. Her program at the Belasco Theater included her well-known solos, *The Negro Speaks of Rivers, Strange Fruit, Hard Time Blues,* and *African Ceremonial,* as well as new works. She was accompanied by four male dancers—James Alexander, Thomas Bell, Joe Comadore, and Alexander Popwell. In addition to the dancers, Primus's show included a narrator, the African percussionist Norman Coker, the Haitian drummer

Pearl Primus in *African Ceremonial,* ca. 1943 (Photographer unknown; Photographs and Prints Division, Schomburg Center for Research in Black Culture, the New York Public Library–Astor, Lenox and Tilden Foundations; reproduced with permission)

Alphonse Cimber, Frankie Newton and his fourteen-piece band, two pianists, and two singers. Yet the show was not a great success and did not receive the favorable reviews of her solo debut. Denby commented that, "Of the serious numbers, 'African Ceremonial' and 'Hard Time Blues' are thrilling dancing. But the other serious ones fail of complete effect because the audience agrees beforehand with the protest they make."[33]

Several months earlier, Denby had praised her dances of social protest at a solo recital. He wrote that Primus "seemed to rely less on the moral sanctions of her themes to awaken sympathy and interest, and more on the buoyant drive of her dance," which was a better tactic because "in the theater, whatever the theme, it is not the theme, it is the actual dancing that really wins the audience's faith."[34] Had the audience (or maybe just this one critic) grown weary of the issues that Primus addressed, thus lessening the impact of her social-protest dances? Or were the Broadway dances just poorly choreographed and/or performed? For Denby, it was not the "theme" but the "actual dancing" that made a social-protest dance a success.

Primus tried again in December of 1944; invited to appear at the Roxy Theatre, she staged a group version (fourteen dancers) of her first solo, *African Ceremonial*. Gordon Heath, who narrated her segment of the show, convinced Primus to commission a soundtrack by Owen Dodson.[35] Primus later decided, to Dodson's dismay, to edit the poetry from her show.[36] In his memoirs, Heath provided a humorous and detailed account of his experiences with Primus on the Roxy stage:

> Pearl and company were invited to appear at the Roxy Theatre in that period when the ornate movie palaces featured vaudeville acts between the showings of the film. Bernhardt and Pavlova, for instance, have gone this route. Our two-week engagement was shared with a tramp comic named Jimmy Savo, well-known to cabaret and musical-comedy goers. He sang "River Stay Away From My Door," frantically trying to push the river back by main force, pleading as if catastrophe would overwhelm him. Which was pretty much the way recording and radio star, Mildred Bailey, the other headliner in the show, sang the blues—so full of "soul" that a large part of her public thought she was black.[37]

Heath's wonderful description of the performance situation encountered by many "serious" concert dancers in the 1940s deserves to be quoted at length because it is all too easy, now that American concert dance has obtained high-art states, to forget its many connections to vaudeville. Heath's recollections also provide valuable insight on the codes of behavior and relationships between Negro and white performers occupying the same theatrical space.

> I wrote and spoke—backstage on the house's microphone—an introduction to our spectacle, beginning, "The dance you are about to witness is really a prayer. . . ." Pearl demurred, wanting to be exact, ethnic, and educative, but the management agreed the ethnology should be played down and the drama played up. They also wanted someone to sing the pop song to accompany the chorus line's number that opened the vaudeville portion of the program. I auditioned and was chosen (over my erstwhile friend George Fisher) to croon "There Goes That Song Again" at the selfsame micro—out of sight again, but amused by the incongruity of the whole bit: Pearl's ballet, drums, African costumes, that cultured introduction, the spangled "Roxyettes" like trained horses at the circus and that pop song—"we fell in love while the organ played, over and over and over and over again"—three times a day for two weeks. The film was "Something for the Boys" with Carmen Miranda, garnished with fruit and cha-cha-cha. The audience applauded everything vigorously but they came primarily for Carmen. The two weeks went smoothly enough. *The management asked the half-clad, black dancers and drummers to avoid proximity to the half-clad, white chorus girls but they knew without being asked.*[38]

In January 1945 Primus appeared at New York Times Hall with the dancer Hadassah (also affiliated with the New Dance Group) and the singer-dancer Josephine Premice in a concert entitled *India–Haiti–Africa*. Denby wrote:

> Authentic neither Hadassah nor Miss Primus really intend to be; but authenticity is the basis of Miss Premice's Haitian songs. Her charming delivery, mixed with dance steps, may have been suggested by Belle Rosette, the Trinidad dancer with whom I believe Miss Premice appeared here, at Louise Crane's brilliant Coffee Concerts some seasons back. (Miss Primus and also Miss Ellis, now a star with Katherine Dunham, were, I think, on Miss Rosette's program, too.) Dance lovers will recall Miss Premice as the charming leading dancer in Dafora's African program last year at Carnegie Hall.[39]

Primus was responsible for the third part of the concert— Africa. Denby praises Premice and the fact that her work is grounded in "authenticity." In spite of the fact that Primus was a Negro from Trinidad and her grandfather was Ashanti, her African dances could never claim authenticity because she was not born in Africa. Yet Primus had obviously garnered respect as well as success, because one month later she shared a concert with her former teacher, Charles Weidman, at the Central High School of Needle Trades.

In the fall of 1945, World War II came to an end; less than a year later, the House Un-American Activities Committee began investigating the activities of alleged Communist sympathizers. Like other artists and writers who had shown some interest in social issues before and during the war, Primus was called before the committee. As a result, her passport was revoked, and she "later was stoned, spat upon and called a 'Red' outside a theater in Harrisburg, Virginia, where she performed."[40]

In the fall of 1946, Ruth Page invited Primus to appear in the Chicago Opera's production of *The Emperor Jones,* starring Lawrence Tibbett. Eugene O' Neill's 1920 play, the basis for the opera, had already been adapted for film by DuBose Heyward and produced in 1933, with Paul Robeson in the title role. O'Neill's play recounts the story of a young Negro who leaves his small church-centered community for employment in the big city. Convicted of killing a man, Jones is imprisoned. He escapes to an island (an unnamed Caribbean site, perhaps Haiti), where he deposes the previous white rulers and sets himself up as "Emperor." The play, which may be read as a cautionary tale against the Negro's acquisition of political power, depicts the inevitable downfall of the Emperor as a result of his vulnerability to primitive island voodoo magic. Primus danced the role of the Witch Doctor, a role originally performed by Hemsley Winfield when the opera premiered at the Metropolitan Opera in 1933. Winfield, who founded the New Negro Art Theater Dance Company in 1931, also staged the dances for what was the first appearance by a Negro on the Metropolitan Opera stage.

Primus continued to tour in 1946–47; she also choreographed and appeared in the musical *Calypso* (later renamed *Caribbean*

Carnival) with a cast that included Claude Marchant and Josephine Premice. Her ballets for this venture on the musical stage were not well received, and the musical had a short run of eleven performances on Broadway. Still, in 1947 she received the New York Newspaper Guild's "Page One Award" for her "faithful and always pleasing interpretations of African culture through the medium of dance."

In April 1948, while appearing at Fisk University in Nashville, Tennessee, as part of a national tour, Primus was offered a grant to study in Africa for approximately nine months by Dr. Edwin Embree, the president of the Julius Rosenwald Foundation.[41]

> The Rosenwald Fellowship Committee gave her $4,000—its last and largest grant. Soon she was on her way to Africa, armed with anthropological field method and a gun. "A small knife for cutting vines, I soon discovered, was more useful than a gun, and the most infallible field method was to approach the natives with honesty and love." On her first trip she covered the Gold Coast, Angola, Cameroons, Liberia, Senegal and the Belgian Congo.[42]

In Nigeria, H. E. Sir Adesou Aderemi II, the spiritual head of the Yoruba people, renamed Primus "Omowale," meaning "child returned home."[43] While in Africa, Primus was often recognized by her movement style as kin, as belonging to that continent. This experience of mutual recognition reaffirmed Primus's belief that African Americans had retained some part of their African heritage, in spite of the traumatic cultural shock of bodies moving along the middle passage into slavery in the Americas.

After her "homecoming," Primus's artistic career changed course. The "real" Africa of the late 1940s that Primus encountered consisted of a varied array of nation-states attempting to articulate, in an early phase of postcolonial struggles, a "modern" cultural identity. Primus, in her essay "Out of Africa," briefly outlined her understanding of the role of dance in African society and the impact of "European life" on traditional cultural values and artistic practices:

> The African danced about everything. . . . Today his struggle is not so much in the understanding of thunder, floods, or fighting

against wild animals, or preparing young people for their passage into the adult life of the tribe. He is vitally concerned with understanding this new European life which is gradually displacing his own. He feels sharply the conflict between the new religion and his own out of which his art forms had developed.[44]

Primus set about restaging the dances and ceremonies she had seen, performed, and notated for American audiences. She often chose the lecture–demonstration format to better explicate the philosophical ideas and religious beliefs underlying the African dances and ceremonies. Performing in museums as well as theaters, Primus created new works based on her field experience, such as *Fanga* (1949), *Yoruba People* (1950), *The Initiation* (1950), *Benin Women's War Dance* (1950), *Fanti Dance of Fishermen* (1950), and *Egbo Escapade* (1950). After her first fieldwork experience abroad (in light of her previous experiences conducting research in Southern rural communities in the United States), Primus assumed a larger ambassadorial task of preserving, performing, and promoting an understanding of African dances and cultures. She believed that "the spirit which was responsible for the dynamic dance and the exciting forms of yesterday is merely underground. . . . sometimes it will spring forth in a seemingly new form. This time, let us hope, the world will open its arms to welcome it and will place it without reservation where it belongs with the greatest."[45]

After 1948, Primus created very few dances in the social-protest or spiritual genres. Having seen with her own eyes people and places she had only heard or read about, Primus's desire for authenticity increased. Her decision to focus on the ethnographic staging of African dances raises questions about her position as an American Negro, anthropologist, and modern dancer in rescuing and promoting African dance. In a letter to John Martin from Africa, Primus wrote: "I am fortunate to be able to salvage the still existent gems of dance before they, too, fade into general decadence. In many places I have started movements to make the dance again important. Ancient costumes were dragged out, old men and women—toothless but beautiful with age—came forth to show me the dances which will die with them."[46]

Primus dissolved her troupe in 1951 in order to study and perform as a soloist. In the summer of 1953 she returned to Trinidad, her birthplace, where she enjoyed a reunion with Mary McBurnie, one of her New Dance Group teachers, and met her future husband, the dancer Percival Borde. Having traveled full circle from Trinidad to the United States, then to Africa, and home again to Trinidad, Primus emigrated once more, from the familiar terrain of modern dance to the world of ethnic and folk dance. Her literal and symbolic return to Africa as the source of her dance work had a profound effect, and she devoted the remainder of her career to celebrating the beauty of African dances as a choreographer, dancer, anthropologist, and teacher.

THE NEGRO SPEAKS OF RIVERS

But there is no good in trying to separate her from race and no reason for it. As an artist ambassador for her race she has something no white dancer can give. Something that is immensely important for her to give. She is intensely Negro. Her skin gleams dark against the silver bracelets and dangling earrings she loves to wear. Her hair is a bush of black which she delights in tying up in rutilant kerchiefs. Her big brown eyes, with their expanse of whites, look out from jungle distances. Her person recalls the far remote land of her ancestry. Her voice bespeaks the composed, college-bred American girl of today.
Margaret Lloyd, The Borzoi Book of Modern Dance

What I find most interesting about Margaret Lloyd's description of Primus is the way in which she perceived Primus's body as a sign for something Other, something primitive from a "far remote land."[47] No doubt well-meaning and complimentary in intent, Lloyd's focus on body parts and race reveal to what extent stereotypical depictions of the Negro had permeated into the social and individual unconscious. How else could one account for the perception of her eyes as looking "out from jungle distances"? Certain attitudes, expressed in reviews and writings about Primus, illuminate how racial ideologies, artistic theories, and bodily practices intersect. Lloyd, like other writers, placed Primus in an awkward and ambivalent position: while her body recalls Africa, her voice bespeaks her college education and her American-ness.[48]

To the extent that Primus appeared "African"—meaning Negroid—in her facial and body characteristics, she did not conform to a theatrical convention that privileged first and foremost white women and then mulattos.[49] Primus could never hope to pass for white or, like Katherine Dunham, a stage and Hollywood film star, ascend to Creole/mulatto status. Not unlike the body of land called Africa in Joseph Conrad's *Heart of Darkness,* Primus's body represented an(O)ther dark site for the projection of primitive fantasies. Helen Tamiris's *How Long, Brethren?* (1937), Charles Weidman's *Lynchtown* (1936), and Ted Shawn's *Negro Spirituals* (1933) are all examples of socially conscious dance pieces about the Negro that predate Primus's work, yet they lacked what Lloyd thinks only Primus can give—her "Negro-ness." Primus literally embodied the suffering and injustices that others could only attempt to portray. Her representations of Negro problems operated not only on a thematic level but also on a physical one.[50] As an authentic Negro, the distinction between actor and role collapses in Primus. She is perceived, unlike Tamiris or Graham, as an "artist ambassador" for her race.

Given this burden of re-presenting and representing the "race," Primus learned, like one of her favorite poets Langston Hughes, to speak for the people in her solo *The Negro Speaks of Rivers.*[51] Created during her Café Society Downtown period, this dance was originally set to piano music by Sarah Malament and the poem of the same name by Hughes.

> I've known rivers
> I've known rivers as ancient as the world and older
> than the
> flow of human blood in human veins.
>
> My soul has grown deep like the rivers.[52]

Primus asked the actor Gordon Heath to recite the poem while she danced. As he recalled in his memoirs:

> In 1944 Pearl Primus asked me to narrate three poems she intended to dance to: Langston Hughes's "I've Known Rivers" and "Our Spring Will Come" and Lewis Allan's "Strange Fruit" (bearing the subtitle, "A Man Has Just Been Lynched"). Pearl's dance erupted with clenched hatred and searing terror—the poem needed no sub-

title. When she was creating "Our Spring Will Come" she grunted and hummed, whispered, sang, and spoke as she gave herself to movement.[53]

The dance was an affirmation of Primus's belief that despite slavery and what Martin had called "cultural isolation," the Negro had been able to retain some memory of a time before his present situation. Like Hughes, Primus chose to speak "of a time and people who are not here":[54]

> I bathed in the Euphrates when the dawns were young
> I built my hut near the Congo and it lulled me to sleep
> I looked upon the Nile and raised pyramids above it.

Primus performed the solo barefoot in a full-length skirt and striped long-sleeve top and wore a scarf on her head. In some photographs, she is captured as dancer in flight or with her arms outstretched as if unseen forces pull at her limbs. Primus has described the movement as being shaped by modern dance techniques and African sculpture; she solicited books, photographs, people, and museums for information and inspiration about Africa for her dances.

> I heard the singing of the Mississippi when Abe Lincoln
> went down to New Orleans, and I've seen its muddy
> bosom turn all golden in the sunset.
> I've known rivers:
> Ancient, dusky rivers.
>
> My soul has grown deep like the rivers.[55]

Hughes's poem, first published in the National Association for the Advancement of Colored People's (NAACP) magazine *Crisis* in 1921, aptly characterizes the sentiment of many Negro Renaissance artists regarding the longevity and richness of the African cultural legacy. Primus and Hughes worked closely during the gestation of *The Negro Speaks of Rivers*. In an interview, Primus recalled that they "would sit and talk about what he envisioned— the rivers that he doesn't even mention in the poem. Rivers of tears, rivers of blood, rivers of milk. All of that I had to know in order to create this work."[56]

Primus later would say that the dance "deals with our people in America, the tears, the beatings, the rape, the running, but also the hope."[57] By using Hughes's poem, she aligned a 1940s modernist dance with the literary and artistic movement of the 1920s and set the stage for her work. In *The Borzoi Book of Modern Dance*, Lloyd calls this solo "one of Pearl's best":

> It is beautiful . . . with undulating rhythms over deep-flowing currents of movement that wind into whirlpool spins. She pivots one knee or circles the stationary leg with the free leg, leaning her body in a long slant away from the traveling foot. The pale soles flash, the brown toes clutch and grasp, the dark fingers spread wide . . . her chaste intensity and passionate imagination carry to a sweeping finish.[58]

The acts of speaking, writing, and dancing are strategies by which American Negroes have attempted to forge social, cultural, and political identities. Excluded from various spaces, segregated in various places, the Negro, presumed to be without history and culture, was now ostentatiously proclaiming that he knew rivers "ancient as the world and older than the flow of human blood in human vein." Primus's dance offers a counterhegemonic narrative of identity by placing the Negro on the grand stage of inherited historical tradition. In this and other dances, Primus drew upon and reaffirmed her diasporic cultural heritage and tradition, using Negro spirituals, Caribbean themes, or African music to inform and authenticate her theatrical "re-presentations." By "speaking" of the timelessness and depth of rivers though the voice of a Negro "I," Primus affirmed the "depth" of the Negro's soul and provided hope that "the Negro problem" would not last forever.

THE POLITICS OF RE-CONSTRUCTING: "THE BLACK TRADITION IN AMERICAN MODERN DANCE"

Like its roots, the artistry of modern dance is "scattered," scattered over a bewildering variety of styles cho-

reographed upon an equally bewildering variety of dancing bodies.

Gerald E. Myers, "Ethnic and Modern Dance"

Southern trees bear a strange fruit,
blood at the leaves and blood at the roots,
black bodies swinging in the summer breeze,
strange fruit hanging from the poplar trees.

Lewis Allan, "Strange Fruit"

After looking at some of the issues confronting Primus as a
Negro dancer in the 1940s, I will now examine how Primus is
now being used by scholars eager to establish a black tradition
and rewrite the modern dance one. In (re)telling of the story of
blacks in American dance, certain historical details are suppressed
or erased while others are stressed. As a result of social and artistic marginalization, the work of some black artists does not fall
neatly within the parameters of the dominant aesthetic or ideological discourse, but circulates, like the segregated Negro performers of the 1940s, literally and metaphorically on the periph-
ery. Admittedly, artistic productions by marginalized subjects can
reinforce systems of oppression and structures of domination, but
they can also contest and pull at the borders separating "blacks"
from "whites," the "haves" from the "have-nots." In the words of
Ralph Ellison: "It is only partially true that Negroes turn away
from white patterns because they are refused participation. There
is nothing like distance to create objectivity, and exclusion gives
rise to counter values."[59]

According to Gerald E. Myers, co-director of the American
Dance Festival's (ADF) reconstruction project, the objective is
"to enhance public appreciation of the role of black American
choreographers in shaping twentieth-century modern dance."[60]
While the importance of researching and performing rarely seen
or "lost" dances is easily recognized, it is equally clear that this and
similarly inspired recuperative efforts are informed by notions of
race and culture that need to be critically examined. What does it
mean to identify a tradition that is labeled "black"? The ADF's reconstruction project honors black concert dance pioneers as part

of the American modern dance tradition, as part of the "bewildering variety of dancing bodies" over which the "artistry of modern dance" is supposedly "scattered." Yet considering the problematic presence of blacks within the modern dance field, what are the consequences and alternatives to formulating *a* "black tradition" as such, within "American modern dance?" I explore this question by problematizing the smooth assimilation of Primus into the canon of American modern dance.

In the dance world and other areas such as education and government, housing, public transportation, and theater, Negroes have faced discrimination and exclusion in the United States. When Myers writes that ADF's reconstruction project "has a story to tell, of how black Americans overcame formidable obstacles during this century to become recognized as modern dance artists,"[61] he is attempting to account for the absences and gaps in what is perceived as the dominant artistic or racial discourse. But this account(ing) of the Negro too often proceeds without radically questioning not only the process of exclusion but also the terms on which inclusion or "recognition" is permitted. In other words, to what extent is the process of "integrating" the "black tradition" functioning to (re)establish certain hierarchical relationships and structural inequalities that are predicated on recognizing the normative value of modern dance and certain modern dancers? As Myers writes explicitly accepting both categories, "[that] there is a black tradition within the growth of modern dance commonly associated with such names as Isadora Duncan, Martha Graham, and Paul Taylor, is a truth that this project emphasizes and elaborates."[62]

If theater is a place for seeing, a site of re-presentation (artistic depictions) and representation (the one that stands in for the many), then it is here that one can begin to address important issues concerning the formation and (re)production of individual and social identities. As Stuart Hall observes:

Cultural identities come from somewhere, have histories. But like everything which is historical, they undergo constant transformation. Far from being eternally fixed in some essentialized past, they are subject to the continuous "play" of history, culture and power. Far from being grounded in a mere "recovery" of the past, which is waiting to be found, and which, when found, will secure our sense of ourselves into eternity, identities are the names we give to different ways we are positioned by, and position ourselves within, the narratives of the past.[63]

Unlike Myers and others who perceive "a truth" about the black tradition that must only be elaborated, Stuart Hall's dialectical approach suggests the process of "recovery" is an archaeological task of sorts which requires not only the unearthing of fossils and artifacts, but also a speculative reassembling of "missing links."

NEGRO. WHITE. SEPARATE BUT EQUAL

"What chance has the modern, intellectual Negro if she is
too close to her race to be a great modern dancer—and
too far removed to be a great Negro dancer?"
    Lois Balcom, *"What Chance Has the Negro Dancer?"*

My task is one of looking back and trying to remember some of the social-protest dances of Pearl Primus from the 1940s— *Strange Fruit, Hard Time Blues, Jim Crow Train.* Primus, because of her affiliation with the New Dance Group, was one of the first Negro dancers to be considered modern by many voices in the white critical establishment. John Martin, who wrote the seminal treatise *Modern Dance* (1933), voted her "number one dance newcomer" ten years later in his *New York Times* column. He wrote that "there is no doubt that she is the most gifted artist-dancer of her race (she is Negro) to appear in the field" and "it would be manifestly unfair to classify her merely as an outstanding Negro dancer, for by any standard of comparison, she is an outstanding dancer without regard for race."[64] Primus was the exception to the rule; yet her ambivalent position as sometimes a modern, but at other times a Negro dancer illustrates some of the ways in which the modern dance was ideologically and physically not only a gendered (female), but a racialized (white) affair.

However, during the 1940s, when Primus began her career, not everyone agreed with Martin's assessment of her talent. For some, the aims and objectives of modern dancer and Negro dancer were mutually exclusive. Lois Balcom, another critic of the period, wrote in her review of Primus's 1944 Belasco Theater debut about the fate of the Negro dancer: "If newspaper reviewers, publicity writers, and popular audiences force her into the typical, predetermined pattern of the 'Negro' dancer instead of letting her work out her salvation as the fine modern dancer which she potentially is, it will be a pity."[65]

Balcom notes the effect of the market on the "pattern of the Negro," but not on that of the modern dancer. Prompted by Primus's earlier success and her current Belasco season, Balcom asks "whether good Negro dance and good modern dance are synonymous or not." One of Balcom's primary concerns was that the aesthetic criteria by which the white modern dancer was assessed were not applied equally to the Negro dancer. Balcom views Primus's racial identity as a problem that manifests itself in choreographic and technical ineptitude rather than a problem of physical structure. Her rhetorical question prompts an enigmatic answer: "Only as she is truest to herself, and that certainly is most Negro, can she be 'most modern.'"[66]

So when Pearl Primus appeared on the dance scene in 1943, her identity as a Negro left a stain, a resistant racial residue that I am tracing in the dust, so to speak, of the writings about her. Her Negro-ness affected the way in which she was perceived regardless of the character who she chose or was chosen to portray. These perceptions were not always adverse. Audre Lorde, a black feminist writer, remembered being deeply affected by Primus's body and words as a high school student:

> But one very pivotal occurrence happened during my second term at Hunter. One day Pearl Prim[u]s came! She was a Hunter High School graduate. She had just come back from Africa, from her first fellowship over there. Pearl Prim[u]s—beautiful, fat, Black, gorgeous! She talked about Africa, and she talked about the African womyn [*sic*]. She talked to us about Blackness, and she talked to us about beauty. Up there with 700 Hunter High School girls, I sat there and ate it up! I couldn't believe what this womin [*sic*] was saying to me![67]

AN AMERICAN DILEMMA

The question of status remains: Is Pearl Primus a modern dancer or a Negro dancer? What do the terms "the black tradition," "modern dance," and "the Negro" signify? The categories and names given and assumed by marginalized subjects raises important historiographic issues. In much of the current work on black dance, certain naming "errors" are supposedly corrected when the Negro dancer is assimilated as a modern. These "errors" in naming are indeed politically relevant sites, not for simple reversals and inclusions, but for formulating concepts of identity and tradition that do not reinscribe or naively mimic existing normatives and social practices.[68] What would it mean for dance research and scholarship to begin, as an alternative point of departure, with the premise that Primus's importance as a figure in American dance history is only known in retrospect, retroactively? Across time and space, her significance, and what she will "signify" for future generations, will continually fluctuate, inevitably increasing and diminishing according to the needs, demands, and desires of those who appropriate her as their own.

Instead of treating Primus's dances as museum pieces, one might ask questions about the social and political circumstances that allow them to be resurrected from the "dead." Contrary to popular belief, all acts of preservation are not necessarily progressive or "positive" moments of cultural affirmation and historical consciousness.[69] The Primus solos chosen for re-construction were dances against segregation, lynching, and cultural denigration. When these solos—and Primus herself—are unproblematically re-presented as part of the American modern dance tradition, the power and status of certain cultural establishments are reaffirmed in the neutralization and absorption of potentially subversive forces.

BACKWORD

Yesterday you asked me a question. You asked me what
I would do if I were handed a bunch of money And I
joked I'd drop dead. And I couldn't answer then. But I've

thought about it carefully. If I were handed a substantial amount of money I'd document my work on film. Yes, on film. A dancer's body goes. . . . . I would document every step, every contraction, every movement, every dance, every leap and jump and turn I know. Many African cultures are dying out now. Film is the great medium that can make them immortal.

Pearl Primus, Dance Magazine

My first encounter with Primus's *The Negro Speaks of Rivers* came in books and photographs. When I attended a lecture by Joe Nash on Black Concert Dance Pioneers, I had my first opportunity to see a videotape of the reconstructed solo performed by Kim Y. Bears of the Philadelphia Dance Company. Finally, on 11 June 1993, I saw the solo performed live at the New York High School of the Performing Arts by Ms. Bears with narration by Primus.

As the house lights dimmed, Primus spoke over the soft African/jazzy fusion music composed by her son, Onwin. But she was nowhere in sight. The stage lights slowly came up to reveal Bears in a wide second-parallel position with the outstretched arms made famous and familiar by photographs. Her costume bore little resemblance to the one worn by Primus in those photographs. I wondered for a moment what the original piano music must have sounded like and how it compared to the more contemporary score that now accompanied the dancer's movements, gestures, and steps.

In the choreography, I recognized some West African dance movements and some "classic" modern dance gestures from dance classes I had taken. I tried to discern the gaps in Primus's memory and notes—places in the dance that were covered over with new material. In trying to imagine Primus's body in place of Bears's, I realized that there are some gaps that can never be filled. As the dance ended, I was left with a strange feeling, because I had been writing about this particular dance and talking about this particular woman, now bowing to an appreciative audience, for so long. "Pearl was worried about audience response to this from those who might remember her performance," Joe Nash later

Pearl Primus in *The Negro Speaks of Rivers,* 1943 (photographer unknown; Photographs and Prints Division, Schomburg Center for Research in Black Culture, the New York Public Library–Astor, Lenox and Tilden Foundations; reproduced with permission)

commented. "See, Pearl's body add[ed] weight to this piece; now a dancer who is ballet trained, there's a lightness that comes forth that's inevitable. Pearl's body determined the effectiveness of her choreography because of that extra little weight she had."[70]

In writing about what was written about Primus and the Negro, I have perhaps succeeded in filling some gaps in dance "history" only to open others. Various questions and voices haunted me from the beginning to the end: What are you writing on Primus? Did you interview her? Did you see her dance? Never having seen her perform "live," I have come to know Primus through the eyes and words of others. There is a rare film in the Dance Collection, New York Public Library for the Performing Arts that captures the young dancer on celluloid, performing a spiritual at the American Dance Festival. The title of the solo is unknown, and the speed at which the dancer's image moves is controlled by the rate at which I turn a hand crank. As the film unwinds from one full reel to make its way over to the empty pick-up reel, as the images flicker over a light bulb and under a magnification lens inside the machine, my desire increases for that which is irretrievably lost. Since the "she" of 1943 no longer exists, and the Negro of yesterday has become today's African American, my task is one of restaging an absence. Like *African Ceremonial,* one of Primus's first attempts at choreographing body movement, this choreography of words is an attempt to re-present and represent a black dancing body that was conceived nearly sixty years ago as a site of resistance to oppression. "She visited libraries and museums," wrote Margaret Lloyd, "consulting the pictures available, taking two or three lines from one book, and half a line from another, slowly piecing together a dance."[71]

My task is not so different.

NOTES

1. I use the word "Negro" because it more accurately reflects a historically specific notion of racial identity that I am attempting to conjure up for the reader. My hope is that in speaking of the Negro, with the risk of seeming somewhat anachronistic and perhaps offensive, I will be able to suggest the distance and proximity between current notions of racial and cultural identification and those of the 1940s. Each time I use the pronoun "he" to refer to the Negro, I request that the reader imagine quotation marks around it and other words, like white and black, which are strategically employed as part of an implicit critique primarily of race, but also of gender.

2. Gunnar Myrdal, quoted in *The Negro in Twentieth Century America,* ed. J. H. Franklin and I. Starr (New York: Random House, 1967), 28. For an insightful critique of this important study of the American Negro see Ralph Ellison's essay, "An American Dilemma: A Review" in *Shadow and Act* (New York:

The New American Library, 1964). Ellison writes: "Myrdal sees Negro culture and personality simply as the product of a 'social pathology.' Thus he assumes that 'it is to the advantage of American Negroes as individuals and as a group to become assimilated into American culture, to acquire the traits held in esteem by the dominant white Americans.' This, he admits, contains the value premise that 'here in America, American culture is "highest" in the pragmatic sense. . . .' Which aside from implying that Negro culture is not American, assumes that Negroes should desire nothing better than what whites consider highest" (*Shadow and Act*, 301).

3. See Stacey Prickett, "Dance and the Worker's Struggle," *Dance Research* 8, no. 1 (spring 1990): 47–61 and Ellen Graff, *Stepping Left: Dance and Politics in New York City, 1928–1942* (Durham, N.C.: Duke University Press, 1997) for more information on 1930s social-protest dancers and dances.

4. Gordon Heath, *Deep Are the Roots* (Amherst: University of Massachusetts Press, 1992), 61. Heath participated in a Committee for Mass Education in Race Relations that included such figures as Langston Hughes, Claude McKay, and Mrs. Paul Robeson. Heath, in his memoir *Deep Are the Roots* (taken from the title of the Broadway play that brought him to national prominence in 1945), wrote: "The Committee planned to use films, theater, and radio to project an image of Negroes as they lived, worked and interacted in America. One result from this project was a radio series entitled 'I'm Your Next-door Neighbor'" (ibid., 76).

5. Pearl Primus, cited in *African-American Genius in Modern Dance*, ed. Gerald E. Myers (Durham, N.C.: American Dance Festival, 1993), 10. For further discussion of the Negro's attempts to achieve political enfranchisement in the 1940s, see Richard M. Dalfiume's essay, "The 'Forgotten Years' of the Negro Revolution," *Journal of American History*, no. 15 (June 1968): 90–106.

6. Judith Delman, "The New Dance Group," *Dance Observer* (January 1944): 8, 11. Also, in October 1933, the Worker's Dance League sponsored a forum entitled "What Shall the Negro Dance About" at the 135th Street YWCA in Harlem. The event was led by Hemsley Winfield.

7. Alain Locke, "Negro Youth Speaks," in *The Black Aesthetic*, ed. A. Gayle Jr. (New York: Doubleday, 1972), 21.

8. Ibid.

9. Langston Hughes, "The Negro Artist and the Racial Mountain," in *The Black Aesthetic*, 169–70. This "vogue" in things Negro included: the "race records" of the 1920s, the blues poetry of Langston Hughes, the folklore collecting of Zora Neale Hurston, the various spiritual and Negro folk song singing groups touring domestically and abroad, Broadway musicals, Josephine Baker in *La Revue Nègre*, and so on. Although the economic depression of the 1930s contributed to a sharp decline in the "vogue," it did not vanish completely, in part because the artistic program of supporting, preserving, and performing Negro culture had been taken up seriously by the Negro himself as a viable means of wielding socio-political power.

10. Quoted in *The Negro in Twentieth Century America*, 28.

11. John Martin, *John Martin's Book of the Dance* (New York: Tudor Publishing Co., 1963), 178; reprint ed. of *The Dance: The Story of the Dance Told in Pictures and Text* (New York: Tudor Publishing Co., 1947).

12. Walter Terry, "The Negro Dances," *New York Herald Tribune,* 28 April 1940, n.p.

13. A significant number of scholars, including Melville Herskovits, Katherine Dunham, John Szwed, and Robert Farris Thompson have researched the retentions of Africanisms in the music and dance of the New World Negro's culture.

14. Primus's immigrant status seems to have been an important factor in her attempt to valorize her African heritage within a "melting pot" American context. Furthermore, her sense of "double-consciousness" as a Negro was perhaps further complicated by the memory of another site of origin—the Caribbean. What was the attitude of immigrants from Trinidad or Haiti toward the American Negroes of the 1920s and 1930s? This area deserves sustained research.

15. Margaret Lloyd, *The Borzoi Book of Modern Dance* (New York: Knopf, 1949; reprint ed., New York: Dance Horizons, 1974), 267.

16. John O. Perpener III, "The Seminal Years of Black Concert Dance" (Ph.D. dissertation, New York University, 1992), 268.

17. Joseph Wershba, "The Gift of Healing Is Not Always a Medical Matter," *New York Post,* 9 August 1960.

18. Pearl Primus, New Dance Group alumni panel, Lincoln Center for the Arts Conference, "Of, By, and For the People," sponsored by the Society for Dance History Scholars and Congress on Research in Dance (12 June 1993). Joe Nash would dance in Primus's company in the latter half of the 1940s; like the actor Gordon Heath, he too recited the poem "The Negro Speaks of Rivers" for Primus's dance solo.

19. Delman, "The New Dance Group." The emphasis is mine.

20. When she later returned to Trinidad, McBurnie started the Little Carib Theatre in 1948 that gave Primus's future husband, the dancer Percival Borde, a place to develop and display his talent.

21. Primus, New Dance Group alumni panel.

22. Holiday first performed it for the club's opening night in 1939.

23. John Martin, "The Dance: Laurels—Award No. 2," *New York Times,* 5 August 1943, n.p.

24. Ibid. Martin, an avid supporter and theoretician of modern dance, had been writing criticism for the *New York Times* since 1927.

25. James Hatch's biography of Owen Dodson, *Sorrow Is the Only Faithful One* (Urbana: University of Illinois Press, 1993), provides further details about the second rally in 1944: "In the center of the stadium, a gigantic red star-shaped platform rested on a huge blue stage. The unions had given Owen [Dodson] access to big names—Langston Hughes, Canada Lee, Abbie Mitchell, Josh White, Marie Young, and Will Geer. Pearl Primus danced and Duke Ellington's orchestra played. For his walk-ons, Owen had seventy-six 'lesser' bodies. Gordon Heath directed the 'voice crew' and James Gelb the lighting. Ray Elliot and Evelyn Araumburo wrote original music for Owen's theme songs designed for the audience to sing along: 'There's a new world a-coming, come on / We've buried Jim Crow, We'll keep him down / White supremacy has no crown / Come on, come on / and on, and on, and on!' " (113).

26. Edwin Denby, "Concert Dancers in Nightclubs," in *Dance Writings* (New

York: Knopf, 1986), 139–40. The emphasis is mine. All of the Denby reviews cited were published in the *New York Herald Tribune,* where Denby worked as a dance critic from 1943 to 1945.

27. George W. Beiswanger, "Asadata Dafora and Company," *Dance Observer* (January 1944): 9–10.

28. Ibid. The emphasis is mine.

29. Denby, "Pearl Primus and Valerie Bettis," in *Dance Writings,* 196. The emphasis is mine.

30. Lois Balcom's review of the same concert, like Denby's, draws aesthetic conclusions that are racially informed. See Lois Balcom, "Valerie Bettis and Pearl Primus," *Dance Observer* (February 1944).

31. Because Primus's body was racially marked, when she moved on stage she inevitably blurred the distinction between art and the natural. Does movement always tell the truth? The distinction I am attempting to make between Primus and Tamiris in dance parallels a distinction made in literature between autobiography and biography. Who, one might ask, is valued more as an author(ity) in speaking about the Negro in art?

32. Considering the period in which Primus studied anthropology at Columbia University, this interest in cultural retentions comes as no surprise since scholars like Melville Herskovits had already laid the groundwork for a study of Africanisms in the cultures of the New World Negro. Herskovits, a pioneer in Afro-American anthropology, greatly influenced the direction of academic research on the Negro in America. Katherine Dunham, who also studied with Herskovits (Northwestern University) and Robert Redfield (University of Chicago), pioneered research on this topic during her Rosenwald- and Guggenheim-funded field work in the West Indies in 1935–36.

33. Denby, "Pearl Primus on Broadway," in *Dance Writings,* 247.

34. Denby, "Pearl Primus," in *Dance Writings,* 222.

35. Dodson had written and staged the 1944 Pageant (at the second Negro Freedom Rally) in which both Primus and Heath participated.

36. Hatch provides details about the Roxy production and the poetic text: "Gordon Heath, narrator for Pearl Primus's dance company in *African Celebration* at the Roxy Theatre, suggested to the choreographer-dancer that she commission Dodson to write a sound track. Owen did, and she put his fourteen short poems into rehearsal—an ensemble of verse nodding in diverse directions to black history. Owen recalled, 'At her opening, Some critic said, "Miss Primus, why do you have all that talk that we have to listen to and watch you dance at the same time?" So without consulting me, she cut it all out. I never heard my words spoken from a Broadway stage'" (Hatch, *Sorrow Is the Only Faithful One,* 317, n. 5).

37. Heath, *Deep Are the Roots,* 61.

38. Ibid. The emphasis is mine.

39. Denby, "India–Haiti–Africa," in *Dance Writings,* 281.

40. Beverly Hillsman Barber, "Pearl Primus: Rebuilding America's Cultural Infrastructure," in *African-American Genius in Modern Dance,* 10.

41. But before Primus left for Africa, she performed in the New Dance Group's "Festival Series—Choreographers and Their Works" at the Mansfield

Theater (23–27 May 1948). She presented *Myth* ("Interpretation of the Melanesian Myth of Creation"), *Santo, Shouters of Sobo, Another Man Done Gone, Strange Fruit, Motherless Child, Gonna Tell God All My Troubles, Great Gettin' Up Morning,* and *Study in Nothing.* See the American Dance Guild's "The New Dance Group Gala Concert" booklet, available at the Dance Collection, New York Library for the Performing Arts, for further information about this concert.

42. "Pearl Primus," *Dance Magazine* (November 1968): 56.

43. Ibid.

44. Primus, "Out of Africa," in *The Dance Has Many Faces,* ed. Walter Sorell (New York: World Publishing Co. 1951), 258. Why is it that the African is so often portrayed as ceaselessly dancing about everything? In the attempt to validate dance as an essential and basic part of human activity, narratives of continuous, non-stop dancing primitives circulated among defenders of the dance in the 1940s and 1950s. In another essay, "Primitive African Dance (and Its Influences on the Church of the South)," Primus synthesized her two fieldwork experiences for Anatole Chujoy's *The Dance Encyclopedia* (New York: A. S. Barnes, 1949), 387–89.

45. Ibid. Edward W. Said offers a brilliant critique of anthropological practice in his essay, "Representing the Colonized: Anthropology's Interlocutors," *Critical Inquiry* 2, no. 15, (winter 1989): 205–25.

46. Primus, quoted in *John Martin's Book of the Dance,* 184–85. Martin also published letters of hers from Africa in his *New York Times* dance column.

47. Lloyd, *Borzoi Book of Modern Dance,* 260.

48. The implicit assumption is that to be African is to be inarticulate (thus one reason why the primitive is always dancing) and uneducated. As John Martin writes in *The Modern Dance* (9) on the subject of primitives: "The simple, understandable actions of daily life which were comprehensible to his limited reason he did not wonder at: if he chose to talk about them he could express himself in a rational manner, by words. But the things that transcended reason, he feared, sometimes he worshiped, but always he was greatly moved by. Therefore he could not rationalize about them, and if he wanted to talk about them, *he had no language though which to express his feelings that transcended understanding. Therefore he danced*" (emphasis added).

49. This is what I would call the Cotton Club, "high yaller" aesthetic.

50. One notable exception to this reading is Primus's solo, *Strange Fruit (A Man Has Just Been Lynched).* In this dance, Primus portrayed a white person who has just witnessed a lynching. From accounts of the dance, Primus did not alter her usual movement vocabulary or style to suggest whiteness. Lloyd commented on Primus's boldness in this and other dances, on the fact that "she has no hesitancy in assuming the male as she does the white identity" (Lloyd, *Borzoi Book of Modern Dance,* 273). Furthermore, wrote Lloyd, "it is noteworthy that she identifies herself with a white person, and has the acumen to see, even in a lynch mob, the possibility of remorse" (ibid., 271). But Primus was less of a tabula rasa than her white female contemporaries. Her assumption of a white theatrical role was complicated by her Negro body, which did not lend itself as readily to "the willing suspension of disbelief" and disappearance into theatrical

narratives for reasons of "theatrical verisimilitude" and other aesthetic conventions.

51. I am drawing what I see as an important distinction between re-presentation (the "one" that stands in for the "many") and representation (the artistic techniques and practices of rendering the real within an acknowledged theatrical frame). Still, I allow the details of what is normally called her "private" or "personal" life to mingle in the narrative with those of her "public" or stage persona. Generally, in writing about Primus, in writing *on* her, I am attempting to avoid what Kobena Mercer has described as the "burden of representation." As he explains, "in a material context of restricted access to the means of representation, minoritized subjects are often charged with the impossible 'burden of representation.' When subordinate subjects acquire the right to speak only one at a time, their discourse is circumscribed by the assumption that they speak as 'representatives' of the entire community from which they came" ("Skin Head Sex Thing—Racial Difference and the Homoerotic Imaginary," in *How Do I Look? Queer Film and Video,* ed. Bad Object Choices [Seattle: Bay Press, 1991], 205).

52. Langston Hughes, "The Negro Speaks of Rivers." From *Collected Poems* by Langston Hughes. Copyright © 1994 by the Estate of Langston Hughes. Reprinted by permission of Alfred A. Knopf, a Division of Random House, Inc.

53. Heath, *Deep Are the Roots,* 60.

54. Patricia Wright, "The Prime of Miss Pearl Primus," *Contact* 10, no. 3 (February 1985): 15.

55. Hughes, "The Negro Speaks of Rivers."

56. Charmaine Patricia Warden, "New Dance Group's Pearl Primus Gala Retrospective," *New York Amsterdam News,* 12 June 1993, n.p.

57. Ibid.

58. Lloyd, *Borzoi Book of Modern Dance,* 277.

59. Ralph Ellison, "An American Dilemma: A Review," in *Shadow and Act,* 301–2.

60. Myers, foreword in *The Black Tradition in American Modern Dance,* 3. In 1987–88, the first year of the project, reconstructions included Donald McKayle's *Rainbow 'round My Shoulder* (1959), Eleo Pomare's *Las Desenamoradas* (1967), Talley Beatty's *Congo Tango Palace* (1960), and three solos by Primus—*The Negro Speaks of Rivers, Strange Fruit,* and *Hard Time Blues.*

61. Ibid.

62. Ibid.

63. Stuart Hall, "Cultural Identity and Diaspora" in *Identity,* ed. Jonathan Rutherford (New York: New York University Press, 1990), 225.

64. Martin, "The Dance: Laurels."

65. Lois Balcom, "What Chance Has the Negro Dancer?" *Dance Observer* (November 1944): 110.

66. Ibid.

67. Audre Lorde, " 'I Am Black Woman, and Poet': An Interview with Audre Lorde," in *Black Lesbian in White America,* ed. Anita Cornwell (Tallahassee, Fla.: Naiad Press, 1983), 42. The interviews were conducted in spring of 1975.

68. Here I would gesture to James Baldwin's idea of a usable past or Cornel West's notion of "subversive memory" to inform future research and re-

construction projects. Baldwin writes: "To accept one's past, one's history is not the same thing as drowning in it; it is learning how to use it" (*The Fire Next Time* [New York: Dell, 1962], 111).

69. As Trinh T. Minh-Ha observes: "The ability to confer aesthetic status on objects and representations that are excluded from the dominant aesthetic is a way of asserting one's position in social space" (*When the Moon Waxes Red* [New York: Routledge, 1991], 230).

70. Joe Nash, "Black Concert Dance Pioneers," lecture given at the Black Theatre in America Conference, New York University, fall 1992.

71. Lloyd, *Borzoi Book of Modern Dance,* 269.

Part 2
Practice

5

African Dance in New York City

Marcia E. Heard and Mansa K. Mussa

OVERVIEW: THE 1920s TO THE 1950s

Although the first permanent community of Africans living in New York date from the early seventeenth century,[1] the history of African dance as a concert art begins some three hundred years later. In the 1920s and 1930s, Efrom Odok, Asadata Dafora, and Momudu Johnson founded groups that taught dances from Nigeria and Sierra Leone.[2] By 1938, their three companies had presented African dance in New York City: Efrom Odok's Calabar Dancers, Momudu Johnson's dance group, and Asadata Dafora's company, Shogola Oloba. Odok, who had emigrated from Nigeria, claimed that his group had been in New York City since 1921, making him the first to present African dances as a concert art in the United States.[3]

Dafora's long-lived company, which remained in operation from 1933 until 1960, had a profound influence on the form, and many important African dancers were named on its rosters.[4] In the late 1930s, Ismay Andrews, a former student of Dafora, began to teach dances from East Africa in Harlem. Nana Yao Opare Dinizulu founded his dance company in 1948, based primarily on work of Dafora dancer Alice Dinizulu. In the early 1950s, Michael Olatunji left Dafora to form his own African dance company, where he reintegrated the dances of Nigeria.

The dances of Guinea were brought to New York City in the late 1950s by the National Dance Theatre of Guinea, better known as Les Ballets Africains. When Les Ballets Africains continued on a tour of the United States, Ladji Camara, one of its drummers, stayed in New York City. He introduced African

Americans to the dances of the Mali Empire and to the d'jembe family of drums. In this, Camara had a great impact on the direction of African dance in New York, and the United States, from 1970 to the present.

Asadata Dafora

Asadata Dafora (1890–1965) came to the United States from Sierra Leone in 1929 and presented his first dance concert in 1933. Following the success of the 1934 work *Kykunkor,* Dafora created several more dance operas that were performed on Broadway, at Carnegie Hall on five occasions, at the Ninety-second Street YM-YWHA, the New York Museum of Natural History, the Brooklyn Museum, the Brooklyn Botanical Gardens, and the Bronx Zoo. He also toured throughout the southern and the western United States and served as choreographer for Orson Welles's production of *Voodoo Macbeth* (1936). He taught many dance and drum artists, including Ismay Andrews, Alphonse Cimber, Norman Coker, Jean-Léon Destiné, Alice Dinizulu, Katherine Dunham, Charles Moore, Michael Olatunji, Josephine Premice, and Pearl Primus. Dafora founded his company, Shogola Oloba, in 1933, and it remained in existence until 1960, when he returned to Sierra Leone. Dafora died in New York City in March 1965.

Ismay Andrews

A former Dafora dancer, Ismay Andrews never traveled to Africa, yet she had the uncanny ability to successfully re-create dances and music from East Africa based upon research. She taught classes at the Harlem Mother African Methodist Episcopal Zion Church, one of New York's major centers of African American religion and culture. Her most accomplished student was Chief Bey, who became a leading African dance figure in his own right. Andrews enjoyed tremendous community support for her dance operations from politicians and community leaders, including the minister and congressman Adam Clayton Powell Jr. She founded a dance company called the Swa-Hili Dancers that

Ismay Andrews and her dance company participating in an American Theater Wing War Service event, ca. 1950 (Photographer unknown; Photographs and Prints Division, Schomburg Center for Research in Black Culture, the New York Public Library–Astor, Lenox and Tilden Foundations; reproduced with permission)

presented re-creations of East African dances on stage, in cabarets, and for the USO. She died in poverty in New York City.

Tonyea Masequoi

In the early 1940s, Tonyea Masequoi came from Liberia to study at the Hampton Institute, a private school for black men and women on the seacoast of southeastern Virginia. He joined the Hampton Creative Dance Group, under the guidance of Charles H. Williams and Charlotte Moton Kennedy, and became instrumental in the introduction of African dance into college settings in the United States. Masequoi became known for his stunning use of stilts in his choreography. The Hampton Creative Dance Group toured throughout the United States and performed several seasons in New York City. In 1964, Masequoi and Dafora performed on the same bill at the New York World's Fair.

OVERVIEW: THE 1950s TO THE 1990s

By the 1950s, African dance had taken firmer root in New York under the stewardship of such artists as Ladji Camara, Nana Yao Opare Dinizulu, Michael Olatunji, Pearl Primus, and Guy Warren. The Black Power movement of the 1960s brought many African American youth in search of self-discovery to the music and dances of Africa. African dance offered the recognition of an ancient, precolonial self and was supported as a viable vehicle of cultural revolution by leaders of the Black Power movement. During this era, African dance classes and performances became staples of African American political events, community center programming, and college courses, a legacy that will continue in the twenty-first century.

Guy Warren

Originally from Acra, Ghana, Guy Warren (born 1923) came to the United States in 1953. Known primarily for his work with jazz artists, Warren was among the first Africans to record an album for dancing: *Africa Speaks, America Answers!* (Guy Warren and Red Saunders, Decca DL-8446, 1957). Among his promi-

Africa Speaks, America Answers! original album cover art, 1957

nent students are drummer Montego Joe and dancer Doris Green. In 1965 he returned to Ghana; in 1994 he appeared in the film *Sankofa.*

Nana Yao Opare Dinizulu

Founded in 1948, Dinizulu's Dancers, Drummers, and Singers drew heavily on the influence of Asadata Dafora (see figs. on pp. 156–57). Nana Dinizulu and Alice Dinizulu formed a school of dance, The Aims of Modzawe, at the Queens, New York, community center.[5] This institution, which serves as the center of information on Akan culture and religion in the United States, sponsors dance workshops led by master teachers from across the United States and Africa. Dinizulu's Dancers, Drummers and

Singers is known for presentations of the South African gumboot dance, a stamping dance that has had tremendous influence on dance traditions in African American sororities and fraternities.

Chief Bey

A former student of Ismay Andrews, Chief Bey (James Hawthorn) has achieved wide renown as a drummer (see fig. on p. 155). He is equally at home on the ashiko, conga, and d'jembe families of drums as well as on such percussive instruments as the sekere, cowbell, and agogo. He founded three dance companies: Royal Household, in the early 1950s; Egbe, in the late 1950s; and Chief Bey and the Five Men, in the 1970s. A fierce taskmaster, he has taught many drummers who have formed their own companies and become accomplished accompanists, including Richard Bird, Billy Bongo, Neal Clarke, and Olukoṣè Wiles. Chief Bey is presently the musical director for the Charles Moore Dance Theater based in Brooklyn, New York.

Olatunji

Michael Olatunji (born 1927) entered the United States in the 1950s as a scholarship student at Morehouse College, a private liberal arts school for black men in Atlanta, Georgia. Upon graduation, he moved to New York City, where he began to perform with Asadata Dafora. Soon after, he formed his own company, Olatunji's Drums of Passion, and made the classic recording *Drums of Passion* (1959). Other successful recordings followed, including *Zungo, Drum Shots,* and *More Drums of Passion.* He was also co-author of a book, *Musical Instruments of Africa* (New York: John Day, 1965). In the late 1960s, Olatunji opened a studio in Harlem, where his students included Darlene Blackburn, a dancer and choreographer from Chicago who later taught Alyo Tolbert, the founder of Muntu Dance Theater in Chicago. Olatunji continues to perform, teach, and lecture about African music and its influences in the Americas, and he maintains a dance company. Prominent members of his company have included Afuavi Derby, Akwasiba Derby, Ruby Pryor, Helena Walker, Chuck Davis, Ladji Camara, and Chief Bey.

Ladji Camara and the Manding Influence

Ladji Camara (born 1923) joined Les Ballets Africains, the national dance company of Guinea, in 1953, and he came to the United States on that company's first tour in 1959. In 1962, he joined Katherine Dunham's company in California for one year, and in 1963 he joined Olatunji's company, where he stayed until 1970. He then formed his own company and school, the Ladji Camara African Dance Studio and the Ladji Camara Drum and Dance Company in the Bronx, New York. Camara has also worked with the Alvin Ailey American Dance Theater and many musical artists.

The predominant African dancing traditions practiced in New York City are those of the Old Mali Empire of the Manding, or Malinke/Bamama-speaking, peoples.[6] Ladji Camara is in large part responsible for bringing the Manding culture, in particular their dance and music traditions, to the United States; he is particularly known for bringing to the U.S. the d'jembe drum, a challis-shaped, single-headed drum.

Former members of Ladji Camara's dance company who founded their own companies are Obara Wali Rahman, Walter Ince, Sule' Gregory Wilson, Hazel Starks, Olukọṣè Wiles, Willamina Taylor, and Jewel Love. Camara's indelible legacy was to foster a shift in African dance in New York from the dances of Nigeria and Ghana to the energy-charged, physically challenging dances and music of Guinea.

Charles Moore

Born in Cleveland, Ohio, Charles Moore (1928–86) moved to New York in 1948 to study with Asadata Dafora, Pearl Primus, and Katherine Dunham (see figs. on pp. 158–60). He danced with Dunham from 1952 to 1960 and appeared as a guest artist with the companies of Alvin Ailey, Geoffrey Holder, and Donald McKayle. He began teaching Dunham technique[7] in the 1960s at the Clark Center for the Performing Arts, the New Dance Group, and the City College of New York as well as in the Caribbean and Europe. In 1972, he formed Dancers and Drummers of Africa, which performed his choreography as well as revivals of Dafora's work, most notably the solo *Awassa Astrige: Ostrich* (1932), which Moore performed to great acclaim. This work showed off his commanding height and lithe clarity of motion. When Moore died, his widow, Ella Thompson Moore, undertook artistic direction and renamed the dance group the Charles Moore Dance Theater. The company stood as the only repertory company to include modern, jazz, and folkloric idioms from the Caribbean in addition to the reconstructed works of Asadata Dafora directed by former Shogola Oloba dancers Zebedee Collins, Lorenzo Newby, Elsie Campbell, and Esther Rolle.

International African American Ballet

Founded in 1977 as a collaborative effort by Obara Wali Rahman, Olukọṣè Wiles, Hazel Starks, John Blanford, Rhoda Morman, and Walter Ince, International African American Ballet (IAAB) quickly became legendary in the African dance world (see figs. on pp. 161–62, 164). The company was appreciated for the exquisite detail in its music, costumes, choreography, folklore, and movement idioms. The founders of IAAB studied or performed with Ladji Camara, Olatunji, and their students. Responding to the Black Power movement and its mandates for excellence, the founding members set about the task of collaboration with clear political purpose. For every dance IAAB created, each member of the company researched a specific area (e.g., costumes or movement idioms) and shared information with the others. Members of IAAB would attend dance classes and rehearsals with instruments in hand. They thought it important that all members of the company be able to play the rhythms they were dancing as well as to dance the rhythms they were playing. Their drummers danced the rhythms too.[8] Bowing to financial and administrative pressures, IAAB disbanded in 1994. Of its founders, Obara Wali Rahman, Walter Ince, and Olukọṣè Wiles continue to teach and perform as independent artists and founders of African dance companies.

Chuck Davis and DanceAfrica

Raised in Raleigh, North Carolina, Chuck Davis (born 1937) danced in the companies of Olatunji, Raymond Sawyer, Bernice Johnson, Joan Miller, and Eleo Pomare (see fig. on p. 165). He was one of the few African American dancers who earned a degree in dance and then chose to pursue African dance as a performance focus. In 1968 he founded the Chuck Davis Dance Company of New York, the first African dance company from America to tour Europe under the auspices of the U.S. State Department. A dynamic presence at a height of 6 feet 5 inches, he teaches African dance workshops based on his frequent world travels. In 1977, Davis invented DanceAfrica, an annual festival showcasing African dance companies in the United States. In 1980, he created the African American Dance Ensemble in Durham, North Carolina.

CURRENT EVENTS

As the twenty-first century begins, many artists are teaching and performing African dance in New York.[9] Prominent teachers include Djoniba, who opened a thriving African dance and music studio at 38 East Eighteenth Street in Manhattan in 1984; Jerome Hunter of the LaRocque Bey Dance Company and School located in Harlem; Doris Green, who invented Greenotation, a means of notating African music in accord with Labanotation;[10] and Mansa Mussa, who teaches African dance at the Dance Theatre of Harlem. Prominent companies include Sabar Ak Ru Afrique, a dance and drum company directed by Obara Wali and Andara Rahman; Willamina Taylor's children's dance company; Kehinde Uhuru's boys' and men's drum ensemble and dance group; Maimouna Keita Dance Company, directed by Olukọsè Wiles and Marie Bass; Picah Dance Company; and Message from Our Ancestors, a company that specializes in West African masquerade traditions. Two important New York publications are *Traditions,* a journal founded by Doris Green and dedicated specifically to the music and dance of Africa, and *Attitude: The Dancer's Magazine,* founded by Bernadine Jennings, which devotes significant attention to African dance events in New York.

Although not based in New York, there are three internationally recognized African dance companies in the United States: Ko-Thi, based in Milwaukee; Muntu Dance Theater in Chicago; and the African American Dance Ensemble in Durham, North Carolina. The most celebrated African dance company permanently based in New York is Forces of Nature, directed by Abdel Salaam (see figs. on pp. 163, 166–67). Founded in 1980 and housed at the Cathedral Church of Saint John the Divine, this company combines martial arts, Horton- and Limón-based modern dance, and African dance techniques to explore the cultural and philosophical foundations of African dance traditions. Performing to great acclaim throughout New York and internationally, their re-creation of historical, mythical, and epic events speaks of Africans both on the continent and in the Americas. In some ways, their varied repertory fulfills the promise suggested by Dafora's 1934 classic, *Kykunkor:* that the dances of Africa hold enormous potential for the modern concert stage.

NOTES

1. See Gilbert Osofsky, *Harlem: The Making of a Ghetto* (New York: Harper & Row, 1971) and Roy Ottley, *Black Odyssey* (New York: Charles Scribner's Sons, 1948) for an extensive overview of Africans living in Manhattan.

2. Johnson, Dafora, and Oduk all danced and choreographed under the aegis of the WPA's Negro Theatre Unit.

3. Poston, *New York Post,* 13 March 1938.

4. Odok's company eventually folded into Shogola Oloba.

5. Although the Dinizulu school of dance began first, LaRocque Bey founded the longest-lived dance school in New York that has continually included dances of Africa in its curriculum. The school is currently under the direction of his nephew, Jerome Hunter, in Harlem.

6. The Old Mali Empire, which flourished from the twelfth to the sixteenth century, extended over the territories of present-day Mali, Senegal, Guinea, Gambia, Burkina Faso (formerly known as Upper Volta), Ivory Coast, parts of Mauritania, Liberia, and Sierra Leone.

7. Katherine Dunham (1909–) pioneered the use of folk dance and ritual as a basis for modern theatrical composition. She established the Dunham Technique built upon African and Caribbean styles of movement, including a flexible torso, precise articulation of pelvis and limb isolations, and the integration of flowing movements from classical ballet.

8. In an interview, IAAB drummer Mansa Mussa stated, "[Dancers have] got to play the music. If you play the music you're going to become a better dancer.

If you dance the music, you're going to become a better player [drummer]. Many are called to the dance but few are chosen for the stage. International is among the chosen few." Interview with author, 24 April 1996.

9. Dance historian Joe Nash has observed that the popularity of African dance seems to be surpassing study of modern dance forms in the United States. Interview with author, 25 April 1996.

10. Labanotation is a system of movement notation for dance developed according to principles of Rudolf von Laban (1879–1958) that employs symbols to record the points of a dancer's body, the direction of a dancer's movement, the tempo, and the dynamics.

Chief Bey, Charles Moore Dance Theater, 1989 (Photograph by Mansa K. Mussa; reproduced with permission of the photographer)

Dinizulu's Dancers, Drummers, and Singers, DanceAfrica, 1979 (Photograph by Mansa K. Mussa; reproduced with permission of the photographer)

Dinizulu's Dancers, Drummers, and Singers, DanceAfrica, 1981 (Photograph by Mansa K. Mussa; reproduced with permission of the photographer)

Charles Moore, Charles Moore Dancers and Drummers of Africa, DanceAfrica, 1978 (Photograph by Mansa K. Mussa; reproduced with permission of the photographer)

Left to right: Jenniene Peebles, Marie Gourdine, Leslie Brothers in *Te Ma Te*, Charles Moore Dance Theater, 1989 (Photograph by Mansa K. Mussa; reproduced with permission of the photographer)

Phillip Bond in *Sacred Forest*, Charles Moore Dance Theater, 1989 (Photograph by Mansa K. Mussa; reproduced with permission of the photographer)

Gregory Ince, International African American Ballet, 1982 (Photograph by Mansa K. Mussa; reproduced with the permission of the photographer)

Oswald Simmonds Jr., International African American Ballet, 1983 (Photograph by Mansa K. Mussa; reproduced with permission of the photographer)

Caren Calder, Forces of Nature, 1986 (Photograph by Mansa K. Mussa; reproduced with permission of the photographer)

Rhonda Morman, International African American Ballet, DanceAfrica, 1981 (Photograph by Mansa K. Mussa; reproduced with permission of the photographer)

Chuck Davis Dance Company, DanceAfrica, 1997 (Photograph by Mansa K. Mussa; reproduced with permission of the photographer)

Amparo Rodriguez, Forces of Nature, 1988 (Photograph by Mansa K. Mussa; reproduced with permission of the photographer)

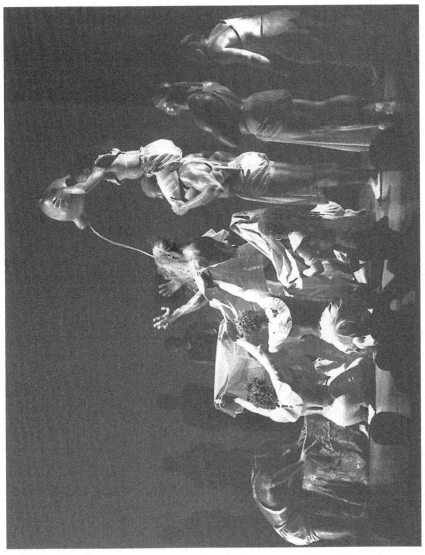

Forces of Nature, DanceAfrica, 1997 (Photograph by Mansa K. Mussa; reproduced with permission of the photographer)

6

From "Messin' Around" to "Funky Western Civilization": The Rise and Fall of Dance Instruction Songs

Sally Banes and John F. Szwed

Listen while I talk to you
I tell you what we're gonna do
There's a brand new thing that's going around
And I'll tell you what they're puttin' down
Just move your body all around
And just shake. . . .
Sam Cooke, "Shake"

"Shake," by Sam Cooke, was recorded at the height of the dance instruction song craze of the 1960s. In this genre—which originated in African American dance and music traditions—choreographic instructions are given or "called" while the dance is in progress. This article will focus on the dance instruction song wave of the 1960s, tracing its roots and its decline. Along the way we will analyze the rhetoric of the song, both in terms of its lyrics and its music.

In her book *Dance Notation,* Ann Hutchinson Guest calls notation "the process of recording movement on paper."[1] The development of written notation for dance since the Renaissance in Europe has been a fluctuating process of analysis in which the dance is described in terms of a body of shared dance values. For instance, Baroque dancing masters in Europe wrote down floor patterns and the ornamentation of footwork and turns with the assumption that arm movements, carriage, and other aspects of dance style were common knowledge, while Laban sought ways

169

to describe scientifically information that was not only quantitative (body parts in use, divisions of time and space) but also qualitative (for example, energy use).

The use of notation for theatrical dancing requires a system that is fully descriptive, since the choreographer's patterns are not necessarily shared by others. Social dancing, however, may be encoded in much more abbreviated ways, partly because of its close relationship with its music and partly because its sequences are redundant in several ways.

However, the dance instruction song is a form of dance "notation" that is part of an oral, rather than written, tradition, and it is popular rather than elite.[2] This popular genre of American song, which clearly has African roots, has appeared in mainstream culture in successive waves, beginning just before World War I with songs such as "Messin' Around" and "Ballin' the Jack." It has spread from the United States to become an internationally known phenomenon. Thus, in the twentieth century, the broad dissemination of African American social dance instruction to audiences of all ethnicities and classes through the mass media— by means of sheet music, records, radio, television, and cinema— has taken its place alongside the dance manual and the private lesson of the Euro-American elite that dated at least from the Renaissance.

The dance instruction song, spread via these modern mass technologies, has a privileged place for the historian of culture and performance, because it is *about* the mass distribution of dance and bodily knowledge and thus has served crucial aesthetic, social, and political functions. It has played an important part in the democratization of social dancing; it has spread African American dance forms and styles throughout Euro-American culture and other subaltern cultures; and it has helped create a mass market for the work of black artists. In short, the dance instruction song has contributed to the formation of a syncretic dance culture— and bodily culture—in multicultural America.

The dance instruction song in mass culture may be traced at least to the beginning of the twentieth century, although it has longer vernacular roots in the African American community.

Even though songs have occasionally been used to teach European dances—the Beer Barrel Polka or the Lambeth Walk—it is important to note that the dance instruction song primarily comprises African American dances, from Ballin' the Jack and the Black Bottom; to the Twist, the Loco-Motion, the Mashed Potato, and the Funky Broadway; to the Hustle, the Smurf, and the Vogue. The song/dance titles range from the internationally recognizable, like the Charleston, the Shimmy, the Madison, the Boogaloo, the Frug, the Limbo, the Jerk, the Watusi, and the Bump, to the more obscure, like the Georgia Crawl, Stewin' the Rice, the Clam, the 81, the Lurch, the Bounce, and the Boomerang. As well, in the African American dance and song tradition, many of these dance instruction songs make reference to "animal" dances: the Bird, the Duck, the Funky Chicken, the Horse, the Pony, the Raccoon, the Dog, the Funky Penguin, the Monkey, and so on.

This genre is so powerful that it has not only spawned various series of dances, like the entire Twist, Jerk, or Dog successions,[3] it has also given rise to a metagenre—a group of songs commenting on or parodying the dance instruction song. These songs create instructions for dances that are physically impossible, either because of the limitations of human physiognomy—for instance, Dr. Hook's "Levitate" (1975), which commands the listener, "I want you to raise your right foot. . . . Awright, now raise your left foot. . . . No no no no no, don't put your right foot back down!"—or because they are far too general and large-scale—for example, Tonio K's "Funky Western Civilization," which, after cataloging the evils of Western history, instructs its dancers to do all sorts of nasty things to one another: "You just grab your partner by the hair / Throw her down and leave her there" or "You just drag your partner through the dirt / Put him in a world of hurt." Loudon Wainwright 3d's "Suicide Song" (1975) gives new meaning to the dance of death by mixing instructions for shaking one's hips with those for cutting one's wrists. It seems that the parodic dance instruction song has been around nearly as long as the genre itself. However, we also want to suggest that one symptom of the dance instruction song's decline during the disco era—the late 1970s and early 1980s—was a disproportionate increase of parodies compared to the number of "actual" or "serious" dance instruction songs.[4]

ROOTS OF THE DANCE INSTRUCTION SONG

Dance instruction songs, in the form of dance rhymes and rhythmic verbal-movement games, were already long-established practices when they were first recorded in African American communities as early as the mid-nineteenth century. One of the fullest and earliest accounts of slave dancing records a portion of a dance song from Virginia: "She *bin* to the north / she *bin* to the south / she *bin* to the east / she *bin* to the west / she *bin* so far *beyond* the sun / and she is the *gal* for me."[5] Thomas W. Talley collected a number of what he called "dance song rhymes" in *Negro Folk Rhymes,* and typical is "Jonah's Band Party," which he saw developed at various occasions as a child:

> Setch a kickin' up san'! Jonah's Ban'!
> Setch a kickin' up san'! Jonah's Ban'!
> "Raise yo' right foot, kick it up high,
> Knock dat Mobile Buck in de eye."
>
> Setch a kickin' up san'! Jonah's Ban'!
> Setch a kickin' up san'! Jonah's Ban'!
> "Stan' up, flat foot, Jump dem Bars!
> Karo back'ards lak a train o'kyars."

(Talley notes that Jonah's Ban', Mobile Buck, Jump dem Bars, and Karo were dance steps.[6])

The roots of this genre reach back to the instructions and commentary by slave musicians at both slave gatherings and white plantation balls; to the African American folk song, game, and dance tradition; and earlier to the close relationship between West African dancing and the musicians' cues.[7] There is a link here with Euro-American forms such as square dancing, quadrilles, and play party games, but there is also strong evidence that there is a hidden history of these Euro-American forms—that in the United States, they were partly shaped by African American interventions, including black musicians, callers, and prompters at square

UNTWISTING
THE TWIST

Preview of Teaching Session by Chubby Checker and Charting of Twist Movements in Labanotation

The Master of the Twist, Chubby Checker, is due to give his all to science — the science of recording dance movement in Labanotation. From 1 to 5 PM on Sunday, Feb. 11, in the Ballroom of NYC's Empire Hotel, Chubby will teach the dance he originated. As he twists away, experts of the Dance Notation Bureau will set down in chart form all the gyrations, thus providing future generations with definitive documentation of this fad-of-the-moment. Afterward, guests will be given a lesson in how to read the Twist — and any other kind of movement — from Labanotation. Tickets, at $3.50, are obtainable from the Dance Notation Bureau, 47 W. 63, NYC 23.

Because up to now it has been used more extensively to record such things as *Swan Lake*, one is inclined to think of Labanotation primarily as a means of preserving ballet choreography. However, it has been used with equal success in recording ballroom steps. The Labanotation and word notes on this page are by Lucy Venable and Billie Mahoney.

Chest (to the right of 3rd heavy line) is slightly fwd. Face ⊂ *(on far right) is looking fwd. and the center of weight* ● *(on far left) is just above the floor. Hands* ⊵ *are closed* ⨯ *and the 1st finger* ⊳ *is stretched.*

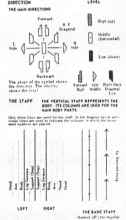

DIRECTION
THE MAIN DIRECTIONS

LEVEL

Forward

R F Diagonal

L Side

R Side

Backward

High (up)

Middle (horizontal)

Low (down)

The shape of the symbol shows the direction. The shading shows the *level*.

Forward High, Side Middle, Right Back Diagonal Low

THE STAFF

THE VERTICAL STAFF REPRESENTS THE BODY. ITS COLUMNS ARE USED FOR THE MAIN BODY PARTS.

Only three lines are used for the staff. In the diagram below additional lines are used to indicate the columns in which the movement symbols are placed.

Head Arm Body Leg Gesture Support (Step) Support (Step) Leg Gesture Body Arm Head

LEFT RIGHT

Read from the bottom up

THE BASIC STAFF

Marked off into regular beats of time

Time passing by

Feet in 4th Position, low level (LF fwd, RF back), have rotated or twisted to the right and weight is on the ball of the foot ⅃ *. Pelvic girdle* ⊡ *has also twisted to the right. In the right arm column the upper arm is diagonal right forward low, and the lower arm is left side middle, while the L arm is half way between the side middle and side low to the left.*

Weight is on RF, low level, the heel just off the floor ⅃ *. L leg is lifted with the upper leg forward low, and the lower leg back middle. Sign on the left* ⊔ *indicates that since the pelvic area is rotated, everything below the waist takes its direction from the pelvic area, while the upper torso keeps its original direction.*

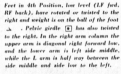

"Untwisting the Twist," *Ballroom Dance Magazine* (February 1962): 8

dances and contra dances, as well as African American games or styles of game-playing.[8]

That the dance instruction songs are related to rhythmic games synthesizing Euro-American and African American traditions is nicely illustrated in a song from the 1960s—Rufus Thomas's "Little Sally Walker," which is a virtual catalog of free-floating, recombinative, formulaic game and song phrases, mixing an Anglo-American traditional children's chanting game with standard African American vernacular dance-calling phrases such as "Put your hand on your hip / Let your backbone slip," all set to a rhythm-and-blues beat.

> Little Sally Walker
> Sitting in her saucer
> Rise, Sally, rise
> Wipe your weepin' eyes
> Put your hand on your hip
> Let your backbone slip
> (I want you to) Shake it to the east
> Shake it to the west
> Shake it to the very one that you love best.
> Little Sally Walker
> I see you sitting in your saucer
> Rise and do the jerk
> I love to see you work.[9]

Roger D. Abrahams recorded girls' jump-rope rhymes from Philadelphia in the early 1960s that were parallel to or derivative of dances of the period, such as the Madison and the Baltimore.[10] Since these girls taught their younger brothers and sisters how to play these games, the interaction between dance and games is difficult to unravel.

There is also a connection between these songs and military marching chants—or cadence counting, or "Jody calls," introduced to the U.S. Army by African Americans—which help coordinate the drill movements of large numbers of troops: "Jody was here when I *left* / You're *right*."

Sheet music renditions of dance instruction songs were printed before the turn of this century. Nearly twenty years before "Ballin' the Jack" (1913), which Alec Wilder calls the first dance instruction song, black audiences were dancing to "La Pas Ma La," introduced by the African American dancer-comedian Ernest Hogan in his Georgia Graduates minstrel show and published in 1895.[11] Less explicit in its choreographic instructions than later songs marketed to whites, "La Pas Ma La" often simply names or calls other dances to be performed, like the Bombashay and the Turkey Trot. According to Marshall Stearns and Jean Stearns, this served as a shorthand for those who knew black dance conventions. But the choreography for the Pas Ma La itself *was* given, if somewhat elliptically, in the chorus:

Hand upon yo' head, let your mind roll far,
Back, back, back and look at the stars,
Stand up rightly, dance it brightly,
That's the Pas Ma La.[12]

But if "La Pas Ma La" was marketed primarily to black audiences, during the first American mass dance craze "season" of 1912–14, many other dances and their notation—in the form of music and lyrics published in sheet music, as well as live demonstrations in Broadway revues and musicals—began to find commercial viability among mass white audiences (that is, both consumers at theatrical spectacles and participants at parties and dance halls). In fact, live performances and sheet music (or instructions, with pictures published in newspapers and magazines) all formed part of a package that provided a network of verbal, aural, and visual demonstrations of the dances.

There were occasional early efforts to reach Euro-American audiences with conventional oral instruction—as in "One Step Instruction" (ca. 1915), a Columbia record of dance music with an instructor interrupting the music to describe the steps. However, these were short-lived failures.[13]

The song "Ballin' the Jack," written for the Ziegfeld Follies of 1913 by two African American musicians, Chris Smith and Jim Burns, describes traditional African American vernacular dance steps, and it is a paradigm of the early dance instruction song. It contains a great deal of information about various aspects of the choreography.

First you put your two knees close up tight
Then you sway 'em to the left, then you sway 'em to the right
Step around the floor kind of nice and light
Then you twis' around and twis' around with all your might
Stretch your lovin' arms straight out in space

Sheet music, "La Pas Ma La," 1895. Note the stereotypical "pickaninny" illustrations lining the edges.

> Then you do the Eagle Rock with style and grace
> Swing your foot way 'round then bring it back
> Now that's what I call "Ballin' the Jack." [14]

Here we have choreographic instructions that describe the structure of the step, call a figure (in the form of an already known

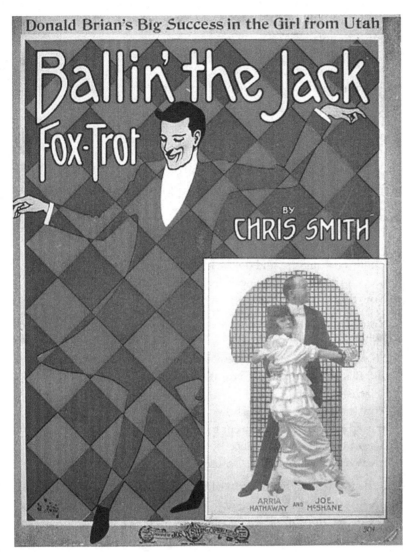

Sheet music, "Ballin' the Jack," 1913

dance, the Eagle Rock), and also give advice on style and energy use ("nice and light," "with all your might," "with style and grace").

Similarly, Perry Bradford's songs "Bullfrog Hop" (1909) and "Messin' Around" (1912) provide explicit choreographic instructions, including some similarities to the later, more widely disseminated "Ballin' the Jack." In "Messin' Around," for instance, Bradford explains:

Now anyone can learn the knack
Put your hands on your hips and bend your back,
Stand in one spot, nice and light
Twist around with all your might
Messin' round, they call that messin' round.[15]

Bradford's "The Original Black Bottom Dance" (1919) encodes instructions in a catalog of other figures, including previous dances by the songwriter:

Hop down front and then you Doodle back,
Mooch to your left and then you Mooch to the right
Hands on your hips and do the Mess Around,
Break a Leg until you're near the ground
Now that's the Old Black Bottom Dance.

Now listen folks, open your ears,
This rhythm you will hear—
Charleston was on the afterbeat—
Old Black Bottom'll make you shake your feet,
Believe me it's a wow
Now learn this dance somehow
Started in Georgia and it went to France
It's got everybody in a trance
It's a wing, that Old Black Bottom Dance.[16]

In addition to the description of the steps and the calling of other figures or dances, the dance explains the timing (like the Charleston, it is on the "afterbeat"), promises positive psychological affect, and makes reference to altered states of consciousness.

Even though these dance instruction songs were published in the form of sheet music, prior to the introduction of recording and broadcast technologies they were part of an oral tradition of instruction through popular performance, at first in minstrel shows and black vaudeville, and then in both black and white revues and musicals. The African American musician Clyde Bernhardt describes a 1917 performance by Ma Rainey and her black minstrel company. In the finale, Bernhardt remembers:

The whole chorus line come stepping out behind her and she dance along, kicking up her heels. The song had dance instructions in the lyrics, and as she call a step, everybody would do it. Soon the whole cast was out on stage, jugglers, riders, singers, comedians, all dancing wild with Ma Rainey shouting and stomping. She call "WALK!" and everybody walked together before breaking out fast. She call "STOP!" and everybody froze. After many calls she finally holler "SQUAT!" and the whole group squatted down with a roar. Including Ma Rainey.[17]

Audiences, that is, learned the dance visually and aurally in public performances, rather than by learning to read cryptographic notation or taking private lessons. Accessible to all, this was a democratic form of dance pedagogy. Eventually, as the mass medium of television edged out live popular entertainments like vaudeville and traveling shows, broadcast programs such as *American Bandstand* and networks such as MTV replaced the live visual demonstrations.

THE RISE OF THE DANCE INSTRUCTION SONG

By the 1920s, Broadway musicals with all-black casts regularly introduced new dance crazes to whites by demonstrating the steps and singing songs exhorting spectators to do the dance, such as the Charleston, danced to the song by James P. Johnson, in *Runnin' Wild* (1923).[18]

The Stearnses give an account of the process by which the African American dance rhyme, a folk form, was transformed into the commercial dance instruction song. At first, the structure was "a *group* dance performed in a circle with a few 'experts' in the center." As these experts improvised, inserted, and invented steps, the chorus on the outside repeatedly executed the steps named in the title of the dance. Often, the dance was simply named, rather than described, and if there was description, it was cursory. Later, however, as the dances reached the commercial market, "editorializing . . . as to its purported origin, nature, or popularity" began to appear as part of the song's format. The group dance with improvised steps metamorphosed into a couple dance with a fixed choreographic structure and order. "Although the verse names new steps, and the chorus describes the main step, the aim is simply to sell the dance," the Stearnses lament.[19]

According to the Stearnses, it was the Tin Pan Alley appropriation of these vernacular African American dances, in the form of the dance instruction song, that fostered their surfacing to the mainstream from black folk culture and, indeed, their survival. But oddly enough, although they were writing at the height of a new dance instruction song craze in the 1960s, the Stearnses claim that by the end of the 1920s, "the days of the dance-song with folk material were passing" and "the demand for dance-songs faded. The practice of including instructions in the lyrics of a song dwindled and gradually hardened into a meaningless formula." They claim that, with the advent of the blues, "dance-songs were forgotten" although the dances themselves persisted.[20]

However, it is our contention that, far from being forgotten or hardening into "a meaningless formula," dance instruction continued in the blues (and beyond). William Moore's "Old Country Rock" (1928) has shouted instructions sprinkled through the record:

Young folks rock.
        Boys rock.
Girls rock.
        Drop back, man, and let me rock.

Now let's go back to the country again
        on that old rock.
Rappahannac, Rappahannac,
        Cross that river, boys, cross that river.

Boogie-woogie pianists continued to simulate the ambience of live dances on recordings up until the 1950s.[21] During the course of the twentieth century, the dance instruction song consistently reemerged in times of heightened racial consciousness or change —times like the 1920s, the 1940s, and the 1960s—as a subtle component of an ongoing cultural struggle between black and white America that includes provisional and partial reconciliations. Even as white America violently resists political and social

progress by African Americans, a steady, subterranean Africanization of American culture continues, and emerging generations of
white youth eagerly learn the bodily and cultural codes of black
America by practicing its dances. Even where whites sang songs
that presented black dances derisively or stereotypically—as in
the case of rockabilly Carl Mann's "Ubangi Stomp" or Johnny
Sharpe and the Yellow Jackets' "Bombie," both of which apply the
"n-word" to Africans—the description and instructional elements
were there nonetheless.[22]

While European Americans had danced to music performed by
African Americans for generations, they did not as a group perform black moves or dance to exactly the same music enjoyed in
the black community. When whites did so, it was either in an ex-
aggerated, stereotyped way, in the context of the blackface minstrel show, or it was an individual matter, done either in the black
community or in private. The dance instruction song "crazes"
seem repeatedly to have served the function of both teaching
and licensing whites to do black dance movements wholesale, to
African American music, in public spaces in mainstream Euro-
American culture.[23] That an African American movement style,
done to a $\frac{4}{4}$ beat, was utterly alien to whites accounts for the ne-
cessity of these songs explicating not only steps, but also aspects
of dance style, even bodily style. (It must be noted, however, that
the dances are doubly coded, for embedded in the instructions
are often allusions to aspects of black culture—particularly to religious experience—that would not necessarily be understood by
the average white listener.) The repeated infusions of black style
into white mass culture, which dance instruction songs enable,
have allowed for temporary resolutions of racial conflict to take
place on a deeply embodied cultural level, paralleling shifts in
political and legal strata. The (as yet uncompleted) democratization of American culture has depended, in part, on the Africanization of American culture. The dance instruction song has been
both a reflection and an agent of that process, although this has
not been unproblematic, as we will discuss below.

TAXONOMY: STRUCTURE AND FUNCTION
OF THE DANCE INSTRUCTION SONG

In order to analyze the dance instruction song in more depth, it is useful to establish a taxonomy of the structure and function of the songs and their component parts. For example, some songs do little more than urge the listener to perform the dance by naming it, like Rufus Thomas's "The Dog" and Van McCoy's "The Hustle." However, the majority of the songs begin with the premise that the listener has to be instructed in at least one or more categories—not only in the steps' spacing, timing, or other particulars of the dance but also in the style as well (that is, in a specifically African American dance style). Although in this section we concentrate on the directions given in the lyrics, a great deal of instruction in these songs takes place through aspects of the musical as well as verbal text.

In the beginning stages of the waves of the 1920s and 1960s at least, the detailed instructions of the songs seem to indicate that the white mass audience/participants needed tutoring in all the moves, postures, and rhythms of black dance. However, in each wave, as it progressed, the songs begin to assume some mastery of the black dance style, naming only figures or other coded instructions; sometimes they even assume mastery of previous dances, naming them specifically as comparative references, as we will illustrate below.

Most of the song structures, despite their apparent simplicity and their repetitions, are quite complex. They contain information about the quantitative and qualitative content of the dance—its steps, gestures, and style—but they also make reference to its novelty, popularity, and/or venerable history; to the dance's psychological affect; to other practitioners of the dance; to the dancer's agency; and to aspects of teaching or learning the dance. They may also make reference to religious practices, sexual pleasure, or altered states of consciousness. Sometimes the songs use the dance as a mask or metaphor for those other experiences; sometimes they overtly frame the dance as a social activity connected with courtship; but at other times they simply offer the listener the chance to learn the dance, with no strings attached. (Strangely, the wording of the instructions given in Irene and Vernon Castle's 1914 book, *Modern Dancing*, seems very similar to that of dance instruction songs, perhaps suggesting that in the process of learning these dances from African Americans, they also absorbed the pedagogical rhetoric.[24])

The dance instruction songs usually begin, almost obligatorily, with a formulaic *exhortation* to learn or perform the dance. These range from the paternalistic ("Listen while I talk to you / I tell you what we're gonna do" ["Shake"]) to the pedagogical ("C'mon baby want to teach it to you" ["Mashed Potato Time"]) to the factual ("Come on let's stroll, stroll across the floor" ["The Stroll"]); from the encouraging ("Come on baby, do the Bird with me" ["Do the Bird"]) to the wheedling ("Come on mama, do that dance for me" ["Come on Mama"]) to the aggressive ("Hey you. Come out here on the floor / Let's rock some more" ["Baby Workout"]) to the tender ("Come on baby, let's do the Twist. . . . Take me by my little hand / And go like this" ["The Twist"]).

It is striking that when inviting the listener to do the dance, narrators of the dance instruction song often sweeten the offer with the promise that the dance will be easy to do. Sometimes, this assurance comes in the form of pointing out that other people have already mastered the dance: "I wish I could shimmy like my sister Kate"; "My little baby sister can do it with ease"; "Goin' to see little Susie / Who lives next door / She's doin' the Pony / She's takin' the floor"; "You should see my little sis / She knows how to rock / She knows how to twist"; "Mama Hully Gully, Papa Hully Gully, Baby Hully Gully too"; "Pappy knows how. . . ." These are aspects of the formulaic part of the song that reflexively calls attention to its *pedagogical function*. In fact, in "The Loco-Motion," Little Eva makes literal the connection with learning, simultaneously guaranteeing user-friendliness, when she remarks that the dance is "easy as a line in your abcs." And the many allusions to little sisters also seem to literalize the idiom that these dances will be child's play. At least as early as "Doin' the Scraunch" (1930), Robert Hicks (a.k.a. Barbecue Bob) promised that "Ain't much to it an' it's easy to do."

These references to teaching and learning also come simply, without any warranties of easy mastery: "Bobby's going to show you how to do the Swim"; "C'mon now, take a lesson now"; "Now if you don't know what it's all about / Come to me, I'll show you how / We'll do it fast, we'll do it slow / Then you'll know the Walk everywhere you go." As the song progresses, words of encouragement and positive feedback are frequent: "Oh, you're lookin' good, now"; "That's the way to do it"; "Well. I think you've got the knack."

Related to the promise that the dance will be user-friendly and the positive feedback offered by coaching is the part of the song — not obligatory but still quite frequent—that speaks to *psychological affect,* either that of the listener or that of the narrator. In "Finger Poppin' Time," Hank Ballard sings, "I feel so good / And that's a real good sign," and in "Bristol Stomp," the Dovells predict, "Gonna feel fine," and conclude the song by noting, "I feel fine." Sam Cooke, in "Shake," claims "Oh I like to do it. . . . Make me feel good now," and Little Eva, in "The Loco-Motion," guarantees, "It even makes you happy when you're feeling blue." The lyric "Twist and fly / To the sky" is one of many invocations of euphoria in "Do the Bird." There is a connection here, to be sure, between the kinetic pleasure of the dance and other forms of ecstasy—sexual, romantic, drug-induced, and religious.

On the other hand, a few songs tell of failures to learn the dances, but always within special circumstances. Some blame their partners, as in "My Baby Couldn't Do the Cha Cha," or in Buddy Sharpe and the Shakers' "Fat Mama Twist," where the singer's girlfriend is too fat to do it. In other songs, the singer is culturally unprepared for the dance: in Frankie Davidson and the Sapphires' "I Can't Do the Twist," the singer (in a fake Spanish accent) confesses he can't do it, though he can do all of the Latin dances; Benny Bell & His Pretzel Twisters' "Kosher Twist" follows much the same pattern, but in Borscht Belt dialect.

Sometimes, at or near the beginning of the song, the narrator makes references to the *popularity, novelty, and/or venerability* of the dance. Although the Stearnses consider this aspect of the song a symptom of commercialization and decline, we see it quite otherwise. This is an African-derived practice, clearly in the tradition of the African American praise song. (Indeed, some of the dance instruction songs—like the "Ali Shuffle"—also function as praise songs for other objects than the dance itself. Similarly, in "It's Madison Time," both Wilt Chamberlain and Jackie Gleason are celebrated with a step.) "Down in Dixie, there's a dance that's new," Barbecue Bob announces in "Doin' the Scraunch"; Blind Willie McTell's "Georgia Rag" sets the scene "Down in Atlanta on Harris Street," and insists that "Every little kid, that you meet, / Doin' that rag, that Georgia Rag. . . . Come all the way from Paris, France / Come to Atlanta to get a chance. . . . Peoples come from miles around / Get into Darktown t' break 'em down." In "The Loco-Motion," Little Eva notes that "Everybody's doing a brand new dance now," while in the background the chorus exhorts "Come on baby, do the Loco-Motion." In "Popeye," Huey Smith and the Clowns tell us that "Everywhere we go, people jump and shout / They all want to know what the Popeye's all about." In "Peppermint Twist," Joey Dee and the Starliters announce, "They got a new dance and it goes like this / The name of the dance is the Peppermint Twist." In "The Bounce," the Olympics assert, "You know there's a dance / That's spreading around / In every city / In every little town." In "Hully Gully Baby," the Dovells characterize the dance's popularity somewhat ominously: "There's a dance spreadin' round like an awful disease." Perhaps in "Mashed Potato Time," Dee Dee Sharp puts the praise of the dance most succinctly: "It's the latest / It's the greatest / Mashed Potato / Yeah yeah yeah yeah." She then goes on to trace the roots of the dance and to bring the listener up to date on its vicissitudes. Similarly, "The Original Black Bottom Dance," "Bristol Stomp," and "Popeye" provide mythic accounts of origins.

Once the dance has been invoked and/or praised, the lyrics indicate the *steps, gestures, and postures*. Usually this information is stated in the imperative mode, as a command: "Just move your body all around / And just shake" ("Shake"); "You gotta swing your hips now . . . / Jump up, jump back" ("The Loco-Motion"); "All right, now, shake your shoulders now / All right, wiggle your knees now" ("Hully Gully Baby"); "You just shake your hips and close your eyes / And then you walk" ("The Walk"); "Shake it up baby" ("Twist and Shout"); "Now you sway at the knees like a tree in the breeze / Then buzz around just like the bumblebees" ("Scratchin' the Gravel"); "Oh, shout you cats, do it, stomp it, step you rats, / Shake your shimmy, break a leg, / Grab your gal and knock 'em dead" ("Shout You Cats"). Sometimes, however, the instructions are more in the manner of a description: "Round and around / Up and down" ("Peppermint Twist"); "We're moving in we're moving out" ("Baby Workout"). Occasionally, this is stated as an invitation: "Now turn around baby, let's stroll once more" ("The Stroll"). At times, the narrator actually counts out the sequence: "One, two, three, kick / One, two, three, jump" ("Peppermint Twist"); "Oh my mama move up (first step) / Honey move back (second step) / Shuffle to the left (third step) / Wobble to the right (fourth step)" ("Baby Workout"). In Charles LaVerne's "Shoot 'Em Up Twist," a freeze is ordered every time a gunshot is heard on the record.

One subcategory of this part of the dance is what might be termed *calling the figure*. As in contra dancing or square dancing, the narrator instructs the dancers to perform a phrase or move that itself has already been named, either during the current dance or by common knowledge because it exists in other cultural arenas (like the dog paddle or back stroke, or hula hoop, or "a chugga-chugga motion like a railroad train"). "It's Pony Time" is a very good example of first teaching, then calling the figure. The narrator explains: "Now you turn to the left when I say 'gee' / You turn to the right when I say 'haw.'" Then he sings, "Now gee / Yeah, yeah little baby / Now haw."[25] Or, in "It's Madison Time," the narrator commands, "When I say 'Hit it!' I want you to go two up and two back, with a big strong turn, and back to the Madison."

As suggested earlier, one way of calling the figure is actually to invoke another dance already popular and, presumably, known and available as a standard measurement. The dance may then simply be repeated: "Let's Twist again / Like we did last summer." Or the song may direct the listener to do other dances as part of the dance being taught (as noted above in "Jonah's Band Party" and "The Original Black Bottom Dance"): "Do that Slow Drag 'round the hall / Do that step the Texas Tommy" ("Walkin' the Dog," 1917); "When I say 'Hold it!' this time, I want everybody to Gully . . . / When I say hold it this time I want everybody to Sally Long" ("Fat Fanny Stomp"); "Do the Shimmy Shimmy" ("Do the Bird"); "Do a little Cha-cha, then you do the Buzz-saw" ("Hully Gully Baby"); "Do a little wiggle and you do the Mess Around" ("Popeye"); "Hitchhike baby across the floor" ("The Harlem Shuffle"); "We Ponyed and Twisted" ("Bristol Stomp"); "Think we'll step back now / And end this with a Shout" ("Baby Workout").[26] Indeed, Bradford's "Bullfrog Hop" is a veritable catalogue of other dance titles:

First you commence to wiggle from side to side
Get 'way back and do the Jazzbo Glide
Then you do the shimmy with plenty of pep
Stoop low, yeah Bo', and watch your step
Do the Seven Years' Itch and the Possum Trot
Scratch the Gravel in the vacant lot
Then you drop like Johnny on the Spot
That's the Bullfrog Hop.[27]

Sometimes the called dance may serve as a model from which to deviate. For instance, in "C'mon and Swim," Bobby Freeman explains how to do it: "Just like the Dog, but not so slow." "The Walk" mentions the Texas Hop, the foxtrot, the mambo, and the congo, but all as dances that are now out of fashion. In a very complex example, Junior and the Classics' "The Dog," the dancer is asked to "do" various breeds of dog—the poodle, the scotty, and others.

Oddly enough for songs that were usually distributed over non-visual channels such as radio or records, sometimes the lyrics indicate that the narrator is also demonstrating the dance along the visual channel, as in "C'mon and Swim" ("Kind of like the Monkey, kind of like the Twist / Pretend you're in the water and you go like this") or as in "The Twist" ("Come on and twist / Yeah, baby twist / Oooh yeah, just like this").[28] The radio or record listener has to fill in the visuals, based on a general knowledge of the appropriate vocabulary and style.

This indication of visual demonstration seems to make reference to earlier times, when dance instruction was routinely done as part of live entertainment in black vaudeville and tent shows, as described above. Long before he became a recording artist, Rufus Thomas was a member of the Rabbit's Foot Minstrels, a black vaudeville group that showed its audiences the latest steps. "I sing, I do a step or two, and I'm a comedian," Thomas later described his act.[29]

On the recordings, the residue of a live show with visual demonstration is evident during the musical break, when the time seems right either for the listener to watch the narrator demonstrate the dance (saving the breath he or she would otherwise need to sing) and/or for the listener to practice the movements just learned. Then, when the lyrics are repeated after the musical break, the listener does not find the repetition boring or redundant, because he or she is ready to test the progress made during the (nonverbal) practice time against the instructions once again.

This is nicely illustrated in the Pearl Bailey/Hot Lips Page version of "The Hucklebuck," in which, partly because of the duet form and the dialogic patter, we have the distinct sense that Bailey is teaching Page how to do the dance. In fact, even before she begins singing, Bailey formulaically initiates the dance event by confiding in Page that she has learned a great new dance. According to their conversation, they are in a club, and not only do they comment on the abilities and looks of the musicians but also Bailey at one point complains that Page is dancing right on her feet. This song seems to record a performance within a performance, for certain lines cue the listener to set up a scene visually that puts Bailey and Page onstage in the club, teaching the audience how to do the dance. That is, in the fictional drama of the song they are a couple getting together on the dance floor in a club, but in the frame they are the featured club performers singing the fictional romance narrative. In any case, they repeatedly sing the chorus together, exhorting the listener to do the dance and describing the steps and other movements:

Do the Hucklebuck
Do the Hucklebuck
If you don't know how to do it, boy you're out of luck
Push your partner out
Then you hunch your back
Start a little movement in your sacroiliac
Wiggle like a snake
Waddle like a duck
That's the way you do it when you do the Hucklebuck.

As the band plays in between the stanzas, and Bailey and Page trade patter, it is clear that they are *doing* the dance, especially when Bailey scolds Page: "No, not now! I'll tell you when. Right here!"

As noted earlier, dance instruction songs teach not only the quantitative aspects of the dance (the steps, postures, and gestures) but also the qualitative aspects. One of these aspects is *timing*. For instance, "The Walk" is very specific in teaching the proper timing for the moves. Walking may be an ordinary act, but turning it into a dance requires the proper rhythmic sequence. So Jimmy McCracklin notes that "We'll do it fast, we'll do it slow," and later regulates the speed even further as he marks the exact moment in the music when the dancer should take his or her step: "You'll then walk / And you'll walk / Now you walk." In "The Harlem Shuffle," Bob and Earl often qualify a step by indicating its proper speed (which, of course, the slow and steady music underscores): "You move it to the right (yeah) / If it takes all night" and they frequently admonish the dancer: "Don't move it too fast / Make it last." In "Slow Twistin'," reminiscent of the "Slow Drag," Chubby Checker and Dee Dee Sharp recommend: "Baby baby baby take it easy / Let's do it right / Aw, baby take it easy / Don't you know we got all night. . . . Let's twist all night! / You're gonna last longer, longer / Just take your time."[30] The music, especially its percussive beat, plays an important role in all the songs in indicating timing.

Another qualitative aspect of the dance is its *spacing;* this too serves as an aspect of instruction. Again in "Slow Twistin'," Chubby Checker and Dee Dee Sharp advise the listener that all one needs is "Just a little bit of room, now baby." Spacing refers not only to ambient space, but also to levels of space, as in "C'mon and Swim": "Just like the Dog, but not so low." It also refers to relations with one's partner, which can be difficult to negotiate. In "The Walk," the narrator warns, "But when you walk, you stand in close / And don't step on your partner's toes." Several songs recommend, once one has learned a step, doing it in "a big boss line" or "a big strong line." In "The Loco-Motion," Little Eva instructs the listeners, once they have mastered the step, to make a chain. This clearly invokes earlier African American vernacular and communal roots, when the dances were done as group folk forms, rather than as couple forms in the dance hall.

Yet another aspect of style is the category of *energy use*—what Laban movement analysts refer to as effort qualities, such as strength and lightness, boundedness and unboundedness, directness and indirectness. This too is a stylistic characteristic that the dance instruction song sometimes teaches. For instance, "The Loco-Motion" tells us to "Take it nice and easy now / Don't lose control," while in "Shake" Sam Cooke gives us quite a few clues: "Shake shake with all your might / Oh if you do it do it right / Just make your body loose and light / You just shake." In "The Duck," Jackie Lee gives some sense of the energy invested in the dance when he describes performing it as "like working on a chain gang" or "busting rocks." Less easy to characterize are other references to *overall style:* the many songs that recommend, for instance, that the dance be performed "with soul."

One of the oldest forms of African American dance instruction is that given by the instruments themselves. The role of drums, for instance, in "talking" to dancers, or in signaling states of possession is a well-known phenomenon, both in Africa and the Americas.[31] The role of instrument as caller or instructor is not so well understood in American dance music, but its presence is undeniable. Barry Michael Cooper describes both horns and singers calling instructions to dancers at Washington, D.C., go-go dances in the 1980s.[32] Dance music critic Michael Freedberg suggests that instruments enact gender roles, both in the blues and in dance music performances.[33]

Dance instruction songs vary in the amount of choreographic information they impart, and they obviously serve a range of functions. Some actually teach the dance from scratch; some serve as prompts or mnemonics, recalling for the listener previously demonstrated and learned dances; some serve to coordinate ensemble dancing; some merely praise a dance or exhort the listener to perform it. It is possible for a dance instruction song to "notate" all ten elements in the taxonomy: exhortation; pedagogical function; psychological affect; popularity, novelty, and/or venerability; steps, gestures, and postures; calling the figure; timing; spacing; energy use; and style. Thus, the amount of information can be quite complete.

DOIN' THE HERMENEUTICS

Certain aspects of the dance instruction song have nothing to do with learning or remembering to perform the dance. In fact, sometimes even what serves as explicit instructions seems also to have subtextual, metaphoric, or "secret" meanings. While the dance instruction songs have partly served to teach the rest of the world African American dances and dance styles, they also allude to other aspects of knowledge and experience. Some of these allusions are highly encoded in terms of African American custom, emerging for white consumers and participants only through familiarity with African American history and culture. That these references are also formulaic and appear repeatedly in the songs, in succeeding generations, shows the extent and tenacity of their roots. They are often unrecognized, sturdy traces of longstanding cultural traditions.

Some of the metaphors of African American dance instruction songs are merely pedagogical in function, since traditional dance language lacks names for the steps. So "mashed potatoes," "ride your pony," "walk like a duck," "walk pigeon-toed" and the like are means of directing the dancers away from the received, conventional steps of Western dance.

Not all the extrachoreographic references have to do with experiences that are uniquely African American. Often, social dancing serves as a metaphor in these narratives for other kinds of partnering—either romantic or sexual. And since dancing—especially to slow music—often involves sustained body-to-body contact between partners, the metaphoric leap can be but a tiny one. When white teenagers danced the Twist, they were accused of moving in overly erotic ways and raised the ire of their parents. The lyrics of "Slow Twistin'" are full of double entendres, underscored by the male–female vocal duet: "Don't you know we got all night. . . . Let's twist all night / You're gonna last longer, longer / Just take your time." Perhaps the extreme case is Ronnie Fuller's "Do the Dive," where cunnilingus appears to be the move taught. In some songs, however, the dance serves not as a metaphor for sex, but as a love potion. Performing the dance itself is guaranteed to bond the partners romantically, as in "Bristol Stomp": "We'll fall in love you see / The Bristol Stomp will make you mine, all mine."

The ecstatic body consciousness of sex, however, is easily conflated with that of another high—from drugs or alcohol. The word "trance" does not only show up in these songs because it rhymes with "dance." Thus, in "Do the Bird," as we have seen, it is not clear whether romance or drugs, or both at once, are in effect when the singer urges:

> Come on take me to the sky above (fly-y-y-y-y)
> Come on baby we can fall in love (fly-y-y-y-y)
> (Do the bird do the bird) You're a-crazy flying
> (Do the bird do the bird) You're going to fly higher.

Similarly, the lines "Let's go strolling in Wonderland," or "Baby, let's go strolling by the candy store," in "The Stroll," also ambiguously suggest some kind of euphoria, whether sexual, drug-induced, or religious.

Yet "Doin' the New Low-Down," while acknowledging rapture —even invoking dreams and trances—specifically rejects other, non-dance forms of euphoria, either chemical or sensual, insisting on a surface reading: for "It isn't alcohol / No yaller girl at all! Thrills me, fills me with the pep I've got / I've got a pair of feet / That found a low-down beat. . . . Heigh! Ho! doin' the New Low-Down."

Another line in "Doin' the New Low-Down" invokes a crucial category of cultural invocations: specifically, African American signs of *religious* references. "I got a soul that's not for savin' now," this song's narrator admits, since his feet are "misbehavin' now." But more often, dance and religion are seen in the dance instruction song not as exclusionary opposites but as integrally linked. In fact, the frequent references in the songs to black religious practices, in particular the shaking or trembling associated with religious possession, suggests that many secular African American folk dances or social dances are derived directly from religious dances; they may even be the same dances performed in a different context. These are movements that originated in sacred rituals in West Africa, were associated with Yoruba, Ashanti, Congo, and other West African spirits, and shaped the syncretic worship formations of the African American church. In fact, instruction in appropriate physical response among Afro-Protestants is seen when ministers direct the congregation verbally ("Everybody raise your right hand and say 'Praise Jesus!' "); and in eighteenth-century Cuba, among Afro-Cuban religious orders, when leaders directed initiates to "open their ears, stand straight and put their left hand on their hip."[34]

Thus the Eagle Rock, mentioned in many of the songs beginning with "Ballin' the Jack," and described by the Stearnses as "thrusting the arms high over the head with a variety of shuffle steps," actually took its name from the Eagle Rock Baptist Church in Kansas City. According to musician Wilbur Sweatman, worshipers at the church "were famous for dancing it during religious service in the years following the Civil War," and the Stearnses note that although the Eagle Rock eventually adapted itself to rent parties and other secular venues, "it has the high arm gestures associated with evangelical dances and religious trance."[35]

Similarly, the Shout often crops up in the steps invoked by dance instruction songs, from "Twist and Shout" to "Do the Bird" to "Baby Workout." Also known as the Ring Shout when done in a group form, this was not a strictly vocal performance, but a religious dance with chants. It involved a rhythmic walk or shuffle in a circle, tapping the heels, swaying, and clapping as one advanced. In several accounts, observers noted that the shouters moved increasingly faster working themselves into a trance.[36]

Indeed, Jones and Hawes explicitly make the connection among children's ring plays, adult secular dances, and religious Ring Shouts in the African American tradition. They include in their chapter on dances the religious Ring Shout "Daniel," which includes lyrics, sung by the leader, strikingly reminiscent of several dance instruction songs:

> Walk, believer, walk,
> Walk, believer, walk,
> Walk, I tell you, walk,
> Shout, believer, shout.
> Shout, believer, shout.
> On the eagle wing,
> On the eagle wing,
> Fly, I tell you, fly
> Rock, I tell you, rock
> Fly the other way,
> Shout, I tell you, shout,
> Give me the kneebone bend,
> On the eagle wing,
> Fly, I tell you, fly
> Fly back home.[37]

Finally, the all-over body trembling called for and described in various songs—and known as the Shake, the Shimmy, and the Quiver, among other dances—bears a striking resemblance to the movements seen, especially among women, during religious possession in gospel churches.[38] Terms like "workout," "work on out," "rock my soul," "turn the joint out," and "tear the house down," as well as the instruction to "go down to the river" ("The Duck"), all make explicit reference to ecstatic forms of African American religious worship.

In addition to these markedly African-derived dance practices, yet another set of associations reveal the presence of African cultural practices in dance instruction songs. Although the songs do give choreographic directions to the dancer, space is often made for *improvisation*. Thus, in "Shake," we are told "Dance what you wanna"; in "C'mon and Swim," we are assured "Do what you wanna, it's all right"; in "The Loco-Motion," we are instructed "Do it holding hands if you get the notion"; and in "It's Pony Time," we learn that "Any way you do it / You're gonna look real fine." These lyrics not only reveal improvisation as a standard component of African American dance, suggesting that during the musical break it will be perfectly appropriate to "go crazy folks for a minute."[39] They also suggest, in a deeper vein, the metaphoric meaning of that improvisation. That is, the songs promise more than simply feeling good; they imply freedom and agency.

It should be acknowledged that the cross-cultural pedagogy of dance has been neither static nor one-way. Hip-hop, go-go, and ska are only the latest African American dance forms assimilated by white America. On the other hand, European dances like the quadrille have been absorbed, albeit in modified form, into the African American repertory.[40] For instance, the Stroll involves forming two facing longways rows of dance partners, as in a European contra dance configuration. However, there is a difference. When each couple goes down the column of space between the rows, they improvise virtuosi inventions in a characteristically African American vein.

One way to understand dance instruction songs is as a kind of summing-up of a musical period. There is considerable self-consciousness about them, and by the time the songs are commercially available it is likely that the original people involved with the dance have moved on to other dances, or will soon do so, as popularization sets in.

What is striking about most of these songs is that they offer a thin reading of the dance that lay behind them. Especially among Euro-Americans, there is a tendency to reduce a complex physical-verbal-musical phenomenon to the merely verbal. Thus, the Shout is often discussed as a kind of folk song. And the same reduction has been worked on rap, where the dance components of the form are almost always ignored in favor of the verbal.[41]

THE DECLINE OF THE DANCE
INSTRUCTION SONG

At the end of the 1960s, popular music was developing at a remarkable rate. Yet, dance per se was not the focus of forms such as
psychedelic music, heavy metal, and art rock. Increasingly, songs
about dances became not merely wannabe dances, but conceptual
dance instruction songs—songs about dances that did not exist.
The genre became something of a joke. *Mad Magazine*'s "Let's
Do the Fink," by Alfred E. Neuman, which came with illustrated
dance steps, was typical.[42] At the same time, however, black and
Latin music continued a commitment to "the beat," so that when
the white gay community encountered strongly grounded dance
music in clubs and ballrooms in the 1970s, it seemed a totally new
phenomenon. It was as if rock had never happened.

When dance music made its comeback as disco, it did so with a
vengeance. New dances were developed apace, but instructional
songs were minimal at best, with exhortation and novelty/praise
functions carrying the weight of the lyrics. The names of dances
were repeated rifflike in songs: "Do the Hustle," "Do the Jaws."
Professional dance teachers returned, and a ballroom formality
replaced the home-made, self-help atmosphere of many earlier
dance eras.

The 1990s are certainly a time of acute racial tension and
heightened race awareness in the United States. And yet, dances
are being invented and reinvented at a slower rate, and no dance
instruction song craze has emerged thus far in this generation.
The Electric Slide, one of the few to have appeared in recent years
(accompanied by a song of the same name by Marcia Griffith
[1989]), was immediately challenged by an older generation of
dancers as a thinly disguised remake of the Madison, especially as
it, too, emerged from the Baltimore–Washington, D.C., area.[43]
Similarly, the Lambada was attacked as a commercially fabricated
generic Latin dance, and its accompanying song was debunked
as plagiarism. The current generation of African American kids
still knows some dance instruction songs, like the currently popular "Tootsie Roll" by the 69 Boys. But these have not crossed

Fink along with Mad, Big Top Records, 1962. Selections by "various artists" included "Let's Do the Fink," "I'll Never Make Fun of Her Mustache Again," "Her Dad's Got Money Cha-Cha-Cha," and "When the Braces on Our Teeth Lock." (Alfred E. Neuman and all related elements are trademarks of E.C. Publications, Inc. © 2000; all rights reserved; reproduced with permission)

over into the mainstream. In hip-hop, one of the few distinctive music forms of the current era, MCs (especially in the early days of the form) may direct dancing and crowd behavior, but usually in an improvised rap, with routinized calls, and seldom in the form of a fully structured song for a distinctive dance. Madonna's appropriation of Voguing from the black gay community in the early 1990s was a sudden, singular—and spectacularly popular— resuscitation of the genre, but it did not spark a new wave.[44]

Dance instruction songs are still with us, though, in truncated, restricted forms. Country and western line dances—a remarkable case of cultural lag—still retain something of the calling of steps used in black popular dancing of the late 1950s and early 1960s (at least in the instructional videos), and aerobics and jazzercise do struggle mightily to get the feel of the discotheque into their routines. But there is a sense here of the end of an era. Two items of nostalgia—"Time Warp" (a camp parody of "Ballin' the Jack") from *The Rocky Horror Picture Show* (1975) and the commemorative scenes from John Waters's 1988 film *Hairspray* indicate that, for the mainstream, the dance instruction song is truly a relic from the past.

CONCLUSIONS

There is a school of mass culture criticism, most notoriously represented by Adorno, that condemns popular music as an opiate.[45] The dance instruction song, however, clearly contradicts that position. Far from assuming a docile listener, it galvanizes audiences into action with both its swinging beat and its lyrics. It is a dialogic form, requiring interaction between artist and auditor. Thus, even though the form of dissemination—especially after the invention of the phonograph—has been mass production or broadcast, the dance instruction song does not promote passivity. Rather, it provides a means for individual agency and creativity, especially with its improvisational component. Moreover, it insists that listener response can be bodily, not just intellectual, participation. Unlike the Castles' gendered ballroom choreography instructions, the dance instruction songs make no gender distinctions in the movements. In fact, unlike the Euro-American style of couple dancing, where the man leads and the woman follows, in the pedagogy proposed by dance instruction songs, women and even girls are often cited as authorities.

The question arises as to whether people actually *listen* to the lyrics and, further, whether listening to the lyrics enables people to learn to do the dance. Several theorists of popular culture claim that people screen out the words in popular music and hear only the rhythm, or the emotional contours.[46] Many cultural critics condemn the lyrics of popular songs, claiming that since the words are banal and predictable to begin with, auditors do not need to pay attention to them.[47] The dance instruction song seems unlike other genres of popular music, in that here it is important to listen to the words, and not just to sense the beat, melody, or emotional content of the song. This is not to say that the words alone supply the entire set of choreographic instructions, for as we have pointed out, the music also directs the dancer. The words are important, even if not all of them need to he heard or understood, because the dance is "overdetermined." That is, listeners may not hear or comprehend every single word (and indeed, not every song makes every word clear enough to understand). Given the various ways people learn to dance, the redundancies, both in terms of the repetition of the lyrics and the parallel teaching across various channels — verbal, rhythmic, melodic, and visual — allow for successful instruction.

The dance instruction song is laced with esoteric references to African American culture — especially to ecstatic religious experiences — that have been inaccessible to most Euro-Americans. Nevertheless, during the course of the twentieth century the dance instruction song, while keeping black vernacular dances alive, has had a mass appeal to white audiences. Through the dance instruction song, white bodies have learned — and loved — black moves, from the practice of performing separate rhythms with diverse body parts, to stances like akimbo arms and bent knees, to specific movements like all-over body quivers or hip rotations. Despite the recondite allusions, there is enough accessible material in the songs, both in the music and the lyrics, for Euro-Americans to learn the dances and the dance style. The genre has become part of mainstream American culture.

We want to close by raising the issue of cultural appropriation. On the one hand, the dance instruction song, besides its own formal pleasures, is an attractive genre for all the reasons we have already mentioned — not only its preservation of vernacular black dance but also its dialogic character, its role in the democratization and Africanization of American culture, and the economic opportunities it has created for African American musicians. By introducing an African American bodily habitus into mass white culture, thereby stirring up racial, generational, and sexual threats, it has even been subversive. On the other hand, the dance instruction song *crazes* have been problematic. They commodified and naturalized the dances, appropriating them for white culture without fully acknowledging their cultural source — their African roots — and sometimes totally detaching them from black bodies and black communities. The dance instruction song crazes created the impression that these dances have no roots — that they always have been and always will be. We hope that this article will in part redress that misperception.

NOTES

This essay was originally published in *New Formations,* no. 27 (winter 1995–96): 59–79. Minor changes have been made for consistency.

The authors would like to thank Roger Abrahams, Robert F. Thompson, Noël Carroll, Laurence Senelick, Michael McDowell, David Krasner, Gerri Gurman and her Memorial High School dance class, Amy Seham, Toni Hull, Juliette Willis, and Margaret Keyes, as well as Brooks McNamara, Richard Schechner, and the faculty and students in the Department of Performance Studies, New York University, for their help with this article.

1. Ann Hutchinson Guest, *Dance Notation: The Process of Reading Movement on Paper* (New York: Dance Horizons, 1984).

2. Alec Wilder, *American Popular Song* (New York: Oxford University Press, 1972), uses the term "dance instruction song." We use his term, but without the quotation marks. Marshall Stearns and Jean Stearns, *Jazz Dance: The Story of American Vernacular Dance* (New York: Macmillan, 1968) call these "dance songs with instructions."

3. "The Jerk," for example, originally recorded by the Larks in 1964, gave rise to a long line of successors: for instance, Clyde and the Blue Jays' "The Big Jerk," Bob and Earl's "Everybody Jerk," and even the Larks' follow-up, "Mickey's East Coast Jerk." See Steve Propes, "The Larks and the Jerk," *Goldmine,* no. 26 (August 1988).

4. For further comments on dance crazes, see Katrina Hazzard-Gordon, *Jookin': The Rise of Social Dance Formations in African American Culture* (Philadelphia: Temple University Press, 1990); and Stuart Cosgrove, "The Erotic Pleasures of the Dance-Craze Disc," *Collusion* (February–April 1983): 4–6. Also, see Jim Dawson, *The Twist: The Story of the Song and Dance That Changed the World* (London: Faber and Faber, 1995); and the 1993 documentary film *The Twist* by Ron Mann (New Line Pictures).

5. William B. Smith, "The Persimmon Tree and the Beer Dance" (1838) reprinted in Bruce Jackson, *The Negro and His Folklore in Nineteenth-Century Periodicals* (Austin: University of Texas Press, 1967), 3–9.

6. Thomas W. Talley, *Negro Folk Rhymes* (New York: Macmillan, 1922), 258–62.

7. Dance instruction songs have also been noted in the carnivals of Haiti and Trinidad, and in Argentinean tango, areas with either a majority of peoples of African descent or with a history of significant African cultural influence.

8. On African American musicians and callers, see Paul Oliver, *Songsters and Saints: Vocal Traditions on Race Records* (Cambridge: Cambridge University Press, 1984), 22.

9. Bessie Jones and Bess Lomax Hawes, *Step It Down: Games, Plays, Song, and Stories from the Afro-American Heritage* (New York: Harper and Row, 1972) discuss the African American version of this "ring play" song.

10. Roger D. Abrahams, "There's a Brown Girl in the Ring," in *Two Penny Ballads and Four Dollar Whiskey*, ed. Kenneth S. Goldstein and Robert H. Byington (Hatboro, Pa.: Folklore Associates, 1966), 121–35.

11. Stearns and Stearns, *Jazz Dance*, 100–102; and Oliver, *Songsters and Saints*, 33–34.

12. Stearns and Stearns, *Jazz Dance*, 100–101, 117. The Stearnses spell the name of the first dance invoked as the "Bumbishay," while Oliver spells it "Bombashay."

13. "One Step Instruction" was part of a newspaper promotion give-away. See *Early Syncopated Dance Music*, Folkways Records RBF 37.

14. Stearns and Stearns, *Jazz Dance*, 98–99.

15. Ibid., 107.

16. Ibid., 110–11.

17. Clyde E. B. Bernhardt, as told to Sheldon Harris, *I Remember: Eighty Years of Black Entertainment, Big Bands, and the Blues*, foreword by John F. Szwed (Philadelphia: University of Pennsylvania Press, 1986), 26.

18. See Stearns and Stearns, *Jazz Dance*, 140–59 on black musicals in the 1920s. Also, see Allen Woll, *Black Musical Theatre: From Coontown to Dreamgirls* (Baton Rouge: Louisiana State University Press, 1989).

19. Stearns and Stearns, *Jazz Dance*, 100–101

20. Ibid., 113–14.

21. Rod Grover, "The Origins of the Blues," in *Down Beat Music 71* (Chicago: Maher Publishing, 1971), 18–19.

22. But see also African American songs that describe animals dancing in Africa, such as the Ideals' "Mo' Gorilla."

23. "Public spaces," however, were, and to some degree still are, segregated: *American Bandstand*, the television show that did the most to spread new dances in the United States, was initially restricted to whites.

24. Mr. and Mrs. Vernon [Irene] Castle, *Modern Dancing* (New York: World Syndicate Co., by arrangement with Harper and Brothers, 1914). Reid Badger, in *A Life in Ragtime: A Biography of James Reese Europe* (New York: Oxford University Press, 1995) describes the relationship between the Euro-American Castles and James Europe, their African American bandleader, and names black dancers such as Johnny Peters and his partner Ethel Williams who taught the Castles African American dances.

25. "Gee" and "haw" (or "hoy") are commands used for horses or mules in

the South. Their use in the 1950s and 1960s suggests that the influence of rural-based "animal" dances was still vital.

26. As we will discuss below, the Shout, contrary to what its title might suggest by way of vocalization, is actually an African American religious dance. See Lynn Fauley Emery, *Black Dance in the United States from 1619 to 1970* (New York: Dance Horizons, 1980).

27. Stearns and Stearns, *Jazz Dance*, 104.

28. There is an obvious sexual meaning here, to be discussed below.

29. Quoted in Roger St. Pierre, liner notes, Rufus Thomas, *Jump Back*, Edsel Records ED 134 (1984).

30. Again, there is an obvious sexual reference here.

31. Morton Marks, "You Can't Sing Unless You're Saved: Reliving the Call in Gospel Music," in *African Religious Groups and Beliefs*, ed. Simon Ottenberg (Meerut, India: Archana Publications, 1982), 305–31.

32. See Barry Michael Cooper, "Kiss Me before You Go-go," *Spin* (June 1985): 65–67.

33. Michael Freedberg, "Dust Their Blues," *Boston Phoenix*, 16 October 1992; and "Rising Expectations: Rick James Gets Down," *Village Voice*, 11 October 1983.

34. Ramón Guirao, *Orbita de Ia Poesía Afrocubana, 1928–37* (Havana: Talleres de ucar, García y cial, 1938).

35. Stearns and Stearns, *Jazz Dance*, 27

36. See Emery, *Black Dance*, 120–26. Also, see Jones and Hawes, *Step It Down*, 45–46, for the distinction between religious and secular shout steps.

37. Jones and Hawes, *Step It Down*, 144–45. After each line sung by the leader, the group responds, "Daniel," and performs a mimetic action.

38. See Stearns and Stearns, *Jazz Dance*, 105 on the various titles of the dances.

39. William Moore, "Ragtime Crazy," quoted in Oliver, *Songsters and Saints*, 33.

40. In fact, the earliest recorded dance calls for European set dances and dance suites were performed by African Americans. See John F. Szwed and Morton Marks, "The Afro-American Transformation of European Set Dances and Dance Suites," *Dance Research Journal* 20, no. 1 (1988): 29–36.

41. This has complex cross-cultural repercussions, especially since, as several theorists have argued, black music and dance (on both sides of the Atlantic) are key agents in the articulation of cultural memory. See, for instance, Paul Gilroy, *The Black Atlantic: Modernity and Double Consciousness* (London: Verso, 1993).

42. Conveniently collected together are the following sets of dance songs without dances: *It's Finking Time! 60s Punk vs. Dancing Junk* (Beware Records LP Fink 1); *Bug Out Volume One: Sixteen Itchy Twitchy Classics* (Candy Records LP4); *Bug Out Volume Two: Sixteen Itchy Twitchy Classics* (Candy Records LP5); *Land of 1,000 Dunces: Bug Out Volume 3* (Candy Records LP 7). A selection from the three Candy discs is available as *Best of the Bug Outs* (Candy CD7).

43. Lena Williams, "Three Steps Right, Three Steps Left: Sliding into the Hot New Dance," *New York Times*, 22 April 1990, sec. 1, 48.

44. On Madonna's appropriation of Voguing, see Cindy Patton, "Embody-

ing Subaltern Memory: Kinesthesia and the Problematics of Gender and Race," in *The Madonna Connection: Representational Politics, Subcultural Identities, and Cultural Theory,* ed. Cathy Schwichtenberg (Boulder, Co.: Westview Press, 1993), 81–105.

45. See Theodor W. Adorno, *The Culture Industry: Selected Essays on Mass Culture,* ed. and introduced by Jeremy M. Bernstein (London: Routledge, 1991).

46. In "Why Do Songs Have Words?" (in *Music for Pleasure: Essays in the Sociology of Pop* [New York: Routledge, 1988]), Simon Frith cites two such theorists: David Riesman, "Listening to Popular Music," *American Quarterly* 2 (1950), and Norman Denzin, "Problems in Analyzing Elements of Mass Culture: Notes on the Popular Song and Other Artistic Productions," *American Journal of Sociology* 75 (1969). Frith notes that this was the typical view of sociologists of rock and pop music in the 1970s.

47. Frith, in "Why Do Songs Have Words?" traces this view back to 1930s Leavisite mass-culture criticism.

7
"Moves on Top of Blues": Dianne McIntyre's Blues Aesthetic

Veta Goler

Almost everyone has a conception of the blues and its heartfelt lyrics of love lost, the challenges of money, or the difficulties of the work world. Blues tunes may elicit sighs of empathy for someone else's troubles or nods of appreciation that someone has given voice to our own. Those "someones" are usually black people. The blues is a black phenomenon, and it is the foundation of most forms of black music. Blues singers and musicians attest to the particular difficulties and triumphs of black Americans through woeful or celebratory songs drawn from their full, and too often tragic, lives. Blues music is one of a number of creative forms through which black people transform difficulty and negativity into beauty as they maneuver through and around life's obstacles. Venerable blues scholar and novelist Albert Murray calls the blues "a highly pragmatic and indeed a fundamental device for confrontation, improvisation, and existential affirmation: a strategy for acknowledging the fact that life is a lowdown dirty shame and for improvising or riffing on the exigencies of the predicament."[1]

The blues, however, is not just a means of coping with adversity. The blues has become a broad form of black cultural expression: an *aesthetic* evident in more than just music. Scholars have theorized about cross-disciplinary cultural expressions that embody African American sensibilities contained within the blues. In the catalog accompanying the Smithsonian Institution's 1989 exhibit *The Blues Aesthetic: Black Culture and Modernism,* art historian and exhibit curator Richard J. Powell describes African

American visual arts as reflecting a "blues aesthetic." This aesthetic, he says, is based in (1) art that is contemporary, that is created in our time, (2) creative expressions of artists who are empathetic with African American issues and ideals, (3) work that identifies with and reflects popular or mass black American culture, (4) art that has an affinity with African/U.S.–derived music and/or rhythms, and (5) artists and/or artistic statements whose *raison d'être* is humanistic.[2] Powell identifies elements of a blues aesthetic in the work of several visual artists, including Romare Bearden, Jacob Lawrence, and photographer Roland Freeman. But Powell's definition is applicable to dance and other expressive modes of African American culture as well.

The blues aesthetic refers not only to characteristics of African American cultural production but also to an important function of black arts. Emory University professor Dwight Andrews considers self-empowerment the impetus and catalytic foundation of the blues and, therefore, other African American music:

> Let us presume that the blues is, in some sense, paradigmatic of all Black music. Now let us consider how one central feature of a blues aesthetic may be extrapolated from the music itself. We must begin by maintaining that the roots of Black music lie not only in the adaptation and synthesis of various African musical practices but also in the African conceptualization of music as power. Music served as a means of communication with the gods; it had the capacity not only to alter the understanding of an existential experience but also to dramatically change the quality of the experience itself. Thus to participate in the creation of music is to have both divine access and power.[3]

Albert Murray rounds out our definition of the blues aesthetic by emphasizing its reliance on the vernacular. In discussing the music of Duke Ellington, Murray talks about the "vernacular imperative to process (which is to say stylize) the raw native materials, experiences, and the idiomatic particulars of everyday life into aesthetic (which is to say elegant) statements of universal relevance and appeal."[4] Popular, or folk culture, is the heart of the blues and the blues aesthetic. The experiences of the "drylongso"—average black Americans—provide the essence of pathos and the joy that come together in the blues.[5]

The blues aesthetic, then, is ultimately about a people's survival with grace and style. It is an approach to life and creativity that claims affirmation in the face of adversity and that brings meaning, power, and a sense of community to African Americans. However, Powell and Murray each identify the blues aesthetic in the work of non-black artists—Powell in the paintings of Jackson Pollock and Murray in the prose of Ernest Hemingway. While the blues and the blues aesthetic developed as an expressive mode of African American culture, because of the tremendous contributions of black people to all facets of American life, American culture is steeped in a blues aesthetic. This reality has been made particularly clear in dance through Brenda Dixon Gottschild's project to illuminate Africanist aesthetics in mainstream, non-black American dance.[6] Given this broader space in which the blues aesthetic is in effect, we can expand the earlier statement thus:

> The blues aesthetic is an approach to life and creative endeavors that claims affirmation in the face of adversity and brings meaning, power and a sense of community to African Americans *in a way that is accessible to, and expressive of, a more universal audience.*

Choreographer Dianne McIntyre accomplishes these ends through rich and dynamic works finely tuned to the blues aesthetic.

Chronologically, McIntyre follows Katherine Dunham and Pearl Primus as the next generation's most accomplished African American woman modern dance choreographer. She dances, choreographs, and teaches as an independent artist, extending her vision and expertise nationally and internationally through various creative efforts, including her work as dance consultant for the biannual National Black Arts Festival held in Atlanta, Georgia. She has created works for the concert stage, theater, opera, film, and television as well as for recording artists. McIntyre directed a company and school, both titled Sounds in Motion, in New York City from 1972 to 1988. Located at the corner of Lenox Ave-

Dianne McIntyre, ca. 1979 (Photographer unknown; Photographs and Prints Division, Schomburg Center for Research in Black Culture, the New York Public Library–Astor, Lenox and Tilden Foundations; reproduced with permission)

nue and 125th Street, Sounds in Motion became a Harlem institution. Now, as an independent choreographer, she continues to work in various professional and educational dance venues. McIntyre is respected as an accomplished artist who has contributed greatly to the black dance community. She has created a distinctive body of work featuring a unique use of music and a dynamic movement idiom, the whole permeated with aspects of a blues aesthetic.

McIntyre's idiom builds largely upon her own brand of theatrical realism. Her movement grammar blends modern dance movement, African American social dance forms, African dance steps, and everyday gesture. Displaying great respect for music, she is considered a "musician's dancer" by her musician colleagues because of her musical sensitivity and knowledge. She incorporates a wide range of musical expression in her choreography and musical choices, including classic and avant-garde jazz, rhythm-and-blues tunes, hymns, and historical black music. McIntyre is responsible for introducing many jazz fans to dance and many dance fans to jazz music.

The body of McIntyre's work for the concert stage can be grouped according to six general approaches: (1) improvisations; (2) celebrations of African American history and culture; (3) works set to existing African American classic music; (4) expressions of African American popular culture, both past and present; (5) works based on African American literature; and (6) celebrations of figures from African American history. For example, slavery is the subject of *The Voyage* (1976). The work's title evokes images of the middle passage, and the dancing conveys attempts of individuals to survive injustices as they attempt to attain freedom. *Up North, 1881* (1975) refers to the migration of black Americans from the rural South to the urban North after Reconstruction. This work expresses the experiences and feelings of Southern blacks as they seek a new and better way of life. *In Living Color* (1988) explores the Gullah culture of the Sea Islands in terms of people's memories and complex issues surrounding cultural change. Her autobiographical *Take-Off from a Forced Landing* (1984) is based on the life of her mother, Dorothy Layne McIntyre, who trained as a pilot in a special U.S. Air Force program during World War II but who found no professional outlets for her skills as an aviator. Another work, *I Could Stop on a Dime and Get Ten Cents Change* (1995), is based on stories McIntyre's father, F. Benjamin McIntyre, told her about growing up in Cleveland in the 1930s and 1940s. Subtitled *A Ball-*

Sounds in Motion in Dianne McIntyre's *The Voyage* (Photograph by Frank Stewart; reproduced with permission of the photographer)

room Drama, the work presents vignettes and monologues about life in Cleveland, such as discrimination encountered at amusement parks, beaches, and roller-skating rinks; gangland shootings by Italian mobsters; and socializing at an after-hours joint called Val's in the Alley.

In *Smoke and Clouds* (1972), an early, abstract work addressing contrasting energies in African American culture, McIntyre juxtaposes the lethargy of hopelessness to the fire of rage and an African American *joie de vivre* born of the need to counter oppression with defiant play. The tone of the dance draws on her childhood memories of Cleveland, her adult life on 125th Street in Harlem, and Romare Bearden's paintings.[7] As the piece begins, we hear "Come on, baby, let the good times roll!" sung by Shirley and Lee as several couples slow dance. Gradually, as if heavily sedated, the dancers slump and fall to the floor. Next they get up, suddenly energized, and begin yelling angrily toward the audience. Their carefree social dancing contrasts with the lethargic weightiness and the karate-like kicks and thrusts. McIntyre weaves a pattern of falling and rising, of apathy, defeat, and resistance, in which rock-and-roll music (which accompanied the initial "unconscious" slow dancing) is opposed by the conga drum and the forceful movement of the dancers as they gain more and more strength. The recorded rock-and-roll music and the live traditional music played on congas converge with the dancers' singing, talking, and yelling. The juxtaposition of musical accompaniments evokes the African American survival technique of finding joy in life, despite oppression, and without abandoning the struggle against that oppression.

According to Powell, the blues aesthetic exhibits an affinity for African or African American music and rhythms. Black music has a special place in Dianne McIntyre's artistry. She named her company Sounds in Motion to reflect her belief that music and movement are essentially the same thing—a concept of the relationship between music and dance that refers to its African lineage. McIntyre describes her early movement explorations as a discovery of how dance is a force in the creation of music and music a force in the creation of dance:

When I first started working with the music, it was almost like a calling that I had. Because I loved the music so much, I wanted people to see it visually, and that's how it began . . . but as I went on and on, I realized that music was so special to me that the dance actually was the music, so that the dancer's body became a musical instrument. So it began more and more to merge with the music, and I found that there is no difference between the dancer and the music.[8]

Eventually McIntyre's goal became to expand the audience's experience of the music and the dance—to enable people *to see music moving and to hear the musicality of the dancers' bodies.* For McIntyre, the respective aural and kinetic expressions of the musicians and dancers combine so that the senses expand and it is possible to see music and hear motion. Dance writer Zita Allen poetically describes the effect as "movement mirroring music mirroring movement in a ricocheting reflexivity."[9]

The kinds of music McIntyre incorporates in her work, and the way she works with the music, also place her within the blues aesthetic. Shortly after arriving in New York City in 1970 with a degree in dance from Ohio State University, McIntyre continued her "dance education" through dance classes; work in dance research at the Dance Collection, New York Public Library for the Performing Arts; and visits to nightclubs to hear "the music."[10] She was most interested in the new music, the jazz of innovative musicians who came to the forefront in the era after John Coltrane's supremacy.[11] Many jazz scholars consider Coltrane, one of the most esteemed musicians of African American classical music (jazz), to be a bridge composer between the bebop and Free jazz (avant-garde) eras.[12] Both the rhythmically and harmonically unrestricted Free jazz era, and the second Free wave, with its emphasis on black self-awareness, appealed to McIntyre.

Although McIntyre utilized recorded music for Sounds in Motion when circumstances or artistry required it, she preferred to use live music for her choreography. Musicians of the Free jazz era often incorporated improvisation in their works, and although McIntyre sometimes utilized improvisation by her dancers in performance, she usually set her choreography. Her interest in Free jazz inspired the development of an improvisation-based choreographic process that allowed music and dance to be created simultaneously. McIntyre utilized this process in creating works for Sounds in Motion. She continues to use this process when making dances today.

The process began with discussions between McIntyre and the composers to get ideas flowing about the theme, story, or basic concept of the project. The composer, often with all of the musicians involved, attended every dance rehearsal. Initially, either McIntyre or the musicians began playing. The other reacted to the initial sounds or movements, and an interplay ensued in which each bounced off the other. While McIntyre was interacting with the musicians, her dancers copied her steps and movements. As they became acclimated to the process, McIntyre's dancers were able to pick up her movements quickly enough so that she was able to set small bits of material at a time.[13] This improvisational collaborative technique was transformed by McIntyre and her composers into a compositional tool. After each rehearsal, the composer and McIntyre separately rehearsed the material they had developed. They came together again to repeat and continue the process until the work, with both dance and music, was fully composed. Early work created in this manner included more improvisation in dance and music than later works, when McIntyre and musicians were able to actually set material through this process. During the 1980s, this process represented McIntyre's standard method of working with musicians in creating pieces performed to live music.

Occasionally, however, a particular recording moved McIntyre to choreograph. In the early 1980s, she conceived a suite that would explore the complexity of the music of James Brown. However, as she worked with her dancers, the shape of the piece changed dramatically. The resultant 1986 work was *Sigh of the Rock,* a women's trio performed to recorded rock-and-roll music of the 1950s. McIntyre chose selections originally recorded by black artists but subsequently popularized by white artists.[14] *Sigh of the Rock* conveys the emotions, strengths, and vulnerability of three African American women through a theatrical staging that alternates depression and struggle with comfort and strength. In this work, McIntyre captures the chaos felt by many black women who quickly move between hope and despair, nurturing and needing support, seeing progress and facing retrogression, and feeling playfully energetic while suffering the fatigue of overwork.

Sigh of the Rock employs abrupt changes in movement and music to emphasize its overall unsettled feeling. The women enter with a rhythmic step sequence. Aggressively bent forward, they accentuate their assertiveness by digging their heels into the floor. Later they scream silently with their shoulders drawn up in anguish. They dance social dances, then press themselves dejectedly against the back wall of the stage. One woman endures a fit of anger, frustration, or madness; the other women comfort her. The piece alternates positive and negative impulses, with the women feeling uplifted one moment and just trying to make it the next.

McIntyre juxtaposes the rock-and-roll music with silence. Short sections of music are repeated again and again, as if the stylus of a turntable were stuck in one groove. At other times, the music cuts off abruptly. The disjointed musical accompaniment emphasizes the women's disaffiliation,[15] and the dancers, finally left with no music, founder and lose their direction. When the music changes, they begin again and rediscover various states of strength and vulnerability.

The blues aesthetic grows out of vernacular experience. Murray calls it a way "to process folk melodies, and the music of popular entertainment as well as that of church ceremonies into a truly indigenous fine art."[16] The vernacular, in the form of African American social dance, is a characteristic component of many of McIntyre's works. These works celebrate social dances and social dance formations, such as rural jook houses, urban neighborhood hot spots, and rent parties. Works in this genre include *Fats Boogie* (1983), which features 1950s social dances; *Last Days of the Down Home Boogies* (1979), danced to 1920s and 1930s music played by the Memphis Jug Blowers and the Washboard Rhythm Kings; and *Long Gones* (1972), performed to the music of the Memphis Jug Band, Bessie Smith, and the Dixie Land Jug Blowers. The text of *Long Gones* situates it at a 1935 rent party. Its title refers to the "old dances" such as the Lindy, Truckin', Charleston, Mess Around, Susie Q, and Camel Walk, which the dancers perform in addition to such acrobatic stunts as cartwheels, barrel turns, and splits.

Another work that celebrates the vernacular experience is *Mississippi Talks, Ohio Walks* (1984). Performed to music written by Olu Dara and played live by his Okra Orchestra, this piece is set in a nightclub in Sugar Tong, Mississippi. McIntyre's syncretic blending of African American social dances with modern dance vocabulary conveys the liveliness of the club and the interactions between its patrons and musicians in a manner at once realistic and theatrical.

A strong element of *Mississippi Talks, Ohio Walks,* and many other works, is McIntyre's use of characterization. McIntyre's solos are often vehicles through which she creates portraits of African American personalities. In *Mississippi Talks, Ohio Walks,* McIntyre dances a solo as an innocent, somewhat befuddled old woman who is compelled by the music to dance. A high point of the work, the "solo" is actually a duet danced with onstage musician Olu Dara.[17] Their movement consists of hand gestures, shoulder shrugs, and eccentric walking and knee bends. The duet, an ingenious blending of performance by musician and dancer, embodies the philosophical connection between music and dance. The title of the work, *Mississippi Talks, Ohio Walks,* also makes reference to this meshing of disciplines. Dara, who hails from Mississippi, "talks" with his instruments, while McIntyre, from Ohio, "walks" in her dancing. Their "walking" and "talking" duet is additionally impressive because it is completely improvised.[18]

In 1991, McIntyre and Dara collaborated on a performance for the Atlanta Jazz Festival's evening of jazz and dance. Social dance and concert dance merged, as African American folk history and popular culture were transformed into artistic expression that reconnected dance art with its popular origin. McIntyre and Dara conceived the concert's title, *Blues on Top o' Blues,* from their perception of a certain elitism within African American communities. They envisioned juxtaposing different strata of black society.

Dianne McIntyre and Olu Dara in Dianne McIntyre's *Mississippi Talks, Ohio Walks* (Photograph by Johan Elbers; reproduced with permission of the photographer)

Dara suggested that they create a piece that would put people "back in touch with their roots."[19] The work was performed to a series of blues songs by Dara: "Work Holler Blues," "The Lullaby Blues," "Bettie's New Blue Dress Blues," "From Time to Time Blues," and "Blues on Top o' Blues." The completed work incorporated movements from traditional African dance, slave work dances, and African American social dances. A climax of the dance came when the improvising dancers and musicians suddenly launched into a unison restatement of music and movement motifs. The audience responded with a vocal enthusiasm usually heard in jazz clubs. At the subsequent Jazz Festival jam session and party, Dara's Okra Orchestra and McIntyre's dancers performed a section from the work. The blending of concert and social dance and music was so complete that at one point, the partygoers encircled the dancers as if the occasion were a rent party and the dance a spontaneous self-expression. When asked about the project, John Armwood, producer of the festival, indicated that, as artists, McIntyre and Dara are important to him because of his interest in the relationship between the development of music and popular dance forms:

> So I set up a situation where on one night people saw an abstraction of that tradition in a formal modern context, and then the next day, with the exact same people, did it all in a social dance context in the form of a party, where the dancers who performed that night danced in the social context also, and the same band performed. People got to see it from both sides, and it was fun. And the band had everybody sweating through their clothes.[20]

Thus, the boundaries between performer and participant, between art and life, between folk and elite were blurred. Work that came out of the community and popular culture was transformed for the stage and, in its informal presentation at the party, came full circle back to the community. The cycle that transformed popular culture into art and art into popular culture was complete.

Blues on Top o' Blues; Mississippi Talks, Ohio Walks; Sigh of the Rock; and *Smoke and Clouds,* like many other of McIntyre's dances, transform the vernacular into art. Through her sensitive embodiment of the blues aesthetic, McIntyre recognizes the troubles and affirms the humanity of black people. Her work reveals the texture born of despair, hope, and perseverance prevalent in different aspects of African American life.

While based in the black experience, McIntyre's dances have a universal scope. An anecdote expresses this fact. After a New Jersey performance in which McIntyre performed a solo, a middle-aged white woman from the area suburbs approached her. She told McIntyre that she had never understood the blues before just by listening to the music, but in watching McIntyre dance, she realized that the blues was not a culturally exclusive phenomenon. The feelings McIntyre conveyed in her movement resonated with this woman, who identified in herself the feelings she witnessed in McIntyre.[21] Clearly, her dances make the blues and other aspects of African American experience accessible to people of other cultures. Through her particular expression of the blues aesthetic, Dianne McIntyre affirms black people, connects their experiences to others, and enriches the lives of audiences everywhere she dances.

Choreographic Works of Dianne McIntyre

CONCERT CHOREOGRAPHY

1999 *Invincible Flowers*
  Music: Lester Bowie.
1997 *A Brand New People on the Planet*
  Music: Olu Dara.
  Susanna Jones
  Music: Olu Dara. Text: Langston Hughes. Premiere: 29 July, Opening Ceremony, National Black Arts Festival, Atlanta, Georgia.
  Too Much in Love
  Commissioned by: Cleo Parker Robinson Dance Company.
  Wade in the Water
  Music: Sweet Honey in the Rock. Premiere: 29 July, Opening Ceremony, National Black Arts Festival, Atlanta, Georgia.

1993   *Red Dance*
      Music: Olu Dara. Premiere: May, Memphis State
      University, Memphis, Tennessee.
      Selected Gems
      Text and vocal sound score: Company.
      Accompaniment: Susan Chess. Premiere: March,
      Ohio State University, Columbus, Ohio.
      Set Me as a Seal upon Thine Heart
      Music: Olu Dara. Premiere: October, Dance Theater
      Workshop, New York City.
      Why I Sing the Blues
      Music: Olu Dara. Premiere: October, Dance Theater
      Workshop, New York City.

1992   *Love Poems to God*
      Music and poetry: Hannibal Lokumbe. Premiere:
      8 June, Schomburg Center for Research in Black
      Culture, New York City.

1991   *Blues on Top o' Blues*
      "Work Holler Blues," "The Lullaby Blues," "Bettie's
      New Blue Dress Blues," "From Time to Time Blues,"
      "Blues on Top o' Blues."
      Music: Olu Dara. Premiere: June, Center Stage
      Theater, Atlanta, Georgia.
      How Long Brethren?
      Original choreography: Helen Tamiris (1937); re-
      created by McIntyre for Federal Theater Festival.
      Music: Amina Claudine Myers. Premiere: May,
      George Mason University, Fairfax, Virginia.

1989   *From Natchez to New York*
      Music: Olu Dara. Premiere: fall, Winter Garden,
      World Financial Center, New York City.
      Jump over the Moon
      "Ecstasy," "Blue Haze," "Summer Dances,"
      "Wildflower on a Precipice."
      Music: Don Pullen. Premiere: fall, Winter Garden,
      World Financial Center, New York City.

Poem in White Light
  Musical accompaniment: Nature sounds. Premiere:
  Cornell University, Ithaca, New York.
1988 *Boogie in Bop Time*
  Music: Mary Lou Williams. Premiere: December,
  Williams College, Williamstown, Massachusetts.
Circle of Soul
  Music: Olu Dara. Premiere: 8 July, Central Park, New
  York City.
The Coming of Eagles
  Vocal accompaniment: Gwendolyn Nelson-Fleming
  and Avery Brooks. Premiere: Harlem Urban
  Development Council, Harlem, New York.
In Living Color
  Music: Olu Dara and Traditional. Premiere: October,
  War Memorial Building, Trenton, New Jersey.
Kingsmen
  Music: Duke Ellington. Premiere: 5 May, Sounds in
  Motion Studio, Harlem, New York.
Running Running
  Music: Lawrence D. (Butch) Morris. Premiere:
  5 May, Sounds in Motion Studio, Harlem, New York.
1987 *Ancient to the Future*
  Music: Art Ensemble of Chicago. Premiere: July,
  Paris, France.
Gratitude
  Music: Don Pullen. Premiere: New York City
  Hospital Authority, New York City.
1986 *Sigh of the Rock*
  Music: Collage of 1950s rock and roll. Premiere:
  10 January, Joyce Theater, New York City.
*Their Eyes Were Watching God (a Dance Adventure in
Southern Blues)*
  Music: Olu Dara and Lawrence D. (Butch) Morris.
  Premiere: 25 June, J.A.M., New York City.

1985 *Fragment*
Music: Olu Dara. Premiere: Philadelphia,
Pennsylvania.
The Queen's Suite
Music: Duke Ellington. Premiere: May, Aaron Davis
Hall, City College, New York City.

1984 *Mississippi Talks, Ohio Walks*
Music: Olu Dara. Premiere: August, Damrosch Park,
Lincoln Center, New York City.
Take-Off from a Forced Landing
Music: Lawrence D. (Butch) Morris and Nat King
Cole. Premiere: 19 June, Joyce Theater, New
York City.

1983 *Blue Thoughts*
Music: Eubie Blake. Premiere: February, Symphony
Space, New York City.
Children of the Air
Music: Cecil Taylor. Premiere: March, London,
England.
Eubie Blake Suite
"Valse Marion," "You're Lucky to Me,"
"Eubie Dubie."
Music: Eubie Blake. Premiere: February, Symphony
Space, New York City.
Fat's Boogie
Music: Fats Domino. Premiere: Dancemobile, New
York City.
Flashback
Music: Anthony Davis. Premiere: June, Small's
Paradise, New York City.
Harlem Night Song
Music: Craig Harris. Premiere: 8 May, Museum of
the City of New York, New York City.
We Are Americans Too
Music: Eubie Blake. Premiere: February, Symphony
Space, New York City.

1982 *Eye of the Crocodile*
    Music: Cecil Taylor. Premiere: 27 May, Judson
    Memorial Church, New York City.
1981 *Duo*
    Music: Charli Persip. Premiere: June, Symphony
    Space, New York City.
    Etude in Free
    Sound design: Dianne McIntyre. Premiere: March,
    Sullivan Hall, Ohio State University,
    Columbus, Ohio.
    It Has Not Always Been This Way
    Music: Amina Claudine Myers. Poetry: Ntozake
    Shange. Premiere: June, Symphony Space, New
    York City.
    Just a Myth
    Music: Various recorded. Premiere: Karamu Dancers,
    Cleveland, Ohio. Sounds in Motion premiere: June,
    Symphony Space, New York City.
    Liquid Magic
    Music: Ahmed Abdullah. Premiere: June, Symphony
    Space, New York City.
    No Wonder
    Music: Recorded rhythm and blues. Text: Toni
    Morrison. Premiere: Sounds in Motion students at
    Sounds in Motion Studio, Harlem, New York.
1980 *I've Known Rivers*
    Music: Gary Bartz. Premiere: 13 June, Symphony
    Space, New York City.
    100% Cotton
    Music and poetry: Oliver Lake. Premiere: 13 June,
    Symphony Space, New York City.
    Suite Music
    Music: Hamiet Bluiett. Premiere: 14 June, Symphony
    Space, New York City.
    Triptych
    "Prayer," "Protest," "Peace."

Music: Max Roach. Premiere: 13 June, Symphony
Space, New York City.

1979 *Last Days of the Down Home Boogies*
Music: Memphis Jug Band and Washboard Rhythm
Kings. Premiere: Atlanta University Center Dancers,
Spelman College, Atlanta, Georgia. Sounds in
Motion Premiere: 8 June, Henry Street Settlement
Playhouse, New York City.

Life's Force
Music: Ahmed Abdullah. Premiere: Carver Center,
San Antonio, Texas.

1977 *Ancestral Voices*
Music: Cecil Taylor. Premiere: February, Alvin Ailey
American Dance Theater, University of California,
Berkeley, California.

Journey to Forever
Music: Ahmed Abdullah. Premiere: 29 May,
Brooklyn Academy of Music, Brooklyn, New York.

Tangent Forces
Music: Doug Hammond. Premiere: 26 October,
Entermedia Theatre, New York City.

1976 *Deep South Suite*
"Magnolias Just Dripping with Molasses," "Hearsay,"
"There Was Nobody Looking," "Happy Go
Lucky Local."
Music: Duke Ellington. Premiere: May, Alvin Ailey
Repertory Company, Theatre of the Riverside
Church, New York City.

Etude for Moving Sounds
Music: Babafumi Akunyun and Hank Johnson.

Going Home
Music: Paul Robeson. From: *Tribute to Paul Robeson.*
Premiere: 18 June, Marymount Manhattan Theatre,
New York City.

Piano Peace
"Piano Peace," "Moon Song," "A Silent Tear."

Music: Mary Lou Williams, Art Tatum, and McCoy Tyner. First performance (work-in-progress): 23 January, Henry Street Settlement Playhouse, New York City.

The Voyage
Music: Traditional slave songs. First performance (work-in-progress): 29 March, La Mama Annex, New York City.

1975 *Memories*
"With Hopes," "With Despair," "With Love." Music: Eubie Blake and Noble Sissle. Premiere: January, Henry Street Settlement Playhouse, New York City.

"Shadows"
Music: Cecil Taylor. From: *Tribute to Syvilla Fort.* Premiere: 3 November, Majestic Theatre, New York City.

Up North, 1881
Music: Louisiana State Prisoners, Rev. Gary Davis, Alabama Sacred Harp Singers, and Fred McDowell. Premiere: 29 May, New York High School of the Performing Arts, High School of Printing Auditorium, New York City.

1974 *Dead Center*
Music: Hank Johnson. Premiere: New Lafayette Theater, New York City.

Free Voices
Vocal accompaniment: Gwendolyn Nelson. Premiere: Lincoln Center Out-of-Doors, New York City.

Union (Union for the Streets)
Music: Steve Solder and Joe Rigby. Poetry: Margaret Walker and Langston Hughes. Premiere: New Lafayette Theater, New York City.

1973 *The Lost Sun*
Music: Gene Casey. Premiere: 27 January, Clark Center, New York City.

1972   *For Four Voices*
      Music: Arthur Williams. Premiere: 27 March,
      Cubiculo Theatre, New York City.
      A Free Thing I
      Premiere: 27 March, Cubiculo Theatre, New
      York City.
      A Free Thing II
      Music: Joe Falcon, Aiye Niwaju, Stephen Reid, and
      Joe Rigby. Premiere: 18 June, Washington Square
      Methodist Church, New York City.
      Long Gones
      Music: Memphis Jug Band, Bessie Smith, and Dixie
      Land Jug Blowers. Premiere: August, Long Island,
      New York.
      Poem: A Collage
      Music: Frank Dawson, Aiye Niwaju, and Joe Rigby.
      Poetry: Ed Bullins, Langston Hughes, Norman
      Jordan, Mari Evans, James Emmanuel, Clarence Reed,
      Margaret Walker, and Fatish Verano. Premiere:
      18 June, Washington Square Methodist Church, New
      York City.
      Smoke and Clouds
      Music: Traditional, Shirley and Lee, Huey Smith, and
      the Jacks. Premiere: 27 March, Cubiculo Theatre,
      New York City.
      The Society of One
      Music: Anthony Wiles, Arthur Williams, and Will
      Crittendon. Premiere: 27 March, Cubiculo Theatre,
      New York City.
1971   *Melting Song*
      Premiere: 6 June, Clark Center, New York City.

THEATER CHOREOGRAPHY
2000   *King Hedley II*
      Text: August Wilson.

Treemonisha
  Text: Scott Joplin. Premiere: Opera Theatre of St.
  Louis, St. Louis, Missouri.
1999 *Death and the King's Horseman*
  Text: Wole Soyinka.
  I Could Stop on a Dime and Get Ten Cents Change
  Director and Choreographer: Premiere Theatre of the
  First Amendment, George Mason University, Fairfax,
  Virginia.
1998 *Blues Rooms*
  Director and Choreographer: Dianne McIntyre.
  Music: Olu Dara.
1996 *The Darker Face of the Earth*
  Text: Rita Dove.
1994 *The Cherry Orchard*
  Text: Anton Chekhov. Premiere: Center Stage
  Theatre, Baltimore, Maryland.
  Othello
  Text: William Shakespeare. Premiere: Center Stage
  Theatre, Baltimore, Maryland.
  The People Could Fly and Still Do
  Premiere: May, Apollo Theatre, New York City.
  What Use Are Flowers?
  Text: Lorraine Hansberry. Premiere: National Black
  Arts Festival, 14th Street Playhouse, Atlanta,
  Georgia.
1993 *Pericles*
  Text: William Shakespeare. Premiere: Center Stage
  Theatre, Baltimore, Maryland.
1991 *Black Orpheus*
  Premiere: Crossroads Theatre, New Brunswick, New
  Jersey.
  Mule Bone
  Text: Zora Neale Hurston and Langston Hughes.
  Music: Taj Mahal. Director of Broadway production:
  Michael Schultz.

1990 *In Dahomey*
      Text: Adaptation by Shauneille Perry. Director:
      Dianne McIntyre. Premiere: October, Karamu
      Theatre, Cleveland, Ohio.
      King: The Musical
      Music: Richard Nelson. Lyrics: Maya Angelou.
      London production
1989 *Miss Evers' Boys*
      Music: Dwight Andrews. Premiere: Center Stage
      Theatre, Baltimore, Maryland.
1988 *80 Days*
      Music: Ray Davies.
1987 *God's Trombones*
      Text: James Weldon Johnson. Premiere: Schubert
      Theatre, Philadelphia, Pennsylvania.
1986 *Black Girl*
      Director: Glenda Dickerson. Premiere: February,
      Second Stage Theatre, New York City.
      Riding the Moon in Texas
      Text: Ntozake Shange.
      Shout Up a Morning
      Music: Nat and Cannonball Adderley. Premiere: La
      Jolla Playhouse, La Jolla, California.
      The Tale of Madame Zora
      Text: Aishah Rahman. Music: Olu Dara. Director:
      Glenda Dickerson.
1985 *Mama Bett*
      Directing debut: Dianne McIntyre. Premiere: Public
      Theatre, New York City.
1983 *Adam*
      Premiere: Henry Street Settlement Playhouse, New
      York City.
1982 *The Last Minstrel Show*
      Premiere: Rutgers University, New Brunswick, New
      Jersey.

Mouths
Text: Ntozake Shange. Premiere: The Kitchen, New York City.

1981 *Paul Robeson*
Premiere: Crossroads Theatre, New Brunswick, New Jersey. Transfer to Off-Broadway and Broadway.

1980 *Boogie Woogie Landscapes*
Text: Ntozake Shange. Premiere: April, Kennedy Center, Washington, D.C.

Take Me Along
Director: Geraldine Fitzgerald. Premiere: Triplex Theatre, Borough of Manhattan Community College, New York City.

1979 *Be-Bop*
Music: Dizzy Gillespie, John Hendricks, Charlie Parker, and others.

Spell #7
Text: Ntozake Shange. Director: Oz Scott. Music: (Lawrence D. Butch) Morris and David Murray

1974 *The Great MacDaddy*
Text: Paul Carter Harrison. Music: Coleridge-Taylor Perkinson. Premiere: February, the Negro Ensemble Company, New York City.

FILM CHOREOGRAPHY

1998 *Beloved*
1996 *Miss Evers' Boys*

TELEVISION CHOREOGRAPHY

The First Day of School
For Colored Girls Who Have Considered Suicide When the Rainbow Was Enuf
Langston Hughes: The Dreamkeeper
Women of Regent Hotel

NOTES

1. Albert Murray, *The Blue Devils of Nada: A Contemporary American Approach to Aesthetic Statement* (New York: Pantheon Books, 1996), 14.

2. Richard J. Powell, "The Blues Aesthetic: Black Culture and Modernism," in *The Blues Aesthetic: Black Culture and Modernism* (Washington, D.C.: Washington Project for the Arts, 1989), 23.

3. Dwight D. Andrews, "From Black to Blues," in *The Blues Aesthetic: Black Culture and Modernism* (Washington, D.C.: Washington Project for the Arts, 1990), 39. Professor Andrews is also a clergyman and an accomplished composer, musician, and scholar.

4. Murray, *Blue Devils,* 77.

5. See John Langston Gwaltney, *Drylongso: A Self-Portrait of Black America* (New York: Random House, 1980) for a history of this term in relation to black Americans.

6. See Brenda Dixon Gottschild, *Digging the Africanist Presence in American Performance: Dance and Other Contexts* (Westport, Conn.: Greenwood Press, 1996).

7. Dianne McIntyre, interview with the author, 17 April 1993.

8. Quoted in Valarie E. Henry, "Moves on Top of Blues: The Passion of Dianne McIntyre," *EightRock* 2, no. 3 (1993): 34.

9. Zita Allen, "Best Feet Forward," *Village Voice,* 10 March 1980, 37.

10. "The music" is a way of referring to jazz that is often used by African American jazz musicians. The term recognizes the relationship between jazz and other forms of black music as well as the historical legacy that links them. At the same time, it avoids the limitations imposed by rigid categorization.

11. McIntyre, interview with the author, 17 April 1993.

12. For detailed studies of avant-garde jazz, see Gary Giddins, *Visions of Jazz: The First Century* (New York: Oxford University Press, 1998); John Litweiler, *The Freedom Principle: Jazz after 1958* (New York: William Morrow, 1984); and Valerie Wilmer, *As Serious as Your Life: The Story of the New Jazz* (London: Allison & Busby, 1977).

13. McIntyre, interview with the author, 17 April 1993; and Olu Dara, interview with the author, 28 October 1993.

14. McIntyre, interview with the author, 19 April 1993.

15. Jennifer Dunning, "Dianne McIntyre at the Joyce," *New York Times,* 13 January 1986, describes the dance as a depiction of the women's "disaffiliation."

16. Murray, *Blue Devils,* 77.

17. Reviewing the work, critic Jennifer Dunning noted "Ms. McIntyre's country-bumpkin solo was a show-stopper, in part due to the sweet, hot and funny repartee between her and the impressive Mr. Dara." Dunning, "Dianne McIntyre at the Joyce," *New York Times,* 13 January 1986.

18. Dara, interview with the author, 28 October 1993.

19. McIntyre, interview with the author, 19 April 1993.

20. Quoted in John D. Thomas, "Armwood's Goal: To Make a Scene for Jazz," *Atlanta Journal-Constitution,* 19 September 1993, N2.

21. McIntyre, interview with the author, 19 April 1993.

Part 3
History

8
Kykunkor, or the Witch Woman: An African Opera in America, 1934

Maureen Needham

Versatile, multitalented as an opera and concert singer, dancer, choreographer, composer, and teacher of African culture, the great but virtually forgotten Asadata Dafora made a huge contribution to the birth of African dance and musical drama in the United States. *Kykunkor, or the Witch Woman,* the work that first brought him fame, premiered in a tiny New York City studio theater in 1934. It was the first opera presented in the United States with authentic African dances and music, performed in an African tongue by a mainly African-born cast. To the surprise of everyone involved except Dafora, who confidently believed that his offspring was destined for the bright lights of Broadway, *Kykunkor* became not only a hit but also one of the top ten theatrical productions of the year.

Austin Dafora Horton was born on 4 August 1890 to John Warner M. Horton and his wife, residents of Freetown, Sierra Leone (present-day Mali). The Hortons were members of the Temeni ethnic group, but their name came from the Nova Scotia family to which the artist's great-grandfather had been attached before settling in Sierra Leone as a freed slave. Dafora came from an educated and accomplished family: his father was city treasurer and his mother a concert pianist who had studied in Vienna and Paris.[1]

Dafora, the name he preferred to be known by, reminisced how he used to run away from home for days at a time, in order to observe festivals far from urban Freetown. Before leaving Sierra

Leone, he toured throughout West Africa. "I never missed an opportunity to see the native dances even though my main interest in life at that time was singing. I wanted to sing opera . . . . But you never know what the future will bring." His firsthand observations of ritual ceremonies were put to good use in his later career as a teacher and specialist in the African performing arts.[2]

Dafora attended the Wesleyan Boys' High School but left to continue his studies in Europe. He spent some time in England and Russia, then went to Milan where he studied voice at La Scala for two years. There he sang a tenor role in an unknown opera, possibly Verdi's *Aïda* or Meyerbeer's *L'Africaine,* both of which were in his repertory. While at La Scala, he met a fellow singer from the United States who suggested that he pursue his career in America. It would be nearly twenty years before he did go. In the interim, he concertized in Germany, France, Italy, and England.[3]

At a certain point, Dafora shifted his primary focus from song to dance. He became a dance teacher while in Berlin. He recounted once how he had attended a performance of African songs in a German nightclub one night in 1910. Overcome with homesickness, he began to dance. The audience was so impressed that the nightclub manager asked him to teach the dances to a troupe engaged to celebrate the completion of the Kiel Canal. Dafora's career from 1912, when he is known to have toured Europe, to 1929, when he made his first appearance in New York City, is a blank, although he may have been involved with a dance troupe toward the end of that period. During World War II, he served with the West African Frontier Force of the British army.[4]

Dafora arrived in New York City sometime in 1929 on tour with a group of African dancers who, like him, were members of the Temeni ethnic group. Ten years later, he told interviewer Waring Cuney that this company had appeared in France and England as well as elsewhere in the United States.[5] In New York, Dafora attempted to establish himself as a singer. The Depression was not a kind environment for expatriate African performers, so he decided to create his own vehicles to introduce Americans to the rich variety of the African arts.

A poster dated 13 April 1933 appears to be the earliest record of the ASADATA African Opera & Dramatic Company, head-

SOMETHING NEW IN NEW YORK

—A NIGHT IN AFRICA—

Asadata Dafora Horton OF SIERRA LEONE WEST AFRICA

Dramatic Tenor and Composer of Native Music & Dances

PRESENTS A SCENE FROM HIS

AFRICAN MUSICAL DRAMA "ZOONGA"

WITH ORIGINAL MUSIC AND DRUMS

This sketch is a portion of the play to be staged on Broadway in the near future, based on the true and original life in Africa. Some of the arias from the African Opera "ZOONGA" will be sung by leading artists.

You cannot afford to miss the thrill of listening to appealing African songs; seeing the War Dance, the Hunters' Dance, the Witch Doctor's Dance, and the Dancing Girls —— such dances have never before been performed in America.

This sketch will be an inspiration to you, an evening of rare entertainment awaits you.
—— See The Real African——

Music and Lyrics by
A. D. HORTON

Directed by
LEON WILLIAMS

LUCILE SCHLEY
SOPRANO

ADELAID SMITH
CONTRALTO

A SADATA DAFORA HORTON

APRIL 13th, 1933 :-: 8-30 P. M.

AT THE

New Y. M. C. A. Little Theatre

180 WEST 135TH STREET   NEW YORK CITY

RESERVED & PATRON SEATS 75 CENTS   GENERAL ADMISSION 50 CENTS

———— Tickets Can Be Obtained At ————

AGNES THORPE STUDIO   ASADATA   McVEY'S   THE LYARTDRA LEAGUE
2259 Seventh Avenue   African Opera & Dramatic Co.   227 West 135th Street   (Morgan & Ramsey Studio)
Y.M.C.A.   228 West 123rd Street, UN. 4-2169   BR. 2-8824   200 West 135th Street. MO. 2-3651

AMERICAN COLOR VIEW PUB. CO. 226 WEST 134TH STREET

Advertisement flyer for *Zoonga,* 1933 (Photographs and Prints Division, Schomburg Center for Research in Black Culture, the New York Public Library–Astor, Lenox and Tilden Foundations; reproduced with permission)

quartered at 238 West 123rd Street. The poster proclaimed "Something New in New York—A Night in Africa." "Asadata Dafora Horton of Sierra Leone" announced the presentation of "a scene from his African Musical/Drama called *Zoonga,*" complete with original music and drumming. Plans were grandiose:

according to Dafora this was an excerpt from a play to be staged on Broadway, even though at that time he could find no backers for the project. The soprano Lucille Schley and the contralto Adelaide Smith were engaged to sing "arias from the African Opera." The playbill also featured African dances, including the War Dance, Hunters' Dance, and Witch Doctor's Dance, as well as a "Dancing Girls" number. These dances, he added, "have never been performed in America." Dafora took credit for the original music and lyrics, but undoubtedly he was the choreographer as well. The performance took place at the opening of the New YMCA Little Theatre on 180 West 135th Street, only a block from where the New York Public Library's Schomburg Center for Research in Black Culture today houses Dafora's papers.[6]

Penciled on the back of this playbill, possibly in Dafora's own handwriting, are directions for Scene 4, which followed the intermission:

"King seating in Palace—Warrior Dancing with Cutlas [sic] as King come in Palace—Drums beat from far coming. Guards dance up and downstage saying "Battio" and all answer "Battio"—King send Captain to Meet Kabbie and bring him in—Kabbie arrive with lots of Noice [sic] with Presents (Dance)—King greet him and Chief with Cabinet greet him too—Slave Girls come in. After dancing put presents down and go offstage—King tell Kabbie he is sending Hunters to hunt for feast. King orders captain to get Hunters— King offer to entertain Kabbie with his favourite Dancing Girl— Kabbie say to King you haven't seen anything till you see my Dancing Girls. In the meantime—Hunters arrive with Kity dancing and go offstage—Kabbie send for his Dancing Girls to entertain King and Guest (all clap with excitement)—After dancing King send for Musu. She come in with Dancing Warriors and her Mother. Warriors say "Battio"—Wedding Ceremony performed after with Musu [who] sings her wedding song, "Bang-bang-te-la-lal" and stop. Medicine Men dance a few minutes, go offstage. Musu finish by singing, "Aha-Lungo-Bore-Oh"—All join with Chorus as curtain drops."[7]

These production notes are important clues to Dafora's artistic development over the next year, when the fully mature opera,

Kykunkor, went into production. The characters are similar: a king, slave girls, warriors, a medicine man, a bride, and a groom. So, too, are the big production numbers that conclude both pieces. Dances are similar—a warriors' dance, a hunters' dance, a witch doctor's dance, and a number for dancing girls. Even some of the cast members were the same: Musu Esami (Frances Atkins) played the part of the bride, and Dafora played the groom.

Dafora recruited his singers and dancers through the Native African Union. Many were apparently students stranded by the Depression, and they performed at private functions in the New York area throughout 1933. The company gained a wider audience when it was invited to perform at Madison Square Garden for the Communist Party production titled the Big Red Bazaar. A newspaper review of the production described *Zoonga* as "a series of skits" that were "interpretations of primitive West African folk songs and dances based upon the customs of the Susu, Kroo, Temini, Nigeria and Senegal tribes." When Anne Kennedy, the manager of the Unity Theatre, urged Dafora to mount the full-length opera he had been longing to stage, it did not take him long to complete it.[8]

At first Dafora had been unable to find financing. His work was criticized by potential Harlem backers as too "highbrow." Dafora later said that the authenticity of his performances did not coincide with the "same old stereotype of African arts," which he derided as the "moving picture and side show idea of Africa." But the Unity Theatre, a studio on East 23rd Street, agreed to a short run, and Dafora's new opera *Kykunkor* opened in early May 1934 to an audience of sixty.[9]

The performance was billed as a "Native African Opera by Asadata Dafora." Set in Kamlawoo, Sierra Leone, the plot was loosely taken from a Mende folktale and divided into three acts. The first act takes place in a village inhabited exclusively by young women who undergo initiation rites and preparation for marriage. When the curtain rises, Otobone (Rimeru Shikeru) directs the women as they pound the grain. Bokari (Dafora), a member of the Temeni tribe, enters. He has come to pick a bride. Otobone shoos the eligible unmarrieds into a hut to prepare for the Bonda, or maidens' dance. Maurice Goldberg, a New York photographer, shot a series of production photographs in 1934 to be used for publicity purposes. The originals, with typewritten and/or penciled comments on the back, are to be found in the Dafora Papers in New York. A photo captioned "The maidens' dance in the native African opera, *Kykunkor or Witch Woman* which is now playing at the Chanin Auditorium, atop the Chanin Building" has a penciled notation that the picture was "taken at the 23rd St. Theatre," which would date it May 1934 (see fig. on p. 253). The scene shows a great variety of movement and action. Of nine people depicted, seven are dancing, and two appear to be elders who oversee the action, yet each individual is caught by the camera in different positions.

Unlike the corps work in traditional Western ballets, synchronous movement is not common to the African dance aesthetic; rather, the beat of the drums calls for movement in rhythmic synchrony so that dancers may extend an arm as far as they choose so long as they move it precisely on the beat and approximate the movement pathway choreographed for that time sequence. Nor do the dancers employ the symmetry so typical of ballet; in African dance, an arm may be flung in any direction while the head will toss in yet another and the torso move as if on its own. Rhythmic patterns consequently may be extraordinarily intricate, with each separate body part creating layers of different accents and tempi.[10]

As seen in the photograph of the maidens' dance, the elders along with other dancers in the background are clapping their hands or stamping their feet. Some have their heads thrown back while others watch the action of two soloists dancing in front of them. One of the soloists looks as if she were traveling forward at great speed: her arms are raised above her head, and her pelvis is arched so as to emphasize her breasts and buttocks, while her left leg is lifted off the ground. Her posture is characteristic of many female African courtship dances. The other dancer, in full spotlight, is also moving with great force, although she seems to be dancing in place. Her left arm is thrown out to the side, while her right has dropped to her hip; her long hair streams outward as she whips her head around in a movement often found in West African dance. Her posture, again typical of West African dance, is asymmetrical, with one hip held higher than the other. Hips may be used in a highly complex rhythmic structure in certain West African dances, with feet, for example, shuffling forward on a one-TWO count, while the right hip rapidly lifts up and then drops down on a syncopated count of one-two-THREE-and-four. Critic Edwin Denby, reviewing a later revival of *Kykunkor* in the *New York Herald Tribune*, commented on the differences between European and African dance: "Its general method is to superimpose on a steady foot rhythm a brief phrase of arm or torso gesture, which is repeated an even number of times and then given up for a new phrase similarly repeated."[11]

According to Denby, in traditional courtship dances it was the custom for the potential groom to dance "a few steps with each of the other girls in turn, circling about each as if to pay her a special compliment; an attention which each rewarded by a lovely smile and a graceful undulation in her steps." Denby described *Kykunkor*'s Dance of Acquaintance of the bride and groom as: "a dance which began with a boops-a-daisy and continued with a figure where she swayed her bright-colored bustle a little on the left or a little on the right, and his arms drew long caressing curves in the air just out of reach behind her—the elegance of their play and the lightness of their rhythm remind me in its spirit of an eighteenth century pastoral" (see fig. on p. 254). After they danced, Bokari selected his bride (Musu Esami) and serenaded her. The attraction between them is mutual, and they brought to the Susu or engagement dance "a series of tender caresses which has the formality of a ritual, passion being isolated." One critic praised "the controlled savagery of movement and gesture which is quite thrilling to watch" in this "especially fine" dance for two. Dafora was characterized as "the smilingist bridegroom this side of the Blessed Isles and a good singer" besides. This observation is borne out by photographs that show the bride and groom standing beside each other with elbows almost touching their waists and their palms facing forward. Dafora is grinning broadly, and his bride smiles sweetly. In another photograph of the same scene the two face each other, with their knees bent and their palms, shoulder high, almost touching each other, as they look directly into the camera. Once again Dafora's smile and his bright gold tooth gleam brightly."[12]

Bokari's retinue, which is considerable, includes wild game and a cow, but the Mende ethnic group, unlike the Temeni, interpret this to be an evil omen. In terror, the women engage in rituals to exorcize the evil spirits and appease the gods before they agree to continue the engagement ceremonies and prepare the bride's trousseau. Afterward, Chief Burab (Tuguese) enters, laden with gifts in honor of his son's impending marriage. He and his retinue are greeted with a performance of the Fugule, the dance of welcome. Greeting dances are common throughout West Africa and were considered one of the most elaborate and hospitable ways to honor travelers of high rank.[13]

The women's dance then leads into a contrasting festive dance, the Aguga, a "dance [celebrating] strength." A photograph of Matta performing the Aguga Dance shows him poised on the balls of his feet, arms bent and raised to the sides, in line with his shoulders, which are so pulled up that his neck appears to be shortened (see fig. on p. 255). His fingers are rigidly extended at right angles to his wrists. He wears a kerchief on his head and a knee-length, plainly colored skirt. His muscular torso is bent forward and twisted slightly to the left. West African dances use the shoulders and upper torso in percussive movements, hunching forward with energy and thrusting the neck at the same time, then rolling the shoulders back on the next beat. In his review of *Kykunkor* in the *Nation*, Lincoln Kirstein described the dancer (probably Matta) who performed this solo as executing "a remarkable series of swift movements of arms and feet, fluently sexual and intense. . . . He exhibits a high potential of concentrated, breathing action, animal and subhumanly skillful."[14]

Critics complimented Turgese as the chief for his "nice comic sense" and touted his acting as "something worth seeing" (see fig. on p. 256). The one sour note was sounded by Lincoln Kirstein who described the actor as "a superb and monstrous black Golliwog King who splutters with benevolent tyranny in French and African, one mad eye whitened, his leopard skins flapping and enormous orange bracelets clacking around his flat feet." Kirstein fantasied that two of the chief's stage attendants were actual slaves in real life who would make backstage "a tricky place for a white man to navigate." In Goldberg's production photographs, a stocky man (who may be Turgese) is placed on a throne or platform of some kind; he holds a pole in his right hand but the carvings on it are not visible (in a 1935 photograph by Harlem habitué Carl Van Vechten, Dafora holds a long staff that ends with a carved, seated tribal figure). His left hand is placed on his knee, and he stares directly into the camera. He would appear to be the Chief Burah, for his regalia and regal dignity have an air of authority. He wears a feathered headdress and elaborate necklaces. His right eye is encircled by white paint, which emphasizes his solemn demeanor and heightens the intensity of his gaze.[15]

In Act Two, Bokari sings to his father of his love for his bride, and predicts that she will bring great wealth to the chief as her dowry. Two photographs of Dafora, which may or may not be from this particular scene but were used for the cover of the program, show him in a similar pose with feet wide apart as if he were stepping forward, body twisted to the side, upper arms rotated inward and held away from the side (see fig. on p. 257). In both photographs his face is unusually expressive, no doubt one of the reasons he was so powerful a performer. Dafora's costume consisted of a wide cloth headband, many strands of beads, armbands on his biceps, an elaborate full-length sarong, and sandals.

Denby, writing in a 1943 review, commented that Dafora had "all the qualities of a great dancer—the verve, the precision, the variety and brilliance within his own dance tradition, the sweetness of stage personality." The African style, as Denby described it, consisted of

> a rather steady rhythm of strong and light beats—the light ones being sole taps, the heavy ones changing the step from one foot to the other. The feet are light and quick, and move from the ankles. The torso is bent forward slightly, the chest is open and the shoulders, relaxed. It is in the arms that the dance ornamentation takes place, and they can move with extraordinary speed, and with great precision, without looking strained. When they fly out, the force of

the gesture is toned down just before the end so that the movement remains graceful and the gesture does not break off.

Denby added that Dafora relied less often on "gentle leaps and turns" and "spinal movements" in his choreography.[16]

After Dafora's solo, the slave girls were presented as gifts to the chief. They danced before their new master, whereupon Bokari persuades his father to free them. One of Goldberg's plates shows a trio of women, who may be the slave girls, since they wear revealing costumes (see fig. on p. 258). They stand in a line, their weight on the left leg which is rotated to the side; the front leg is bent and the toes of the right foot are forward. The arms are extended hip-high in front, with the palms pushing downward as the torsos sway slightly toward the back. The women are smiling and laughing. Their costumes are made of leopard-cloth skirts, zebra-skin belts, beaded brassieres, and headdresses. They wear long beaded necklaces and multiple layers of ankle bracelets. None of the women dancers, unlike the male singers and dancers, came from Africa, but were recruited from Harlem neighborhoods. They were assigned what the *Amsterdam News* described as "beautiful euphonic African names," but evidently none of the women, except Musu Esami who played the bride, had ever appeared on the stage before. Kirstein dismissed the women as "little brown girls with straightened hair and more than a hint of Cotton Club can-cans."[17]

At this point the marriage ceremony commences. Otobone describes in song her fondness for the young bride who must now leave her for new lands. A photo of Otobone shows her with right arm enfolding the bride and her left hand clasping her right hand (see fig. on p. 259). The young woman plaintively leans her head on Otobone's shoulder.

Bokari enters and kneels before them. In a photograph of the wedding scene, the bride and Otobone remain in close embrace. The bride is festively dressed in a long pale underskirt, topped by a colorful print tunic with a vine-like design. She wears multiple beaded necklaces and many bangle bracelets on her upper arms, wrists, and ankles, as well as an elaborate head scarf. Otobone wears a headdress, beads, bangles, and a full-length dress in a bold printed pattern. The groom has changed as well. Along with the sarong and sandals from Act One, he wears a scarf draped over his bare torso and a finely beaded headband that covers his fore-head. He falls on his right knee, in a traditional courtship posture, and extends his arms toward the bride (see fig. on p. 260). She regards him shyly, as if loath to leave the protecting embrace of her guardian. Otobone is thanked in song for her care and devo-tion. The groom begins to dance, and the bride joins him in the Apomba, or wedding dance.

Suddenly Kykunkor, the witch woman, enters and invokes the gods in song (see fig. on p. 262). Her hair is disheveled, and white paint covers her eyebrows, cheeks, and mouth. She frightens the guests who fear that disaster lies close at hand. The witch woman is emissary for a jealous rival who has sent her to cast a spell over the groom. In a highly dramatic scene, she screams a curse, and Bokari slowly sinks to the ground as his life ebbs away. He falls unconscious, center stage, despite the loud cries and pleas to the gods by the members of the wedding party, who crowd and crouch around him.

Immediately a "devil dancer" is called in to exorcize the evil spirit with the Oummoie Dance, but the magic is unsuccessful. Obviously a higher power is needed, so the witch doctor is sum-moned. He was played by Abdul Essen and billed as an "authen-tic witch doctor of the Aussa tribe of Africa" (see fig. on p. 261). A photograph shows him wearing beads, a large hoop earring, a leopard-skin headband, an amulet on his upper arm, and a grass skirt. Dabbed on his cheeks were strokes of white paint, and he wore a goatee.

The witch doctor enters, playing on a reed pipe, calling upon the gods even as he invokes Allah (performer Abdul Essen was actually a Muslim). Reviewer John Martin wrote: he "beats him-self in the breast and utters guttural animal sounds, until by force of his grotesque ecstasy he succeeds in casting out the devil."[18] While the groom lies prostrate on the ground, the witch doctor leans over him solicitously, placing a black carved mask at his side and trapping the evil spirit in a cow horn (see fig. on p. 264).

Using his considerable magical powers, he summons the witch woman to return. Her eyes open wide in terror as she gazes at the fetish he holds above her. His face writhes in contortions that indicate his intense concentration (see fig. on p. 263). The two engage in a contest of strength, but in the end she is forced to swallow the evil spirit lying dormant in the horn, which causes boisterous merriment among the spectators (see fig. on p. 265). The groom is saved from death, and the wedding ceremony can continue.

Abdul Essen's performance was considered a high point of the opera. Writing in the *World Telegram*, Emmanuel Eisenberg praised "the incredible performance of Abdul Assen [*sic*] as the witch doctor. The violence, extravagant use of the voice and barbaric passion create an overwhelming characterization which will leave one limp with emotion and admiration." An anonymous critic for *Musical America* called Essen's "outstanding" performance one of "thrilling and blood-curdling intensity . . . played as by one possessed." Julian Seaman in the *Daily Mirror* called him "one of the most amazing players I have ever seen," while Henderson in the *New York Sun* spoke of the "passionate emotion of immense power" he brought to the role, and urged "every actor in town" to the Unity Theater. John Martin wrote that this "amazing scene . . . is likely to remain long in memory," an opinion that most critics shared. Writing in *Esquire*, Gilbert Seldes described Essen's shrill laughter, shrieking, moaning, cursing, and wrestling "in an awful agony with the spirit of evil," adding, "No more than myself, you do not believe in black magic; you are a theatregoer and know that everything will come out right. But this terrific savage rite engrosses you so that you share in the triumph when the dead man is raised to life again."[19]

Once the groom returns to life, the celebrations begin anew in Act Three. The program notes described the order of events: "The festival starts in real earnest. There is first the AGUNDA, the dance of joy; then the EBOE, the jester, dances. The BATOO, or dance of challenge follows, then the war-dance, and then the JABAWA or festival dance." The last act of the opera resembled other traditional ethnic group dance-dramas in that it featured acrobatics and dancing combined with music, song, and the spoken word. The finale was not unlike the Italian operas that Dafora may have seen or performed at La Scala. As the description of the action makes clear, the finale incorporated a number of elements from the original 1933 version of *Zoonga*. The opera closes with the young men and women performing the Jabawa, or festival dance, with the elders clapping the beat (see fig. on p. 266).

Dafora had called his work an "opera," a categorization that few critics accepted unreservedly. Gilbert Seldes called it a "spectacle, dramatic dance, opera, or study in folklore." John Martin, also uneasy with the term "opera," preferred to call it a "ritual drama," on the grounds that the music was secondary to the dance. The reviewer for *Musical America* followed his lead, describing the production as "a primitive African ritual drama." Garland, after referring to it as "a native African opera," then demurred: "actually it is a ritual drama but opera is what it is called." Henderson felt it should "properly . . . be classed as a folk drama, developed from native songs and dances of Africa." Emmanuel Eisenberg reported that it was "an apparently authentic African dance opera." John Mason Brown, writing in the *New York Post,* described the production as "a baffling but invigorating mixture of folklore, ritualistic dancing and what the program describes as Native African Opera," while Julian Seaman in the *Daily Mirror* called it a "dance drama."[20]

Dafora seems to have some misgivings about the term and chose to call his 1937 *Bassa Moona* and 1938 *Zunguru* "dance dramas," although he created two more operas, *Batanoa* in 1941 and *Battalokar* in 1953. By the 1940s he was known primarily as a dance specialist, and his productions were typically billed as festivals of dance and music. When he returned to Sierra Leone in 1960, Dafora was hailed as an "internationally heralded African Dancer and Choreographer." His obituaries uniformly praised his activities as a dancer and choreographer but omitted to point out his involvement with the creation of the first "African opera" produced in the United States.[21]

Perhaps another reason that critics were unsure about defining the spectacle as an opera was because the emphasis on solo arias (the high point of European opera) was modest compared to the focus on dance. For the African, where there is music, there almost invariably is dance. In addition the "orchestra," as it was billed, consisted of four drums, which, again, did not fit with Western notions of operatic accompaniment. For example, Martin argued that *Kykunkor* was not an opera, because "the musical aspect was secondary. There are, to be sure, several enchanting songs, and an unceasing background of rhythmic drumming by three extremely skillful drummers."[22]

Few, however, questioned the authenticity of the music, and all praised highly the sensitive drumming of the four musicians: Abrodun Salako, Uno Eno, Sakor Jar, and Ezebro Ejiho. For John Mason Brown, it was "the four tireless drummers at one side of the crowded stage who give the most astonishing and compelling performance of the evening." Julian Seaman evoked the spell cast by the music: "Save for the reed pipe used by the Witch Doctor, supplemented by the eerie and tremendous twittering of the voice, like some frightened night bird of the wild, no tonal instrument is used throughout the entire production. But the drums beat an incessant rhythm, weaving a curious pattern in percussion, and the singers chant and moan. Weirdly lovely is the effect, for the soft syllables of the tribal dialect melt into the slurs and melancholy cadences of this peculiar scale."[23]

Not everyone was quite so entranced. Henderson, for instance, found the singing "absorbing" but "untutored"; the anonymous critic for *Musical America* pointed out the incongruity of the "chorus in the background singing in plain diatonic harmony what more closely resembles 'Nearer My God to Thee' than anything else. These incongruous musical interludes come occasionally and even though they may be adaptations of English hymn tunes gleaned in some time past from missionaries, they are very irritating to a Western ear which does not expect its own harmonies and tunes—banal ones, at that—from a portrayal of savage mysteries. Much more congenial is the occasional singing of plaintive and weird chants which seem consistent and lyrical." Kirstein, too, confessed to being "puzzled" by the mixture of West or North African songs combined with "traces of Methodist missionary hymns and the effective, if hardly legitimate, interpolation of some melodies from Martinique." On that ground, he dismissed the music as a "salad sound." Composer Paul Bowles spoke of this inconsistency in a review of a later production:

> As long as the music used as its basis the eight drums of varying dimension, which were slapped, patted, and pounded or struck with sticks, the illusion of West Africa was very well preserved. The rhythm was mostly a somewhat unvaried six-eight beat rapidly with occasional unexpected accents. The song consisted of rhythmical and unrhythmical cries uttered by separate groups at the same time, and this made a pattern of sound which was convincing in its authenticity. When any sort of sustained melodic line was introduced, however, the atmosphere was automatically destroyed by the fact that the voices all used the European tradition of voice production. These "cultured" voices brought everything right back to New York where it decidedly did not belong; and then the musical associations ran amok, suggested anything from Stephen Foster to "Aloha Oe."[24]

For those who criticized the music, the juxtaposition of Western melody with African rhythm was profoundly disconcerting.

Dafora compared his function as composer to that of a weaver who made use of the music of the Mende ethnic group, perhaps meaning that the syncopated drum patterns were the warp and woof of his musical fabric. "Africans," he told the *New Yorker,* "instead of having music written down on paper, they have it in the head, they have it in the body. Then the drum signals, and they dance. They dance the feeling of the moonlight—the moon shines in Africa just like daybreak." Although Dafora taught the music to the cast, the production's music director, Marguerite Kennerly Upshur, a Harlem pianist and teacher, scored it. The drums were not notated but left to the lead drummer to cue. The drummers were from the Mende ethnic group.[25]

Despite general reservations as to how the production should be categorized, it was considered a great success by musical and literary celebrities of the time. Leopold Stokowski, the renowned conductor of the Philadelphia Orchestra, Lawrence Tibbett of the Boston Symphony, composer George Gershwin, novelist Sherwood Anderson, novelist Theodore Dreiser, and the eminent literary critic Carl Van Doren saw the show; Stokowski, Tibbett, and Gershwin saw it more than once. Indeed, even without publicity, *Kykunkor* filled the theater and scored a greater success than Virgil Thompson's *Four Saints in Three Acts,* which, as Gilbert Seldes observed, "had its Hartford premiere triply covered by each newspaper, and yet was unable to make a long run." Part of *Kykunkor*'s appeal, according to Henderson, was to musicologists interested in the antecedents of Southern black music and possible African retentions. According to some observers, musicians and dancers came "in quest of sources," which suggests that Gershwin and others found much to emulate in Dafora's work.[26]

In fact, only months before *Kykunkor* opened, George Gershwin had just begun composing *Porgy and Bess.* He worked on the score throughout the spring, even as he attended several performances of Dafora's *Kykunkor,* continuing over the summer in South Carolina. Just as with Dafora's work, *Porgy and Bess* was billed as "a folk opera" when it opened on Broadway. Although contemporary musicologists have yet to explore Dafora's impact on American musicians and composers of his time, it is quite likely that *Kykunkor* influenced George Gershwin during the all-important genesis of *Porgy and Bess.*

Kykunkor was born in "an informally rigged up studio theatre on East 23rd Street" called the Unity Theatre. Audiences had to climb dingy stairs to get to it and once inside discovered that the so-called theater was only a loft with "a makeshift platform" at the site of a former beauty parlor. The show went on despite the total lack of advertising or advance publicity, and it was booked for only eight performances. About sixty people paid thirty-five cents to see the opening night presentation on 6 May. Fewer came the next night and fewer still the next.

However, on 9 May 1934, when John Martin's review appeared in the *New York Times,* 425 people crowded into the tiny loft, and some 200 were turned away at the door. The next day, ticket prices were raised from thirty-five cents to $1.50, with standing room for fifty cents. The police became apprehensive of overcrowding, since the hall was licensed for 150 spectators and twice that were nightly filling the space. People were sitting on hard wooden benches and on the platform itself. John Martin remembered that "famous actors, conductors, dancers, were quite content to sit on top of the unused piano or even to huddle in the unventilated space euphemistically referred to as standing room."[27]

The fire department threatened to closed the show, so the entire production moved to City College, then located at Lexington Avenue and 23rd Street, but the auditorium was felt to be "too large for an intimate opera." As more and more critics published glowing reviews, the "tiny but elegant" Chanin Theatre on 14th Street opened its doors to Dafora's opera. Located on the fiftieth floor of the Chanin Building, the theater was sold out nightly to a "chic and select" audience. Gilbert Seldes protested that critics were forced to purchase tickets rather than receive complimentary ones, "and none of your nonsense about low prices—$2.50 plus tax." Still, as he observed, "the place was crowded and the swells were there." Finally, in fulfillment of Dafora's dream, *Kykunkor* moved uptown to premiere at the Little Theatre on West 44th Street on 15 June.[28] Here, against all odds, *Kykunkor* had a three-month run, much of it to sold-out houses. As Emmanuel Eisenberg summed it up in the *New York World Telegram:* "This is a success story and a remarkable one."[29]

Even some sixty years later, Asadata Dafora's historical impact on American musical theater has been considerable, for it is generally acknowledged that he opened the way for African Americans to be accepted as serious performers on the concert stage. His impact on other musicians and composers, especially George Gershwin, who was immersed in writing *Porgy and Bess* during this period, has yet to be evaluated. However, it is incontrovertible that *Kykunkor* provided a positive model of African music and dance for those who attended its performances. Furthermore, present-day dance productions by numerous U.S.–based African American troupes are modeled extensively on Dafora's original *Kykunkor,* with its winning combination of music, drama, and dance in festive African settings.

NOTES

1. The *Dictionary of Blacks in the Performing Arts,* ed. E. Mapp (Metuchen, N.J.: Scarecrow Press, 1978) is the only source to give Dafora's birth date as

4 August 1890, although it gives his forenames as John Warner. The *Biographical Dictionary of African-American and African Musicians* (Westport, Conn.: Greenwood Press, 1982) gives his date of birth as 1889, and the "Scope and Contents" inventory notes for the Asadata Dafora Papers at the Schomburg Center for Research in Black Culture, New York Public Library, gives this as 1890, as does Anatole Chujoy's *Dance Encyclopedia* (New York: Barnes, 1949). A 1960 article in the Freetown newspaper the *Ten Daily News* ("The Native Returns," 4 June, 1960) gives his birth name as Austin and his father's initials as J. W., which would make it likely that his father's name was John Warner. I have followed this source, since it is the only contemporary evidence with this information, and Dafora himself included this clipping in his papers. Margaret Lloyd, in a 1945 interview with Dafora, gives his birth name as "Austin Horton," noting this was also the name of his great-great-grandfather ("Dancer from the Gold Coast," *Christian Science Monitor,* 26 May 1945, n.p.). Unless otherwise noted, all press clippings are from the Dafora Clippings File, the Asadata Dafora Papers at the Schomburg Center for Research in Black Culture, New York Public Library.

2. "The Native Returns."

3. Margaret Lloyd, "Dancer from the Gold Coast," *Christian Science Monitor,* pt. 1, 26 May 1945, and pt. 2, 9 June 1945. See also "The Native Returns." "Beat Me, Daddy," an unidentified clipping in the Dafora Papers, mentions that Dafora toured Russia in 1910. See also the inventory of the Asadata Dafora Papers.

4. Inventory, Asadata Dafora Papers: "Africa," *New Yorker* (19 May 1934); K. K. Martin, "America's First African Dance Theatre," *Odu* 11 (January 1975): 11. See also Lloyd, "Dancer from the Gold Coast."

5. New York Public Library, Schomburg Collection, Writer's Program, New York City; "An Interview with Asadata Dafora," by Waring Cuney, 25 July 1939, 1. At the end of the interview, located in the file "Negroes of New York, 1939: Biographical Sketches," Cuney describes the African population then living in Harlem.

6. Dafora was quite active in the New York–New Jersey region during 1933. In the file "Correspondence, 1933–63," an undated letter from a Mr. S. A. Allen of the New York Urban League requested Dafora to perform for free, which indicates that the artist was known at that time as an African specialist. On 25 November 1933, Dafora did appear at Town Hall for an Urban League benefit along with his company, billed as "Horton's African Dancers," and Bill Robinson. In the same folder is the playbill for the 13 April 1933 performance. MSS 48, Dafora Papers.

7. The original spelling has been retained, but numbers 25 through 39 have been dropped and hyphens substituted for ease of reading. Some punctuation has been added.

8. "African Dancers and Singers Appear in Recital in Harlem," *New York Age,* 21 October 1933. The critic also mentions that Dafora has appeared several times at the Little Theatre at the Harlem YMCA, the Experimental Theatre on the east side of Manhattan, and at Mountain Lakes, New Jersey. My thanks to Nicole Underwood for providing me with this citation. See also K. K. Martin, "America's First African Dance Theatre," 121.

9. Dafora was interviewed by Cuney in 1939 ("Interview," 2). The opening date is not certain: K. K. Martin ("America's First African Dance Theatre," 199) says April, but the Inventory of the Dafora Papers (2) gives the date as 6 May 1934. John Martin's famous review in the *New York Times* on 9 May 1934 does not give a specific date, but Martin's later article "The Dance: African Lore," published 13 May 1934, says performances had been going on for eight days and would end after one more evening. An unsigned piece in the *New Yorker* ("Africa," 19 May 1934) states that it opened on 6 May. See also Martin, "America's First African Dance Theatre," 121.

10. These observations are taken from my study of Ghanaian dance performance and technique with Professor Adinku, University of Ghana, while he and I were colleagues on the dance faculty at the University of Illinois during the 1970s. They are further based on extended viewings of African dance films, particularly *The Dancers of Sierra Leone*, filmed by the Reverend Paul Dillingham while on assignment to Sierra Leone in the mid-1960s. (A print of this film, donated by the author, can be viewed at the Dance Collection, New York Public Library for the Performing Arts.)

11. Similar postures of the young women can be seen in Michel Hunt's *The Dance, Art, and Ritual of Africa* (New York: Pantheon, 1978), plates 17–18, 185, 200, 212. Edwin Denby, "The Dance: Saga of Rhythm," *New York Herald Tribune*, 5 April 1945.

12. Edwin Denby, "A Glimpse of Real African Dancing," *New York Herald Tribune*, 21 December 1943. Gilbert Seldes, *Esquire* (August 1934): n.p.; *Musical America*, 25 May 1934; "African Opera Fifty Stories off the Ground," *Daily News*, 24 May 1934. A set of Maurice Goldberg's photographs of the original production is in the Dafora Papers.

13. Photographs of Togan ceremonies welcoming Chief Ewe are published by Michel Huet in *The Dance, Art, and Ritual of Africa*, plates 72–74.

14. Lincoln Kirstein, "The Dance: 'Kykunkor': Native African Opera," *Nation* (13 June 1934): 684.

15. Burns Mantle, "African Opera Fifty Stories off the Ground," *Daily News*, 24 May 1934; W. J. Henderson, "Native African Opera Moves," *New York Sun*, 21 May 1934; Lincoln Kirstein, "The Dance: 'Kykunkor': Native African Opera."

16. Edwin Denby, "The Dance: In Brightest Africa," *New York Herald Tribune*, 14 December 1943.

17. Martin, "America's First African Dance Theatre," 120. Reviews of that time claim that none of the women performers had stage experience, but Musu Esami, who played the bride, had previously appeared in *Zoonga*. Kirstein, "The Dance: 'Kykunkor': Native African Opera."

18. Martin, "The Dance: African Lore."

19. Emmanuel Eisenberg, "'Kykunkor' Hits the Top," *New York World Telegram*, 24 May 1934; *Musical America*, 24 May 1934; Julian Seaman, "Jungle Dances," *New York Daily Mirror*, 19 May 1934; W. J. Henderson, "Native African Opera Moves," *New York Sun*, 21 May 1934; John Martin, "The Dance: African Lore," *New York Times*, 13 May 1934; "Tom Toms and Witch Doctor on Broadway," *Time* (16 June 1934): n.p.; Robert Garland, "Native African Opera

Proves Entertaining," *New York World Telegram,* 19 May 1934; Gilbert Seldes, *Esquire* (August 1934).

20. See citation above for newspaper critics' comments.

21. "The Native Returns."

22. Martin, "The Dance: African Lore."

23. John Mason Brown, "Africa Comes to Manhattan—The Unusual Dancers and Drummers Now Performing at the Unity Theatre," *New York Post,* 19 May 1934; Seaman, "Jungle Dances."

24. *Musical America,* 24 May 1934; Kirstein, "The Dance: 'Kykunkor': Native African Opera." Bowes is quoted by Denby, "The Dance: Saga of Rhythm," *New York Herald Tribune,* 5 April 1945.

25. *New Yorker* (19 May 1934).

26. Seldes, *Esquire* (August 1934). An unsigned article in the Dafora papers, "Ritual Dance and Primitive Drama Combine in Kykunkor," (n.d., n.p.) refers to the current production at the Little, which would date it sometime after May 1934. Henderson, "Native American Opera Moves." Dafora's obituary was published in the *New York Times,* 7 March 1965, and *Dance Magazine* (April 1965).

27. See the unsigned article "Tom Toms and Witch Doctors on Broadway," 16 June 1934. See also Mantle, "African Opera Fifty Stories off the Ground"; "Africans"; John Martin, "Au Revoir to Dafora," *New York Times,* 22 May 1960.

28. "Ritual Dance and Primitive Drama Combine in Kykunkor," (n.d., n.p.); John Martin, "Native Cast Gives an African 'Opera,'" *New York Times,* 9 May 1934; Martin, "The Dance: African Lore"; Martin, "Companion Piece to 'Kykunkor,'" *New York Times,* 31 July 1934; Seldes, *Esquire* (August 1934); Henderson, "Native African Opera Moves"; Mantle, "African Opera Fifty Stories off the Ground"; Brown, "Africa Comes to Manhattan"; Eisenberg, "'Kykunkor' Hits the Top"; *New Yorker* (19 May 1934); Garland, "Native African Opera Proves Entertaining"; "Tom Toms and Witch Doctor on Broadway," 16 June 1934; Kirstein, "The Dance: 'Kykunkor': Native African Opera."

29. Emmanuel Eisenberg, "'Kykunkor' Hits the Top."

The maidens' dance in *Kykunkor* (Photographer unknown; Photographs and Prints Division, Schomburg Center for Research in Black Culture, the New York Public Library–Astor, Lenox and Tilden Foundations; reproduced with permission)

253

Asadata Dafora and Musu Esami as the bridegroom and bride in *Kykunkor* (Photograph by Maurice Goldberg; Photographs and Prints Division, Schomburg Center for Research in Black Culture, the New York Public Library–Astor, Lenox and Tilden Foundations; reproduced with permission)

Matta in the Aguga Dance in *Kykunkor* (Photographer unknown; Photographs and Prints Division, Schomburg Center for Research in Black Culture, the New York Public Library–Astor, Lenox and Tilden Foundations; reproduced with permission)

Turgese as the chief in *Kykunkor* (Photograph by Maurice Goldberg; Photographs and Prints Division, Schomburg Center for Research in Black Culture, the New York Public Library–Astor, Lenox and Tilden Foundations; reproduced with permission)

Asadata Dafora as the bridegroom in *Kykunkor* (Photograph by Maurice Goldberg; Photographs and Prints Division, Schomburg Center for Research in Black Culture, the New York Public Library–Astor, Lenox and Tilden Foundations; reproduced with permission)

Slave girls in *Kykunkor* (Photographer unknown; Photographs and Prints Division, Schomburg Center for Research in Black Culture, the New York Public Library–Astor, Lenox and Tilden Foundations; reproduced with permission)

Musu Esami and Rimeru Shikeru as the bride and Otobone in *Kykunkor* (Photograph by Maurice Goldberg; Photographs and Prints Division, Schomburg Center for Research in Black Culture, the New York Public Library–Astor, Lenox and Tilden Foundations; reproduced with permission)

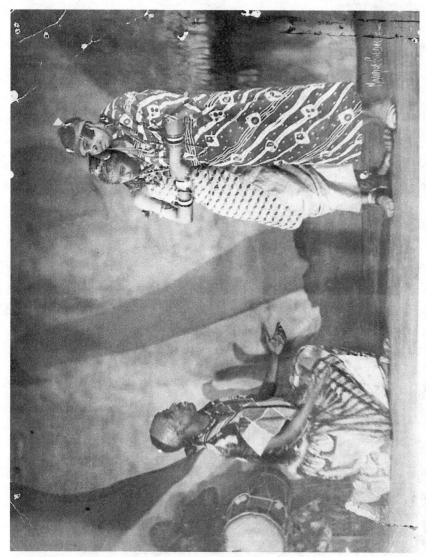

Asadata Dafora, Musu Esami, and Rimeru Shikeru as the bridegroom, bride, and Otobone in *Kykunkor* (Photograph by Maurice Goldberg; Photographs and Prints Division, Schomburg Center for Research in Black Culture, the New York Public Library–Astor, Lenox and Tilden Foundations; reproduced with permission)

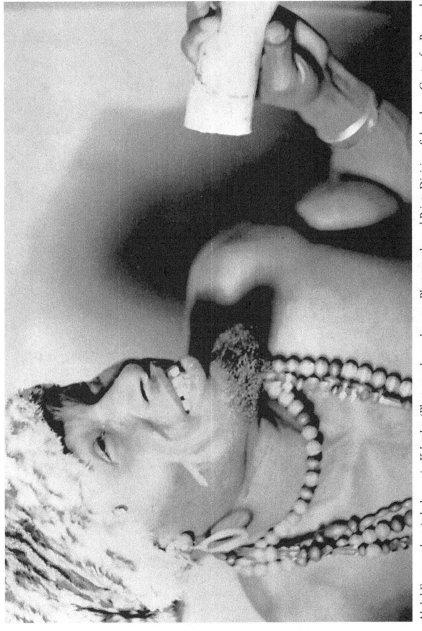

Abdul Essen as the witch doctor in *Kykunkor* (Photographer unknown; Photographs and Prints Division, Schomburg Center for Research in Black Culture, the New York Public Library–Astor, Lenox and Tilden Foundations; reproduced with permission)

Unidentified dancer as the witch woman in *Kykunkor* (Photographer unknown; Photographs and Prints Division, Schomburg Center for Research in Black Culture, the New York Public Library–Astor, Lenox and Tilden Foundations; reproduced with permission)

Abdul Essen as the witch doctor in *Kykunkor* (Photograph by Maurice Goldberg; Photographs and Prints Division, Schomburg Center for Research in Black Culture, the New York Public Library–Astor, Lenox and Tilden Foundations; reproduced with permission)

Abdul Essen and Asadata Dafora as the witch doctor and bridegroom in *Kykunkor* (Photographer unknown; Photographs and Prints Division, Schomburg Center for Research in Black Culture, the New York Public Library–Astor, Lenox and Tilden Foundations; reproduced with permission)

Abdul Essen and unidentified dancer as the witch doctor and witch woman in *Kykunkor* (Photographer unknown; Photographs and Prints Division, Schomburg Center for Research in Black Culture, the New York Public Library–Astor, Lenox and Tilden Foundations; reproduced with permission)

265

Asadata Dafora and Musu Esami as the bridegroom and bride in *Kykunkor* (Photographer unknown; Photographs and Prints Division, Schomburg Center for Research in Black Culture, the New York Public Library–Astor, Lenox and Tilden Foundations; reproduced with permission)

9

Between Two Eras: "Norton and Margot" in the Afro-American Entertainment World

Brenda Dixon Gottschild

INTRODUCTION

From 1933 until 1947, Margot Webb and Harold Norton performed on the Afro-American vaudeville circuits of night clubs and theaters in the Northeast and the Midwest. Known professionally as "Norton and Margot," they were one of the few Afro-American ballroom teams in history.[1] Their career was emblematic of the frustrations, paradoxes, and double standards that existed for Afro-American artists in the United States. As a ballroom team, they faced the same obstacles as a Dean Dixon or a Marian Anderson: they were traveling on a white road posted with "No Trespassing" signs for the Afro-American. They followed on the heels of the 1920s, which was the golden era of Afro-American vaudeville, of the Cotton Club–type posh nightclub, and of "Black Broadway." They preceded by two decades the civil rights era of the 1960s, when more opportunities became available to Afro-Americans in mainstream (or white) show business. Norton and Webb belonged to the swing era of the 1930s and the 1940s. However, due to the nature of their performance style and the racial tenor of their times, they were either too early or too late for success. It is in this sense that they existed between two eras.

Had they been Lindy Hoppers, tap dancers, or an exotic act, they might have gained opportunities in white show business. For example, Afro-American dancers like Bill "Bojangles" Robinson who achieved mainstream popularity exhibited qualities con-

Harold Norton and Margot Webb in a studio portrait, ca. 1930 (Reproduced with permission of Margot Webb)

ventionally associated with "Black Dance": speed, eccentricity, "natural rhythm," fast footwork, or exoticism. They succeeded by adhering to a repertory that acknowledged the accepted stereotypes of a society based on racial discrimination and segregation. In contrast—and like their Afro-American counterparts in opera, ballet, and classical music—Norton and Webb adopted a white repertory. This was a radical move for an era in which America questioned the potential of Afro-American achievement in Western disciplines, and even doubted the existence of romantic love in the Afro-American male–female relationship. The wheels of minstrelsy remained in motion, and many acts performed in black-face in both white and Afro-American vaudeville. Widespread lynchings and segregation were the main concerns of the Afro-American community. Demeaning racial stereotypes were rife in both the sociopolitical and the cultural realms.

In this atmosphere, an Afro-American tap act could be booked on the Loews circuit or at Radio City Music Hall. However, a romantic ballroom team performing a white repertory of waltz, tango, rumba, and bolero numbers was ahead of its time. Western art forms were reserved for whites only. Norton and Webb never reached Broadway or any other major white outlet in America. They were invisible—unnoticed and mainly undocumented—to white audiences. Like many Afro-American performers, they were "dancing in the dark," as far as the white world at large was concerned. For example, tap dancers Aaron Palmer and Earl "Groundhog" Basie may have been esteemed by their colleagues, many of whom said they surpassed mainstream talents like Bill "Bojangles" Robinson. Nevertheless, there is no documentation of their work save the superficial mention of them in interviews recorded by Marshall and Jean Stearns in *Jazz Dance*.[2] Their unique contributions are forgotten. Norton and Webb, too, are prototypes of this invisible category of Afro-American performance; namely, the world of the touring vaudeville entertainer whose horizons were limited by one-night stands, the two-to-five-show-a-day format, and lack of exposure in white show business.

Paradoxically, because of the rarity of ballroom dancing by an Afro-American team, Norton and Webb could be booked regularly on Afro-American entertainment outlets when a ballroom act was solicited. They were preceded by Thelma and Paul Meeres, who performed as "Meeres and Meeres" in the 1920s. The Meereses' act was more a novelty and ethnic repertory than ballroom dance and included Native American and Caribbean dances performed in "authentic" costume. Fredi Washington and Al Moore were a team for a short time, but they went on to other show business careers. Washington, who had created the role of Peola (the light-skinned Afro-American who decides to pass for white) in the original 1934 film version of Fannie Hurst's novel *Imitation of Life* returned to the stage to pursue a career as an actress. With the exception of teams such as "Anise and Aland" and "Ross and McCain," both contemporaries of Norton and Webb, other Afro-American teams were tap, acrobatic, exotic or novelty acts.

Norton and Webb toured extensively on the East Coast and in the Midwest, performing on the Afro-American vaudeville circuits that ran tours from New York to Philadelphia, Baltimore, and Washington, D.C., and from Chicago to points west. These were the standard touring routes taken by most Afro-American entertainers after the demise of the Theatre Owners Booking Association (referred to hereafter as TOBA), the first circuit for Afro-American talent, which thrived from the 1910s to the early 1930s. Due to the extreme racism to which they would have been subjected, Norton and Webb refused to perform on tours going south.

Their popularity was documented in the Afro-American press of the era. They received regular coverage in the 1930s and the 1940s in such publications as the *Afro-American, Amsterdam News, Norfolk Journal and Guide, Pittsburgh Courier,* and *Chicago Defender*.[3] These newspapers represented a network of Afro-American publications that reflected a world shaped by discrimination. The Afro-American world was a microcosm of the white world, providing goods and services, arts, and cultural outlets for inhabitants of the many Afro-American communities throughout the nation.

Besides newspaper documentation, oral interviews conducted for this study revealed the popularity of this team in the Afro-American world. Norton and Webb were remembered by musicians, former students, and fellow dancers for their romantic image and their smooth, sustained performance style, supported by their strong foundation in ballet technique.[4] Both studied ballet. Their teachers included Russian émigrés who fled the Bolshevik Revolution and brought classical ballet to popularity in America. Webb studied at the Louis Chalif studios in midtown Manhattan. Chalif was a popular teacher of the era, and he published *The Chalif Textbook of Dancing,* a five-volume work detailing his techniques and ranging from ballet to ballroom to Greek dance.[5]

Norton and Webb did not entertain the dream of a ballet career, since the possibility of an Afro-American entering ballet did not exist. Ballroom dancing, with its lifts, spins, and pas de deux format, was akin to their ballet training and became the resting place for their "dream deferred." Comments on their performance in both the white and Afro-American press described them as a sophisticated, elegant "class act." However, ballroom dance as a popular genre was on the wane by the mid-1940s, along with the big band music that accompanied it. The decline of the swing-era nightclub and vaudeville circuits resulted in the team's retirement by 1947.

Like most of their vaudeville colleagues, the team was multi-talented, because having more than one ability offered more than one job opportunity. But for them, dance was not a stepping stone to another career, as is often the case with chorus girls and dancers of lesser talent. For Norton and Webb, ballroom dance was their calling, their special craft, and they took other types of bookings in a futile attempt to survive between ballroom engagements. The team was dissolved from 1943 to 1945, due to the scarcity of engagements during the wartime era. In 1946 the lure of their ballroom-dance art called them back from family and semiretirement, and they gave their specialty one more chance. Finally, the team of "Norton and Margot" retired in 1947.

WEBB'S ENTRY INTO SHOW BUSINESS

The permutations of irony created by institutionalized racism were highlighted in the fortune—or plight—of the Afro-American female vaudevillian. If she were light enough, or white enough, to suit the tastes of the clientele, the Afro-American female had a chance for success or, at least, for a regular salary. Often she performed in "cotton clubs" or "plantation clubs," which existed in cities large and small across the nation and which provided all-black entertainment for white-only clientele. Added to this irony was the fact that white celebrities and the well-to-do attended posh night spots located in Afro-American urban enclaves, the Harlems of America. The surrounding areas were inhabited by Depression-poor, non-white proletarians who could not afford entry to these clubs and who would have been refused entry even if they had presented the necessary admission price. At the height of the Depression, the Afro-American entertainment industry was a lucrative enterprise.

Given this setting, Webb's entry into show business as a chorus girl in 1932 was typical for the light-skinned Afro-American female performer of her era. Her career was launched not principally from a love of the dance, but as a viable way of earning a living during the Great Depression. Comparable stories are told by many others, including Josephine Baker and actress Fredi Washington.

EARLY CAREER OF NORTON AND WEBB

Margot Webb, née Margaret Smith, was a native New Yorker who left Hunter College in her junior year to make a living in show business. She met Harold Norton in 1933. They were booked separately in a Ralph Cooper revue in Philadelphia. Cooper, the emcee and bandleader, thought it would be a crowd-pleasing gimmick if Webb, young and beautiful in face and figure, were to do a fan-dance solo in addition to her work in the chorus line. According to Webb:

I was so embarrassed because I had to take off everything and put on some kind of little skin-tight thing the color of my skin, which, of course, in those days was like going out on stage nude—which Sally Rand did—with a little G-string, of course. . . . [The entire routine] was based on her popularity. . . . [White performers] weren't always copying us; we were copying them, too. Whatever was acceptable in the white world was carried over into Black show business. So the fan dance was very popular.

Cooper had seen Webb practicing *en pointe* and hit upon the idea of a novelty fan dance on toe:

I knew how to do the toe dance, but I didn't have the slightest idea how to use the fans. Those fans are not easy to use. They're great big things. . . . They look very simple. I was flabbergasted! Those fans! I couldn't get them to go—my wrists wouldn't go fast enough. However, Norton helped me with the routine. . . . I never saw a man who knew so much [about dancing]. . . . He knew how to handle the fans front and back. . . . He rehearsed with me for a few days, and it was all right in the show. I was no Sally Rand, but I looked good, and that's the only way it went over.[6]

Cooper further suggested that the two of them team up and work out some routines together. This was common practice: to "team up" for the duration of a show, or longer, to increase performing and payroll possibilities. They continued their individual work in the Cooper revue: Norton as Spear Dance soloist and Webb as chorus girl and fan-dance soloist. They began rehearsing together between shows, trying out the steps, routines, and partnering of ballroom work. In that same year they had their first performance as the team of "Norton and Margot" at New York's Club Harlem.

Webb cannot recall the exact length of this engagement, but it was extended and ran approximately one month. Allowed to use the nightclub space, free of charge, for daytime rehearsals (an advantage in working nightclubs that was not possible in theaters), they continued rehearsing, developing a repertory of two or three numbers. Many of the best ballroom teams of the era were Latin, such as the De Marcos (Italian American) and Veloz and Yolanda (Hispanic). Webb's first name, Marjorie, was modified to Mar-

Harold Norton and Margot Webb in a studio portrait, 1933 (Reproduced with permission of Margot Webb)

got, giving the team a Latin sound. Occasionally, in further pushing the Latin image, the "t" was dropped from her name. The name change was more than a matter of image. In some cases, a team of Latin origin could be hired in environments where Afro-Americans were not allowed to perform.

Norton was a versatile and well-trained performer. He had grown up in show business, and his performance background was extensive. According to Webb, he could perform a range of popular styles, including tap, softshoe, acrobatic, and trapeze work—as well as ballet and interpretative work. He was also an accomplished teacher. In the beginning he did not choreograph their dances but bought routines from established white choreographers. According to Webb:

> We could have the dance instructor come up in the afternoon [to the club where they were performing] and teach us . . . [and we would] pay him by the hour or by the routine—it was up to us, as a rule. If we got someone white from downtown he usually was rehearsing a big show similar to the [shows at the] Latin Quarter or one of those places. He would come up and make this extra money—stage a number for you—work with you for as many hours as you wanted. . . . Say you paid him $250 for a routine. You could pay it in installments.[7]

Their first choreographer was Jean De Meaux, who taught them the suave, downtown adagio style. De Meaux also staged shows for Harlem night spots like Small's Paradise, the only lavish Harlem club with a floor show and chorus line that catered to an Afro-American clientele.

Music arrangements cost from $50 to $75 apiece. The team's first arranger was Armand Lamet, whose arrangements they took with them when they left New York for their first bookings on the road. Webb asserts that a good arrangement had a potential performance life of two to three years. De Meaux and Lamet worked together with the team in rehearsal: De Meaux tailoring the movement to fit the best lines of their bodies, and Lamet setting the musical arrangement to the movement.

Once on tour, they made use of some of the fine Afro-American arrangers who were members of the bands that played for them.

In Chicago both Jimmy Munday and Wilbur de Paris of the Earl Hines band made arrangements for them. The team fared best with sophisticated bands like those of Earl Hines, Noble Sissle, Ovie Alston, and Teddie Hill—orchestras capable of interpreting a variety of music, including a traditional repertory of ballads and light classics, and not limited to the jazz repertory and the new swing sound.

THE PROFIT MARGIN

Newspaper articles on the team appeared regularly in the Afro-American press. Some of these were intriguingly concocted examples of exaggeration and fabrication. Norton and Webb did not discourage the stories. Exaggeration garnered publicity and surrounded the matter of salary in a protective net of goal-oriented subterfuge. It was common knowledge that Afro-American performers did not draw top salaries but, as Webb explains, "In order to make people think you were doing well, you had to exaggerate, the same as everybody else did."[8] The rationale behind this strategy was that a rumored high salary on the show business grapevine might make it easier to command a better salary on the next engagement. According to Webb:

> If we were in a show with the Berry Brothers . . . they might have gotten the top salary—we knew that, and they knew that, and everybody else in the show knew it; so we would have to take second best. If . . . there wasn't anyone in the show of the caliber of the Nicholas Brothers or the Berry Brothers, then we would get the top salary. . . . We would be considered second also to stars like Adelaide Hall, Valaida Snow, or George Dewey Washington. We wouldn't know what they were getting, but we'd assume they were making almost twice as much as we were.[9]

The following specimen contracts give a sense of the Norton and Webb salary range, which remained stable throughout their performing career. On a basic, shoestring salary (averaging $150 weekly, with a general range from $100 to $175), the team was obliged to keep up appearances in order to continue receiving top bookings. Travel expenses were not always included in their contracts. Publicity photographs, musical arrangements, and costumes consumed most of their profits.

PUBLICITY

At the beginning of their career, the team thought they had a chance to make it to the top of their profession and to better salaries. As Webb states, "Not knowing the world outside [the white world] too well, we always felt we could get to the big white clubs, and we never did."[10] From indications in both the white and Afro-American press, Norton and Webb seemed to be headed for greater opportunities. For example, articles in such newspapers as *Billboard* and the *Chicago Defender* indicated that, as Afro-Americans adopting a white dance style, their act would be an innovative addition to a white revue. Their training and interpretations gave a novel twist to a traditional form.

Their repertory consisted of approximately three to five "working numbers" from a total repertory of eight or nine dances. In each, the ballroom dance technique remained constant and consisted of lifts and spins linked together by steps—waltz steps for a waltz, rumba steps for a rumba, and so on. As is the case with ballroom teams, Norton and Webb's innovation lay in their particular variations on the basic vocabulary. They adopted not only a white movement genre, but also the costume, makeup, and aura created by such famous white teams as the De Marcos and Veloz and Yolanda.

Webb believes they could have expanded the scope of their repertory had they been allowed to perform on white circuits. Although they received critical journalistic acclaim for their full repertory, including their waltz interpretations, the Afro-American public—and those whites who came to Afro-American clubs for a stereotyped evening of entertainment—posed a problem. According to Webb, the average nightclub customer in America preferred the team's jazz numbers, liked their Latin numbers, but were cold to the waltz interpretations.

It was while touring in Europe and working as an independent act on white vaudeville circuits abroad that Norton and Webb developed their waltz and Latin repertory. Webb states, "There were certain Black owners who had big places who really were not in love with ballroom dancing. Now, if we had been able to do a fire dance. . . ."[11] Conversely, there were Afro-American clubs that could not afford them due to budget limitations or a floor space unequal to the needs of the ballroom style. Yet, according to Webb, there were some Afro-American audiences that were receptive to the waltz interpretations. For example, audiences at the Howard Theatre (part of the Howard University intellectual community in Washington, D.C., and a more bourgeois group than the Apollo clientele) and at the Afro-American–owned Amytis Theatre in St. Louis were two exceptions.

In the swing-era spirit of star sensationalism, publicity articles often contained fallacies about the team. As mentioned above, publicity was useful with regard to salary and bookings. For example, a 1934 *Chicago Defender* article contained compelling but false tidbits about Norton's growing up in England and having graduated from "White Plains University," and Webb as "a native of French Guinea."[12] Webb's photogenic face made her a perfect subject for photo-plus-gossip items. In addition, she received coverage and financial recompense for advertising commercial products on the Afro-American popular market. For example, a 1935 issue of the *Norfolk Journal and Guide* ran an advertisement featuring the light-skinned Webb promoting "Dr. Fred Palmer's Skin Whitener Ointment," a product she never used.

On the other hand, some seemingly far-fetched items were true. According to Webb, there actually was a balloon dancer, the purported girlfriend of Chicago mobsters, who adopted the name "Margot" in an obvious attempt to draw audiences to her on the strength of Webb's popularity in the Chicago nightclub world.[13]

NORTON AND WEBB IN AFRO-AMERICAN SOCIETY AND COMMUNITY

The press and the grapevine were corollaries in Norton and Webb's quest for bookings. In addition to attracting publicity through newspaper coverage, the team participated in community and society functions and were well-known by word-of-mouth in Afro-American communities in New York and Chicago.

In 1938, Webb began writing a gossip column for the *Chicago Defender*'s New York office. That same year she received publicity for several activities independent of the team's ballroom work, including appearing in fashion shows, crowning local award winners, and the like. This was the year after the team returned from Europe. Ironically, after constant billing in the Afro-American press as internationally famed artists, they obtained few engagements on their return, which is why Webb participated in the paraprofessional functions mentioned above. In still another auxiliary performance capacity, she trained beauty contest competitors in the art of walking, modeling, and body placement.

The team also performed at community benefits and for Afro-American society functions. As an underpaid performer, Webb remembers the benefits with particular distaste. These were charity performances for homeless children, the handicapped, the policemen's mutual aid societies, the NAACP, and so on. Performers could not refuse to do these engagements without gaining a bad reputation, but it meant another output of free time and labor in the already crowded agenda of two dancers trying desperately to gain a foothold on the ladder of success.

The many clubs, congregations, and ladies' guilds that formed a basic part of Afro-American community life hired celebrities like Norton and Webb to perform as guest stars, usually at an annual dance, a holiday celebration, or a debutantes' ball. Occasionally, Norton staged a routine for gowned or costumed amateurs, with himself and Webb as the featured dancers. This same function was expected of white ballroom teams like Veloz and Yolanda, and dates back to the origins of ballroom-dance-as-art as a spin-off from ballroom-dance-as-society-function, a legacy of Vernon and Irene Castle.

In 1936, Norton and Webb opened their dance studio in Harlem. This move was an important extension of their practice of drawing upon Afro-American cultural and community values to expand their professional horizons. A significant aspect of the Afro-American lifestyle of the era was musical training and dance lessons for children. If by 1940 most households were proud of having a radio in the living room (usually the large floor models designed after the Stromberg–Carlson example), still, the piano in the parlor was a cultural symbol. It meant that some family member had studied and could entertain guests with light classics or the "boogie-woogie." There were dancing schools in Harlem well before Norton and Webb opened their studio. Three well-known ones were the schools of Charles Anderson, Grace Giles, and Emma Kemp. Like Norton and Webb, they could teach routines to nightclub performers and, perhaps, invite Broadway dancers coming uptown to learn the Afro-American genres; but generally it was the rare, downtown-based Afro-American studio that drew a white professional clientele. Basically these Harlem schools catered to children and usually offered at least one recital a year—with music, costumes, and decor to satisfy the parents. According to Webb, the most successful Harlem schools were the ones that staged the largest end-of-the-year recitals, using the largest number of students, whether or not they were ready to perform.

For Norton and Webb, running a studio presented a problem. First, they continued their performing and touring careers, keeping the studio running in their absence by hiring substitutes who were also professionals like themselves. Second, they concentrated on training rather than recitals and therefore did not attract the many children whose parents were as interested in the recital as in the training process. The Depression compounded their problems. With most clients barely able to pay for lessons, Webb contends that the studio charged whatever people could afford to pay, taking on children and adults for lessons days, evenings, or weekends in private or group classes. In contrast to the $250 they paid for a routine tailored to their needs, they were paid less than $10 for teaching step routines to the infrequent white dancer who needed material and came to them. Consequently, Webb took on a summer-camp dance position during this period, teaching in the Catskills while Norton ran the studio.

In spite of a European tour, local bookings, and the difficulties of gaining a following of students, the studio survived for almost two years. The lack of continuity finally caught up with them, and they closed the school in 1938. Webb continued teaching, between performance engagements at the Harlem Branch of the YWCA, where Vivian Roberts, a popular dance teacher of the era and one of Webb's former instructors, was head of the dance program.

Some of Norton and Webb's students who entered the world of professional dance included the comedy team of "Slap and Happy"; the twin ballerinas Marion and Marjorie Facey (whose careers in ballet were ruptured by discrimination, although Marion Facey ran a ballet school at Carnegie Hall Studios from the late 1960s through 1980); and Archie Savage, who became a dancer-choreographer in Hollywood and was in the film version of *South Pacific*. According to the Facey sisters:

> We were so impressed with Margot because she was such a beautiful woman and also she represented something that we wanted. . . . We were aware of the ballroom dancing and the glamor of it. . . . Norton and Margot represented the fantasy, the aura of that particular period which is still the kind of thing that draws young people today into theater.[14]

WEBB ON TOUR

When the team of Norton and Webb performed on the Afro-American East Coast circuit—Washington, D.C., Philadelphia, and Baltimore—they worked as part of a "unit." The basis of the traveling unit was the band, usually a large group like that of Louis Armstrong, "Fats" Waller, Chick Webb, Ovie Alston, or a similar outfit. The composition and format of the unit was the same as that of the TOBA shows on the Afro-American circuits in the West and the South. This format included comedians, tap dancers, solo singers, and chorines. There was generally a large opening number, solo acts, and a major production number with a theme (often the jungle or the plantation), with showgirls parading costumes and chorus girls dancing precision routines. Everyone joined in the finale. First, all the individual acts presented an eight-bar finale solo; then the entire cast joined together in chorus, performing some popular dance step in unison, such as the Shim Sham, Shorty George, or Trucking.

Socially, Webb often kept aloof from other performers. As a dancer who had to keep in top form and, later, as a married woman whose husband was not her dancing partner, she composed her post-performance social life in a low key. When the team was booked in a nightclub where the final show was not over until about 2 A.M., there was little problem in turning down late-hour social invitations in order to be able to rehearse, shop, visit, or simply "work out" the following day. If the team was booked into a theater, the entire day was spent there, in any case. It may have been possible for musicians to burn the candle at both ends; for a dancer, fatigue detracted from performance. As a daytime person and a teetotaler, Webb did not maintain a regular social life with musicians on tour. This isolation was reinforced by her partner's personality. Webb compared Norton to Balanchine in the rigorousness of his demands. He managed all the business, contractual and choreographic arrangements for the team; in return, he demanded a performer in top shape, emotionally ready, and physically able to dance as he required. He was disliked in some circles and was known as a rigorous perfectionist with a hot temper, who did not bite his tongue and took no nonsense from any-one—white or Afro-American—and was not averse to engaging in physical confrontation to make his point.

This is not to indicate that performers were not Webb's friends but, simply, that her relationships with entertainers were usually working relationships. Webb had her own family life, private and separate from her performing career. In addition, she had interrupted her academic ambitions to enter show business. By 1947, these two forces won out over her dancing.

CONCLUSION

As many times as the team of Norton and Webb seemed on the brink of success, so many times some twist of fate blocked their progress. They came too late for the 1920s period of Afro-American popularity spawned by the Harlem Renaissance and too early for the integrated period of the civil rights era, when Afro-American acts were accepted in white show business. In their political naiveté they performed in Nazi Germany in 1937, and they planned to follow this with possible engagements in Scandinavia, Romania, and Egypt; but these bookings were curtailed by the momentum of the coming world war. Forced out of Germany by Hitler with little notice except a one-way ticket home, they returned to America and, like many performers who spent time abroad, they found that their absence resulted in a loss of contacts. Bookings were even more difficult to arrange. Although both the white and Afro-American press reacted favorably, there was no room at the top for them. During the 1940s, like other Afro-American dancers of the swing era—and like the swing bands that accompanied them—Norton and Webb found their careers grinding to a halt.

Styles come and go in vernacular dance, song, and music. Specialty techniques such as toe-tap dancing (tap dancing *en pointe*), roller-skate rope dancing (jumping rope while dancing on wheels), and other eccentric and acrobatic forms have disappeared beyond the same horizon as ballroom dance. The disappearance of novelty forms was in some ways attributable to the hard-edged, stereotypical appeal of the flash tap acts, the last and most scintillating fad genre of the swing era. In a bulldozer effect created by speed, relentless rhythm, and sheer force, these acts, so commercially popular with the white mainstream, overwhelmed and obliterated more subtle genres including the little-known, lyrical, romantic style of Norton and Webb. In their leap to fame, the flash acts self-destructed and marked the tail end of a golden era of Afro-American vaudeville dance. Just as the 1910 generation of Afro-American witnessed, with relief, the gradual demise of another popular genre, the "Coon" song; and as James Reese Europe's Afro-American orchestra, which accompanied the seminal, white ballroom team of Vernon and Irene Castle, dissolved and was forgotten; so the big bands declined from swing-era popularity into postwar obsolescence by the onset of the 1950s. In addition, tap dance, ballroom dance, and chorus lines virtually disappeared. With big-name stars like Cab Calloway and Ethel Waters unable to find work, it was inevitable that a team like "Norton and Margot" would cease to exist. In 1947, after a comeback the previous year, the team disbanded permanently, and their show business career ended with as little fanfare as it had begun.

Chronology

1922–28	Margaret Webb, a native New Yorker attending public secondary schools, performs as a semi-professional on weekends and in the summer with Afro-American chorus lines in white-only clubs and burlesque houses in the greater New York–New Jersey area.
1929	Webb enters Hunter College and continues performing semiprofessionally.
1932	Due to the pressures created by the Depression, Webb leaves Hunter College after her third year to earn a living in show business. She performs in Manhattan, Brooklyn, Saratoga Springs, and Montreal in revues choreographed by such major Afro-American "dance directors" as Leonard Harper and Clarence Robinson.
1933	Webb meets Harold Norton when both were performers in a Ralph Cooper revue in Philadelphia. "Norton and Margot's" first engagement was at New York's Club Harlem, former site of Connie Immerman's famous nightclub, Connie's Inn.
1934–38	The team tours extensively, both in the Midwest and the Northeast. They play in theaters from Chicago going west, performing for a week at a time in cities such as St. Louis, Louisville, Omaha, and Kansas City and in such small towns as Elkhart, Indiana. They have extended bookings at the Grand Terrace Cafe, performing with the Earl "Fatha" Hines Band. In addition to theater bookings, they play Cotton

Club–type nightclubs whenever possible late in the evening. (The last theater show was over by 10 P.M.; nightclubs might begin the floor show at the same hour, with subsequent shows at midnight and occasionally at 2 A.M.) On the East Coast, they have the same performance format of theater/nightclub bookings. However, the East Coast theaters are in Afro-American communities and cater to an Afro-American audience, while the Midwest theaters are former white vaudeville palaces that are booking Afro-American units by the mid-1930s due to the demise of white vaudeville. In addition, the Midwest theaters are in the white sections of town and play to white-only audiences.

1936–38   In addition to touring, the team opens a dance studio in central Harlem. They teach classes for children and adults and choreograph routines, often for white nightclub performers. Duties are shared with other performer-teachers while the team is on tour. They finally close the school due to the pressures of maintaining both the school and their performing careers.

1937   (June–August) Norton and Webb are part of the Cotton Club Revue that tours abroad with the Teddy Hill Band. They perform at the London Palladium, the Moulin Rouge, and the Théâtre des Ambassadeurs in Paris.

1937   (September–December) The team performs as an individual act booked on European variety bills in France, Italy, and Germany. They are described in the Afro-American press as the team "who broke the jim-crow barrier of Hitler."[15] When Hitler tightens his ban on non-Aryans, Norton and Webb are expelled from Germany and given free boat passage home from Hamburg in December 1937.

1939–40   With fewer bookings for the team of Norton and Webb, Webb works with dancer Al Moore for several ballroom bookings in 1940. She also returns to Hunter College to work toward a bachelor's degree in French. She marries William P. Webb Jr. Also, she shares bookings with dancer Al Vigal in an exotic act that runs for an extended engagement in Montreal.

1941   Norton and Webb perform at Dave's Café in Chicago and tour nightclubs in the Midwest. By this time, the Midwest white vaudeville theater circuit has dried up as a source of employment for Afro-Americans. The theaters became total film houses, showing feature films, newsreels, cartoons, and so on. On their return from the Midwest, the team tours the Northeast Afro-American vaudeville circuit.

1942   Webb works as a soloist and as occasional ballroom partner of Al Moore. Her solo work included a "La Conga" specialty and a jazz toe dance. Both are performed at the Apollo Theatre in Harlem.

1943–45   The team dissolves, and Webb retires from show business.

1946–47   Norton and Webb stage a comeback. They open in September 1946 at Harlem's Club Baron. Only a few bookings follow. The team disbands permanently in early 1947. Webb enters graduate school at Columbia University's Teachers College, bringing her performance career to an end.

NOTES

This chapter was originally published in *Dance Research Journal* 15, no. 2 (spring 1983): 11–20, under the name Brenda Dixon-Stowell. Minor changes have been made for consistency. This chapter is an early version of material that appears in Brenda Dixon Gottschild's *Waltzing in the Dark: African American*

Vaudeville and Race Politics in the Swing Era (New York: St. Martin's, 2000) and is reprinted here with the permission of the publisher.

1. Hereinafter referred to as Norton and Webb, except when the proper name of the team itself is cited.

2. Marshall Stearns and Jean Stearns, *Jazz Dance: The Story of American Vernacular Dance* (New York: Macmillan, 1968; reprint ed., New York: Schirmer Books, 1979), 87–89, 342–48.

3. For a sampling of particular issues, see Brenda Dixon-Stowell, "Dancing in the Dark: The Life and Times of Margot Webb in Aframerican Vaudeville of the Swing Era" (Ph.D. dissertation, New York University, 1981), bibliography, 784–88.

4. Interviews, correspondence, and/or conversations were conducted by the author with the following people: Marion and Marjorie Facey, ballet teachers and former students of Margot Webb; Howard "Stretch" Johnson, former Cotton Club dancer; John Williams, swing-era and contemporary bassist who played with the Louis Armstrong and Teddy Wilson bands among others; Ralph Cooper, former dancer, bandleader, emcee, and actor, who introduced Margot Webb to Harold Norton; Louis Williams, former tap dancer, who worked in the team of "Pops and Louis."

5. Louis Chalif, *The Chalif Textbook(s) of Dancing*, 5 vols. (New York: The Chalif Normal School of Dancing, 1914–25).

6. Margot Webb, interview with the author, 19 November 1977. The following excerpts are from the same interview.

7. Brenda Dixon-Stowell, "Interview with Margot Webb," unpublished transcript and audio tape, April 1978, 9. Dance Collection, the New York Public Library for the Performing Arts.

8. Webb, interview with the author, 27 August 1980.

9. Ibid.

10. Webb, interview with the author, 17 September 1980.

11. Ibid.

12. "Margot-Norton Set Nite Lifers Ga-Ga with Dance Thrills," *Chicago Defender*, undated clipping [1934]. Webb Collection.

13. "Can't Steal My Dance Is Margot Yarn," *Chicago Defender*, undated clipping [ca. 1934–35].

14. Marjorie and Marion Facey, interview with the author, 7 October 1980.

15. *Afro-American*, 18 November 1937.

10

Katherine Dunham's *Southland:*
Protest in the Face of Repression

Constance Valis Hill

> The man who truly loves his country is the man who is
> able to see it in the bad as well as the good and seeing the
> bad declaim it, at the cost of liberty or life.
> *Katherine Dunham, prologue to* Southland

In 1951, at the dawning of a decade that would be known for its suffocating conformity and political intolerance, Katherine Dunham created *Southland,* a dramatic ballet Americana about what was by then the century-long practice of lynching. In the program notes to the ballet, which premiered at the Opera House in Santiago de Chile, Dunham wrote, "This is the story of no actual lynching in the southern states of America, and still it is the story of every one of them."[1] She spoke the prologue on stage, in Spanish:

> Though I have not smelled the smell of burning flesh, and have
> never seen a black body swaying from a southern tree, I have felt
> these things in spirit.... Through the creative artist comes the need
> to show this thing to the world, hoping that by exposing the ill,
> the conscience of the many will protest."[2]

Southland, a protest as much against lynching as against the destructive powers of hatred, was created before the Selma march of 1965, the Freedom rides, the student sit-ins; before the Montgomery bus boycott of 1955; and before the lynching of Emmett Till. Unlike the 1960s, artistic expression in the late 1940s and 1950s provoked suspicion and outright repression. It was a time when dissent itself seemed illegitimate, subversive, un-American. The story of *Southland* tells of the consequences of social protest in the 1950s, the decade once described as "the happiest, most stable, most rational period the Western world has known since 1914."[3] But it also reveals the temperament and perhaps the very soul of protest expression rooted in the African American political struggle, an expression that was for Dunham both a public act and private *rite de passage,* affirming how dancing is a healing process as well as a political act.

THE 1940s

In the postwar years, Dunham was at the height of a stage and film career that had been launched on Broadway with *Cabin in the Sky* in 1940. Fame seemed limitless for the woman most remembered as "decked out in singular hats and dresses, daring to wear feathers, bright colors, soft fabrics,"[4] though the woman who was making brilliant-textured transformations of indigenous Caribbean dances was still limited by racial discrimination. There was the ongoing critical debate as to whether she was a serious artist or a popularizer, whether comment and integrity in her work were "sacrificed to conform to what Broadway expected the Negro dance to be."[5] There was Dunham's perennial double-image, in which she was simultaneously viewed as "the hottest thing" on Broadway and "an intelligent anthropologist of note."[6] Perpetual intimations of a split personality appeared in such headlines as "Schoolmarm Turned Siren," "Torridity to Anthropology," "Cool Scientist or Sultry Performer?" and "High Priestess of Jive."[7] However, the clever phrases invented to cheapen her talent and tarnish her beauty diminished neither her popularity nor her creative output. The Katherine Dunham School of Dance and Theatre opened in New York in 1944, and throughout the 1940s—from club work at Ciro's in Hollywood and the Martinique Club in New York to musicals in Chicago and performances in Mexico City, London, Paris, and Rome—Dunham and her company of singers, dancers, and musicians were on what seemed a perpetual tour across America and around the world.

Touring did not keep Dunham out of touch but instead only

heightened her awareness of America where, simultaneous with the optimism of postwar prosperity, there was the ever-presence of Jim Crow in transportation, education, and public accommodation. Though lynching was rampant and went without condemnation in the South during the 1930s, it declined in the 1940s. However, violence continued against blacks, countless and perpetual acts of violence that were part of an overall pattern of retaliation against postwar egalitarianism.[8] From 1936 to 1946, forty-three lynchings of mostly Southern blacks were reported, though the lynchings went unprosecuted. The most notorious lynchings were the 1944 drowning of a fifteen-year-old black youth in the Suwannee River, an act that the boy's father was forced to witness, and the quadruple killing in 1946 of two black men and two black women in Monroe, Georgia.[9]

America's fight against Nazism and Fascism abroad highlighted the hypocrisy of racism at home and provided a catalyst for African Americans, whose long-suppressed anger and outrage sought new expressions of protest. In dance, for the most part, social protest was accepted. About her 1943 solo *Strange Fruit,* an interpretation of the Lewis Allan poem that presented the residual emotions of a woman who witnessed a lynching, Pearl Primus recalls, "In the forties you could protest, in fact, I was most encouraged."[10] Primus openly stated at that time that the "'Negro problem,' so-called, in reality was a problem of democracy" and asserted that as people in other countries fought against Hitler's suppression of minorities, so they needed to fight against fascist ideas in the United States.[11] Talley Beatty, whose 1947 *Southern Landscape* dealt with the terrorization of black and white share-croppers in the South during the Reconstruction, confirms, "I thought everybody back then was doing protest dances."[12] Nor was Dunham a stranger to political activism during the 1930s and 1940s. Touring in a segregated society such as America's presented problems she faced head on, from curtain speeches to segregated audiences to a staunch insistence on finding decent housing for her company. "There comes a time when every human being must protest in order to retain human dignity," Dunham announced to a segregated audience in Louisville in 1944, explaining she would not return but that she hoped the war abroad for tolerance and democracy would change things in America.[13] Sometimes there were outrageous confrontations, such as the story company members tell about how Dunham, in a segregated theater in the South, turned around and showed her rear end to the audience, saying, "Until people like me can sit with people like you," the company could not and would not perform.[14]

However, by the late 1940s the times were changing, as overt expressions of dissent were suddenly construed as being politically incorrect. The political climate was chilling with the Cold War and a new Red Scare so powerful that many social causes identified with liberal principles could be tarred with the fatal brush of being called subversive. The politics of anticommunism exerted such a cooling effect on all progressive causes that even blacks in government who actively opposed segregation were accused of disloyalty.[15] In 1949, the House Un-American Activities Committee (HUAC) continued to investigate members of the movie industry and then escalated its assault against Paul Robeson, who in bold counterattack challenged HUAC's "ominous silence" in the face of the continued lynchings of black citizens.[16] Katherine Dunham was abroad with her company at the time, but she was neither safe from nor immune to the onslaught of news from America that both haunted and assaulted her.

She remembers hearing about the lynching of an American Southern black youth and, during an airplane ride over the Nile River, she wrote, "The mud that turns in the Mississippi, is it able to cover those black bodies, or would any river do?"[17] In a bar in Genoa, company members were threatened and insulted with racial slurs by American sailors in an incident that brought them late to a cocktail party given by Ambassador Pell. And in the summer of 1950 in Brazil, Dunham was denied entry into one of the better hotels because she was black, a bitter reminder of the pervasiveness of color prejudice.[18] It was the fall of 1950, the aftermath of the Eighty-first Congress, which became the graveyard for the NAACP's thirty-two-year fight for federal anti-lynching legislation. In response to this travesty, Langston Hughes's character Simple, expressing the reactions of the black community, declared the federal government could find the means to pass espionage and security legislation, "yet cannot and will not and won't pass no bill to keep me from getting lynched if I ever look cross-eyed at a white man when I go down south."[19] It was amidst hearing news about the trials of the Martinsville Seven and Willie McGhee, in which black youths in Virginia and Mississippi convicted of raping a white woman were sentenced to death,[20] that Dunham's response to America from afar took shape in *Southland*.

THE MAKING OF A PROTEST DANCE

Commissioned by the Symphony of Chile, and with a premiere in Santiago set for January 1951, *Southland* was researched, composed, choreographed, designed, and rehearsed in the last months of 1950 in Buenos Aires.[21] The musical score by Dino di Stefano, a Jesuit priest based in Argentina, was an orchestral arrangement of African American spirituals, blues music, and popular American songs. Designed by John Pratt, Dunham's husband and artistic collaborator, the set's centerpiece was a sprawling magnolia tree in full bloom that evoked the warm and sunny American South. However, while Dunham, speaking the prologue, praised America for its youthfulness, she probed its dark underside:

> There is a deep stain, a mark of blood and shame which spreads from under the magnolia trees of the southland area and mingles with the perfume of the flowers. This is not all of America. It is not all of the south, but it is a living, present part.[22]

The curtain opens on a chorus standing before the portals of an antebellum Southern mansion.[23] "Is it true what they say about Dixie? Does the sun really shine all the time?" they sing, and the mock nostalgia of "Swanee River" and "Carry Me Back to Old Virginia" contrasts with the ecstatic force of the spirituals "Steal Away" and "Dry Bones."[24] The Southern mansion gives way to the magnolia tree where fieldhands on their way to work dance a suite of plantation dances, leaving behind a pair of lovers, Lucy and Richard. Their tender pas de deux, in which he reaches up into the tree to pluck a magnolia blossom, combined dramatic gesture with dance movement. What Dunham described as "a mixture of mime and motion" in her dance drama was an ingenious mixing of fact and fiction. She meticulously researched the history of lynching in the United States by consulting the records on file at the Tuskegee Institute. She then wrote a detailed scenario and working script, complete with dialogue written in Southern dialect, as the following segment from the "Love Scene" for Lucy and Richard demonstrates:

HE: Lucy.
SHE: Huh?
HE: Come ova heah, Lucy.
SHE: (small cry of joy as she dances to him) Oh.
HE: Love ain't a big enough word for what I has for you, gal. (When she is in his arms) De whol' worl' ain't big enough to hol' it. (When she reaches for flowers) Here, gal, let a big fella help wid dat. (Carries her to flowers).[25]

The script was used by dancers for rehearsal and discarded when the dialogue was replaced with motivated action. The names of the characters in the script were the actual names of the dancers playing them—the characters of Lucy and Richard, for example, played by company members Lucille Ellis and Ricardo Avales. The dance movement was created through a collaborative rehearsal process in which Dunham worked with dancers onstage while di Stefano composed at the piano. Newly choreographed scenes were supplemented with well-known dances from the company repertory. The square dances and patting jubas in the opening plantation scene, for example, were long-standing numbers from Dunham's *Americana* suite from the 1930s and 1940s. Dunham's dance drama, then, recontextualized historical "facts" and dancers' biographies, new dramatic choreography and old musical numbers, thereby enabling dancers to more truthfully internalize, or embody, the materials. To borrow dance scholar VèVè Clark's term, it was a kind of "method dancing" that motivated a complete transformation into the world of "the play,"[26] a play that was a thinly disguised exposé of truth.

After the "Love Scene," Lucy and Richard separate, and a white couple, Julie and Lenwood, tumbles out from behind the magno-

Julie and Lenwood struggle. Julie Robinson Belafonte and Lenwood Morris in Katherine Dunham's *Southland*, Paris production, 1953. (From the archive of Julie Robinson Belafonte; reproduced with permission)

Julie teases Lenwood. Julie Robinson Belafonte and Lenwood Morris in Katherine Dunham's *Southland*, Paris production, 1953. (From the archive of Julie Robinson Belafonte; reproduced with permission)

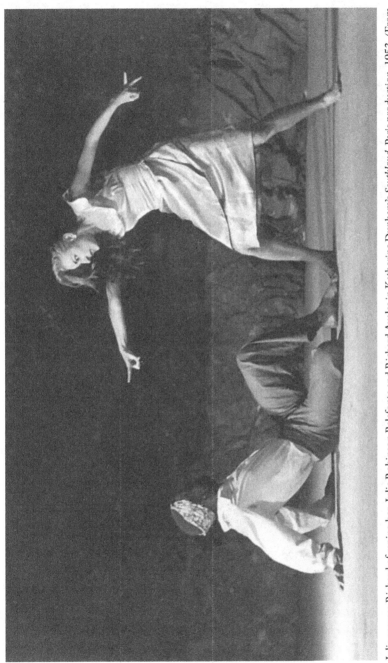

Julie accuses Richard of raping her. Julie Robinson Belafonte and Richard Avales in Katherine Dunham's *Southland*, Paris production, 1953. (From the archive of Julie Robinson Belafonte; reproduced with permission)

Julie screams for help after accusing Richard of rape. Julie Robinson Belafonte in Katherine Dunham's *Southland*, Paris production, 1953. (From the archive of Julie Robinson Belafonte; reproduced with permission)

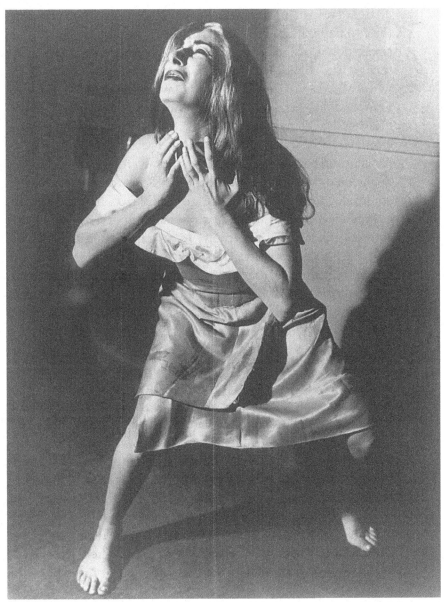

Julie demands the lynching of Richard. Julie Robinson Belafonte in Katherine Dunham's *Southland*, Paris production, 1953. (From the archive of Julie Robinson Belafonte; reproduced with permission)

lia tree. The role of Julie was played by the only white dancer in the company, Julie Robinson Belafonte, with a bleached-blonde streak down her long brown hair to represent Southern white society; the role of her boyfriend Lenwood was played by Lenwood Morris, wearing a red wig and whitened makeup. Julie and Lenwood are drunk, and he takes her teasing as a sexual insult. Chasing her around the tree, he catches her by the hair and in the ensuing *apache*-styled duet, he beats her viciously, strutting away like a proud cock to leave her unconscious. Julie is discovered by the fieldhands who flee in fear, though Richard remains. He lifts her head, and she opens her eyes to see his face. In that moment, between feeling the humiliation of being discovered in that state and recognizing the opportunity to capitalize on it, Julie decides to make him the perpetrator of her attack. Pointing an accusing finger, she cries out the word "Nigger!" and skillfully draws in an imaginary crowd, inciting them to believe she's been raped. Dancing a *habanera,* she strips her blouse, whips her hair, and then twists it around her neck to advocate his lynching. Trapped by this imaginary crowd-turned-lynch-mob, Richard cowers on the ground in complete animal fear. He mimes being kicked offstage by the white mob, moving into an offstage pool of red light. Onstage, Julie dances herself into a fury born of hatred, fear, and guilt as, offstage, the pool of flaming red light intensifies as the mob hangs and burns the black man. It is only when Richard's body, swinging by his neck from a branch of the magnolia tree,[27] swoops toward her in full view that Julie feels the full impact of her lie. Fascinated by what she sees of herself in the disfigured body, she rips off a piece of Richard's charred shirt and, on her exit, she meets Lucy face-to-face: one woman clutches the burnt cloth, the other holds the magnolia blossom. The chorus, turning into a cortège of mourners, gathers up the remains of the body as Lucy dances a searing adagio solo that is filled with back-spiraling descents to the floor and recovers. Ellis recalls that Dunham, coaching her, said, "Lucille, feel you are that child again and you just lost something you had, come out completely limp and innocent."[28] Lucy dances and weeps; and in her final descent, she wraps herself around the legs of Claudia McNeil, who sings:

Southern trees bear a strange fruit,
Blood at the leaves and blood at the root.
Black bodies swaying in the southern breeze
Strange fruit hanging from the poplar trees

Pastoral scene of the gallant south
The bulging eye and the twisted mouth
Scent of magnolia sweet and fresh
Then the sudden smell of burning flesh

Here is a fruit for the wind to suck
For the rain to gather for the crows to pluck
for the sun to rot for the trees to drop
Here is a strange and bitter crop.[29]

The second scene opens with the "Basin Street Blues" and takes place, writes Dunham in the scenario, on "any street where, because of color, creed or forced inferiority, people are relegated to the frenzied cynicism that substitutes for the deprivations of their daily lives."[30] In a smoky cafe inhabited by couples dancing, men gambling, and a blind man begging,[31] the funeral cortège passes bearing the body of the lynched man. Singing a funeral dirge, the chorus moves across the stage dragging Lucy, whose arms are wrapped around the legs of the bass singer. For a moment, everyone is motionless. Then cards fall from the hands of a gambler; a woman weeps silently, and couples tighten their embrace to grind slowly and disjointedly, like somnambulists, while a man opens his knife and continues to plunge it into the floor, retrieve it, and plunge it again.[32] The blind man suddenly stands straight up. "Seeing" what the others feel but cannot define, he follows the funeral procession, "seeking the answer which all of us who love humanity seek more than ever at this moment."[33]

THE PUBLIC RESPONSE

It was not only the graphic depiction of a black man swinging by his neck from the end of a rope that made *Southland* so shocking; as Dunham says, "It was the whole thing."[34] She remembers on opening night that some in the audience wept, while others, members of the diplomatic corps, sat rigid. If the ballet ended on a

Backstage view just before the lynching of Richard. Katherine Dunham's *Southland*, Paris production, 1953. (From the archive of Julie Robinson Belafonte; reproduced with permission)

Chorus sings after the lynching scene. Katherine Dunham's *Southland,* Paris production, 1953. (From the archive of Julie Robinson Belafonte; reproduced with permission)

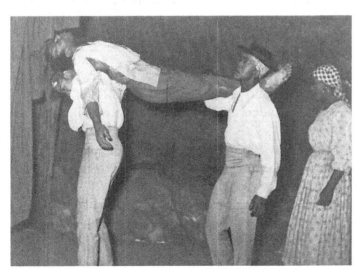

Cortege of mourners carry Richard's body. Katherine Dunham's *Southland,* Paris production, 1953. (From the archive of Julie Robinson Belafonte; reproduced with permission)

note of mournful resignation, with the fieldhands carrying off the body, would Dunham have gotten the response she was delivered the next morning? A reporter from the Communist newspaper in Santiago, who asked to secretly meet her in the hotel garden, told her that the review that he wrote of *Southland* was the only review she would receive in Santiago. Every newspaper in Chile depended on America for newsprint, he explained, and members of the press were "informed" that all newsprint would be withdrawn if anyone dared to write about *Southland*. It wasn't only the explicit violence of the first scene that was intimidating, but also the implicit threat of violence in the second scene. Dunham remarks about the last scene in *Southland*:

> If you were at all sensitive, you would pick up this thread of violence. The guy with the knife—a 1960s type—and the crap players, they were mean; they wouldn't take it very long. And we do get the feeling of something going to happen, not the feeling it's hopeless. I should think that any white person, whether they belonged in that setting or not, would feel particularly uneasy."[35]

It was January 1951, ten months after Senator Joseph McCarthy had claimed there were 205 known Communists in the State Department.[36] That an American artist, a black woman in a foreign country known for its strong Communist base and anti-American sentiment, had dared to expose America's darkest side, was a flagrant betrayal of her country. This action appeared totally out of character for the Katherine Dunham so often perceived as the glamorous entertainer. She recalls, "People who thought I was having such a success as a figurehead goddess, whatever that was, couldn't understand how I could do a thing like that onstage."

The paranoia aroused at the American embassy in Chile—which was under the ambassadorship of Claude G. Bowers, whose 1929 book *The Tragic Era* justified the Ku Klux Klan as being organized "for the protection of women, property, civilization itself"[37]—can only be imagined. While reprisal on the part of the State Department was indeed insidious, it was at first invisible. *Southland* was immediately suppressed in Santiago: the company was forced to leave within days. There were no more reviews; nothing more was written, and nothing was publicly said; what followed was a cold and sustained silence. Dunham had been warned, after all, by officials who attended rehearsals in Santiago to remove "the lynching scene." Since she insisted on presenting the ballet as conceived and rehearsed, there would be no more calls or invitations from the members of the embassy who had wined and dined her. The intention of the ensuing silence was to pretend that *Southland* had never happened. Nevertheless, word about the ballet traveled quickly over the Andes. When the company returned to Argentina, there was also a cold silence from the embassy in Buenos Aires, and it was a silence Dunham clearly understood. In the company's second command performance in Buenos Aires for Eva Perón, *Southland* was not performed, nor was it performed in the rest of 1951 during the company's tour through South America, nor in all of 1952. "Dunham's whim," as her impresarios deemed it, was a financial hazard that was to be avoided.

However, by the end of 1952, in preparation for the company's Paris season, rehearsals for *Southland* started again in Genoa, Italy. Anticipating criticism and possible repression, Dunham sent John Pratt ahead to inform the American embassy in Paris that she intended to perform the ballet. Arriving in Paris with the company, Dunham was besieged by members of the press who wanted to know more about her "lynching ballet." They knew she had been heavily criticized and ousted in Santiago, and they asked Dunham what she thought the Americans might do if she performed *Southland* in Paris. A few days before the opening, Dunham tried to see American ambassador James Clement Dunn, but he was supposedly out of town. She spoke instead with his cultural attaché, who reportedly told Dunham, "We trust you and your personal good taste, and we know that you wouldn't do anything to upset the American position in the rest of the world." Pressing for a definitive answer as to whether or not she should present *Southland*, Dunham says, "He wouldn't go any farther. So I did it."

Southland opened at the Palais de Chaillot on 9 January 1953 to a swarm of radically bipartisan reactions. There were praises in the French Communist newspaper *L'Humanité* for the ballet's remarkable powers of expression and its contribution to "the emancipation of the blacks by rising against the racist assassins," and complaints in the conservative *Le Monde* that "Katherine Dunham had changed since those wonderful evenings in Paris. . . . What has happened to the anthropologist we once admired?"[38] A *Paris Presse* review refused even to acknowledge Dunham's creation of *Southland*.

The critical responses, as she later wrote, sounded to Dunham like "the repeated rhythm of an out-of-gear piece of machinery" and ranged from pronouncements such as "cerebralism," "Sorbonnism," and "betraying racial origins in emphasizing the orchestra instead of the tam-tam" to "beauty," "unforgettable theatre," "courage," and "going beyond the folkloric and anecdotal into the realm of classicism."[39] While *Southland* marshaled criticism from radio commentators, who advised Dunham not to show blacks hanging on the stage, several of the Communist newspapers felt she had not gone far enough to show her anger and wanted to see the burning of the body on stage.

There were as many congratulations as criticisms for Dunham's breaking away from the limiting categories that had been placed on her by the French. However, she was deeply grieved by the criticism, especially from her friend, the noted art historian and critic Bernard Berenson, who saw the production in Paris. Berenson's rejection of *Southland* symbolized the American response: "I know and respect all of your feeling towards the State, many of which I have," Dunham wrote in a response to Berenson after the Paris opening:

> But I have not been approached by either communists or the communist press who I believe do not see anything, either in the ballet or in the material, for anti-American usage. . . . In my heart of hearts . . . I know this has done more good for the American government than perhaps even they know. It has proven to the world that the thing of which they are being accused every day, due to the acts of such people as Senator McCarthy, has not yet become a fact and that freedom of speech still remains one of our basic principles."[40]

Southland was never again performed after the Paris production. Dunham says, "I didn't do it after Paris. I was personally
spent. I didn't have the spiritual strength, because it takes that."
She was burned out, not only from battling critics but from fighting her own company which, she discovered, had never wanted to
perform *Southland:* "I was surprised at their reaction because they
didn't want me to do it at all. Their idea in leaving America was
to lose any feelings of racial difference, to try to forget what the
whole thing was about. And when I first mentioned it, they asked
why was I doing it. They had never really known me, I discovered." Dunham remembers talking to the company, for days that
seemed like an eternity, about a situation to which they had shut
their eyes. She explains: "It's not easy to take a company who had
defended themselves all their lives, and then been protected because of the constant touring, from the indignities of their color.
They felt they were untouchable and were afraid of losing that.
And this took them down to the very bottom, to a reality they
felt they had never known."[41]

However, members of the company had a different perspective.
"Why bother getting into something so deep when everything
was fine, the ballets we were doing were expressive enough," says
Lucille Ellis, who joined Dunham's company in 1938. "We were
not ready to go into anything that was racial because it was back
to a history we wanted to rest. Paris had accepted us, we weren't
going to change the world."[42] Ellis remembers that when Dunham explained to the company who the principals were, how the
characters would react to each other, and that Julie was going to
play a white girl, "all of a sudden, some members of the company
realized that Julie was white—they never thought about that before."[43]

Says Julie Robinson Belafonte about creating the role of the
"white trash" girl, "The only way I could do it, because I almost
didn't, was to analyze it as an acting problem and transpose my
hatred of this person I'm playing into the character."[44] It was
the word "nigger"—the only word spoken in the ballet, and by
Julie—that triggered hostility and confusion within the company.
At a midnight rehearsal, which the entire company witnessed,

Belafonte remembers how Dunham, directing the moment when Julie opens her eyes and sees Richard, said:

> All right, open your eyes and you're in shock. All of a sudden, you could be somebody. And you start to think how you could use this situation. You've got it, you're going to accuse him of rape and tell everybody a lie. Yes. Now with all your everything, and in an accusing way, scream out "Nigger."[45]

There was no way Julie could say the word out loud; weeping, she begged Dunham to let her find a way to get the word across without speaking it. "When the word finally came out, I couldn't believe it was coming from my own body," says Belafonte. It was only when she overheard a dancer remark, "Do you hear the way she says 'Nigga'? Nobody would say it that way if they didn't really mean it,"[46] that she realized how *Southland* forced members of the company into an awareness of their own color prejudices and fears.

"It meant that color came into play, shades of color," Lucille Ellis explains, "because some dancers were white and some were lighter than others."

> And then Julie and I had to stay apart in rehearsals to acclimate to our roles because we weren't those same people. And she was afraid to hurt my feelings and I was afraid to hurt hers. We were all walking on eggs.[47]

Most difficult was that right after performing *Southland*, the company on the same program had to turn around and perform a lighter piece from the repertory, like *Minuet* or *Cakewalk*. Ellis remembers, "Out of the depths of hell, we were coming back to 'Oh, fine,' and the transition of personal emotions was very difficult."[48] *Southland* put a strain on the entire company. They worried about whether they could do it, whether or not they were doing the right thing, whether it would ruin the company's reputation, whether it would ruin Dunham. Says Ellis:

> *Southland* took our security blanket away. If we were run out of the country, where would we be? We were in limbo. Until finally, we

said we can fight it—we can do what we want to do, because this is what it's all about. And that's how we all came together."⁴⁹

THE AFTERMATH

Though she was never called before the House Un-American Activities Committee, Dunham was not spared the most devastating of reprisals from the State Department. In the 1950s, when the U.S. State Department began sending representative American artists abroad as cultural diplomats—a policy that was, ironically, a direct outgrowth of the Cold War—Dunham was continually denied both support and subsidy and was never chosen to officially represent the United States.

In 1954 the José Limón Dance Company was chosen as the first State Department–sponsored dance touring company to perform in South America. In Montevideo, the Limón company's opening was booked on the same evening as Dunham's opening. It was a seeming surprise to the embassy, which hosted a cocktail party for Limón to which Dunham was not invited and insisted that Dunham's impresario attend the Limón premiere and forego Dunham's. In Greece, with an engagement next in Lebanon, Dunham learned that the State Department almost succeeded in getting the theater owner in Lebanon to say the theater was occupied, which would have made the company sit for days in Greece at their own expense until the day before the Lebanon performance.⁵⁰

In San Francisco in 1955, from the high cost of keeping the company going and the dancers decently housed to the exorbitant fees that had to be paid to the theater and musicians' unions, Dunham faced the company's greatest financial crisis. "I have been closer these days than ever to complete annihilation," she wrote to Berenson. "When we arrive in New York, I shall put my case before the proper authorities and try to obtain some sort of government aid."⁵¹ Still battling segregation, she began a lawsuit against the landlords who leased an apartment to Dunham and Pratt and then changed their minds after discovering they were an interracial couple "disgracing their respective races."⁵² Dunham changed her mind on the lawsuit, thinking it petty compared to the recent lynching in Mississippi of Emmett Till, which, along with the other difficulties encountered in San Francisco, had led her to believe that very little had changed since *Southland:* "I am thoroughly discouraged by and about America and what is happening here,"[53] she wrote.

In Australia in 1956, a representative of the Chinese Opera invited Dunham to visit the People's Republic of China. The invitation was an honor as well as a breakthrough in cultural relations, while also providing a convenient travel stop for the company, which had subsequent engagements in Manila and Tokyo. Dunham's request to go to China was obstinately refused by the U.S. embassy, which told her she could go if she was willing to give up her passport and pay a $10,000 fine for each company member. Dunham reasons, "I think it was because they would not want anything as attractive as a black company, as we were, to go. It would give us too much prestige." It was not until the late 1960s that American contact with China resumed. By then, it was claimed that a United States ping-pong team had made the first breakthrough in communication with Red China.

In the 1960s, the State Department continued to give Dunham the excuse that the company was too large and therefore too expensive to sponsor. Dunham, to no avail, offered to send as few as five dancers and two pianos abroad, despite the fact that Alvin Ailey's company of dancers, singers, and musicians toured the Far East and Australia for thirteen weeks in 1962. Duke Ellington's Orchestra was treated to an extravagant State Department–sponsored tour through Europe and the Middle East in 1963.[54] For Dunham, these inconsistent policies, embarrassing oversights, and reports that she was under secret investigation by the F.B.I. indicated an intentional blackballing. "I had fallen from grace. I never had aid from the State Department. I had all sorts of encouragement and cocktail parties wherever we went, but never financial aid."[55] Physically exhausted and financially bankrupt, the Katherine Dunham Dance Company gave its last performance at New York's Apollo Theatre in 1965.

PROTEST AS A SEARCH FOR IDENTITY

Artistic confrontation and struggle is a way of life; it is neither a badge pinned on and taken off, nor a placard carried and put down. Dunham's commitment "to expose the ill so that the conscience of the many will protest" is a deep one, as she wrote to Berenson about *Southland:* "Somewhere in me are roots stronger than I am based more on intuition than reason, and which walk hand-in-hand with my own will and judgment so that I seldom falter in an act, and if I do I am almost always regretting and ashamed."[56] Not to confront, not to respond to the social injustices of her people was to sin: it was a lesson Dunham learned early in childhood, when in a courtroom she unwittingly abetted in the loss of a custody suit between members of her family and bitterly learned that: "There is no absolution in innocence and even unwilling collaboration was at least stupidity, which has no place in uprightness; and that betrayal of the trust of others and pride of self is more guilt-engendering than just plain, willful sinning."[57]

Propelled by a search for truth, *Southland* is rooted in the African American struggle for self-definition in a society that has often refused to acknowledge its humanity. From the innocent Lucy to the trusting fieldhand Richard; from the gospel-like chorus to the "seeing" blind man searching for answers; from the Basin Street Blues people, who absorb the tragic lynching through the sheer power of their dancing, and the knife-thrower who fiercely refutes it, to the chorus that in the end is practically triumphant, the characters in *Southland* struggle to confront and transcend their historical restrictions in an attempt to affirm meaning in their lives. They refuse to allow the racist perception of black humanity to be reduced to the sum total of their brutalization.[58] They are what makes *Southland* such a powerful protest expression.

Dunham wrote to Berenson, "I have turned every possible searchlight and inner eye on *Southland* and I must say I feel absolutely innocent. It was a thing to me of great beauty, an expression of the passion in me. I grieved the unkind remarks, but I would have more deeply grieved had I betrayed myself."[59] The act of creating *Southland* was absolutely crucial to Dunham's well-being, just as the act of performing it was to her dancers, however painful it was. Dunham believes that "a person who dances should know why they dance, and to do so, they must have an historical background."[60] Dancing is a way to knowing, hence it is an affirmation of self and of one's culture. The "fiction" of *Southland*, the artwork itself, becomes the healing agent for the more brutal "fact" of it. As Lucille Ellis confirms for the company, "*Southland* was the beginning of knowing the quality of life and the human element. It made us all respect life and people. It made you feel you must do something. And in the doing, you finally begin to find yourself."

Southland was silenced, though Dunham was not. Nor were those she touched. "She was my Toussaint L'Ouverture," Talley Beatty says about the woman who made him a dancer and gave him the courage to choreograph from the center of his own experience. Though *Southland* was suppressed, and never even performed in the United States, its fierce spirit and bold theatrical form prefigured such black protest expressions of the late 1950s and 1960s as Beatty's *Road of the Phoebe Snow,* Donald McKayle's *Rainbow 'round My Shoulder,* Eleo Pomare's *Blues for the Jungle,* and Alvin Ailey's *Masekela Langage.* These protest expressions by African American artists followed Dunham's conviction: "Your daring has to backed up with a willingness to lose that point. To make a bigger point, you might have to lose one. I like to avoid confrontations if I can. But if I cannot, I want to be totally prepared to solve them or eliminate them, one way or another."[61]

Although *Southland* instigated the dissolution of Dunham's company, it laid the moral groundwork for subsequent expressions of affirmation and dissent and will forever embolden all those who dare to protest in the face of repression.

NOTES

This chapter was originally published in *Dance Research Journal* 26, no. 2 (fall 1994): 1–10. Minor changes have been made for consistency.

1. Katherine Dunham, "Program: *Southland* in Santiago de Chile, World Premiere, January 1951," in *Kaiso! Katherine Dunham: An Anthology of Writings*, ed. VèVè A. Clark and Margaret Wilkerson, (Berkeley: University of California Press, 1978), 118.

2. Ibid.

3. Quoted by Leon F. Litwack, "The Nifty Fifties," in *Advancing American Art: Painting, Politics and Cultural Confrontation at Mid-Century*, ed. Taylor D. Littleton and Maltby Sykes (Tuscaloosa: University of Alabama Press, 1989), 2. Litwack does not identify the writer except to say that his observation was published in *Commentary.*

4. VèVè A. Clark and Margaret Wilkerson, eds., "Dunham the Woman: Perspectives," in *Kaiso!* 5.

5. John Martin, "The Dance: Tropical Review," *New York Times*, 26 September 1943, sec. 2, 2.

6. Katherine Dunham, "Thesis Turned Broadway," in *Kaiso!* 55.

7. John Martin, "Schoolmarm Turned Siren or Vice Versa in *Bal Nègre* at the Belasco," *New York Times*, 17 November 1946, sec. 2, 9; "Torridity to Anthropology," *Newsweek* (27 January 1941): 62; Dorathi Bock Pierre, "Cool Scientist or Sultry Performer?" *Dance Magazine* (May 1947): 11; "High Priestess of Jive," in Katherine Dunham, *Scrapbooks: Clippings, Programs and Photographs*, vol. 5, *1937–49*, Dance Collection, the New York Public Library for the Performing Arts.

8. Howard Smead, *Blood Justice* (New York: Oxford University Press, 1986), xii. The Tuskegee Institute conservatively reports that between 1937 and 1946, 200 blacks were rescued from threatened lynchings, 21 blacks alone in 1946; see *Crimes against Lynching: Hearings before a Subcommittee of the Committee on the Judiciary United States Senate* (Washington, D.C.: U.S. Government Printing Office, 1948), 50.

9. The January 1944 lynching of an unnamed fifteen-year-old Negro youth in the Suwannee River, and the quadruple lynching of Roger Malcolm, Malcolm's wife, George Dorsey, and Dorsey's wife in Monroe, Georgia, on 20 July 1946 are cited in *Crimes against Lynching*, 10, 50.

10. Pearl Primus, telephone interview with the author, 23 March 1993.

11. Primus, in 1944, quoted by Bragiotti and cited in Beverly Hillman Barber, "Pearl Primus: Rebuilding America's Cultural Infrastructure," in *African American Genius in Modern Dance*, ed. Gerald E. Myers (Durham, N.C.: American Dance Festival, 1993), 10.

12. Talley Beatty, telephone interview with the author, 2 July 1992. Beatty was one of the nine original dancers in Dunham's dance company; *Southern Landscape* was created after Beatty left Dunham to form his own group.

13. "Miss Dunham's Comment to the Louisville Audience at Memorial Auditorium, October 19, 1944," in *Kaiso!* 88.

14. Julie Robinson Belafonte, interview with the author, 14 April 1993, New York City. "People forget," writes Agnes DeMille about Dunham: "Now people can go anywhere, stay anywhere, but in the thirties and early forties, it was terrible for blacks, particularly on tour . . . every city she went to posed the same problem: how should she house and protect her company and keep

them out of dreadful rooming houses and filthy hotels. . . . The dimensions of this persistent problem and the amount of trouble it caused her have never been discussed, but they were significant" (*Portrait Gallery* [New York: Houghton Mifflin, 1990], 45).

15. William H. Chafe writes that any program that deviated from a 100 percent conservative Americanism might have been attacked as reflecting a Moscow party line: "If you believed in civil rights, you were critical of America's racial customs and therefore an ally of those who, from abroad, also criticized American racism" (*The Unfinished Journey: America since World War II* [New York: Oxford University Press, 1991], 108).

16. Martin Duberman's *Paul Robeson* (New York: Knopf, 1988) provides a detailed account of Robeson and the 1949 Peekskill riots.

17. Katherine Dunham, interview with the author, 29 January 1993, East St. Louis.

18. VèVè Clark, "Katherine Dunham: Method Dancing or the Memory of Difference," *African American Genius*, 8.

19. Langston Hughes in Robert Zangrando, *The NAACP Crusade against Lynching, 1909–1950* (Philadelphia: Temple University Press, 1980), 204.

20. On 2 February 1951, the seven black defendants known as the Martinsville Seven—Joe Henry Hampton, Howard Hairston, Booker Millner, Frank Hairston, John Taylor, James Hairston, and Francis Grayson—were executed at Richmond, Virginia, for allegedly having raped a white woman. On 8 May of the same year, Willie McGee was executed by the state of Mississippi, after having been convicted of raping a white woman, Mrs. Willamette Hawkins. Though evidence indicated Hawkins forced McGee into a relationship he later tried to sever, once the charge of rape had been raised, Mississippi was incapable of legitimizing the concept that a white woman sought a sexual relationship with a black male. The racist stereotype of the black rapist served to justify execution of black defendants who had been convicted in trials that mocked proper judicial procedures. Herbert Shapiro, in *White Violence and Black Response* (Amherst: University of Massachusetts Press, 1988), documents the chilling details of McGee's trial and execution. Dunham remembers following the news of the trials, which lasted from 1949 to 1951. By March 1950 the seven youths, who were convicted in Virginia on 8 January 1949, were in the midst of applying for a change of venue, the details of which are documented in "Hampton v. Commonwealth," *58 South Eastern Reporter, 2d Series*, 290.

21. Dunham dancer Lucille Ellis recalls that *Southland* was produced by special arrangement with the Symphony of Chile and performed on the company's day off. Dunham arranged to have the theatre open, prepared a special concert of three premieres (*Southland* and two shorter dances), and had the audience invited through special invitation. "It was regal—the Embassy and all the dignitaries were there," Ellis recalled in a telephone interview with the author on 8 June 1993.

22. "Program: *Southland*," in *Kaiso!* 117.

23. The singers in the chorus included Freddye Marshall, Gordon Simpson, Milton Grayson, Ural Wilson, Claudia McNeill, and Delores Harper and acted

as what Dunham described as a "Greek chorus" reflecting the action in song and mime.

24. The program, prologue, and scenario for *Southland* is reprinted in "Program: *Southland*" in *Kaiso!* 117–20. Details of the ballet were recounted during the author's interview with Katherine Dunham on 29 January 1993 in East St. Louis, at which time Ms. Dunham described the action of the ballet while playing a tape of di Stefano's musical score. Unless otherwise indicated, descriptions of the ballet come from the interview with Ms. Dunham.

25. Katherine Dunham, unpublished script for *Southland*.

26. "Method dancing" is aptly termed and elaborated on in VèVè Clark's "Katherine Dunham: Method Dancing or the Memory of Difference," in *African American Genius*, 5–8.

27. Ricardo was literally swung by the neck onto the stage; Dunham remembers on opening night, "He was dying for air and choking," because the stagehand forgot to put on his harness.

28. Ellis, telephone interview with the author, 8 June 1993.

29. Based on the 1943 poem by Lewis Allan, the song "Strange Fruit" was made popular by Billy Holliday; Lillian Smith's best-selling novel *Strange Fruit* (1944) dealt with the topic of interracial sex and romance, not rape, and caused quite a sensation.

30. Katherine Dunham, "Program: *Southland*" in *Kaiso!* 120.

31. The character of the blind man in the Santiago production was played by a Haitian priest by the name of Sisemone, who also drummed for Dunham's dance company.

32. After the chorus's dirge, the music changes back to jazz, but in a minor key. Dunham says, "It was never perfected, they should do what they're doing but with an understanding of the futility of their situation. It should have hatred in it, like the knife that showed it." Dunham, interview with the author, 29 January 1993.

33. Ibid. Julie Robinson Belafonte adds that "the character of the blind man is one of searching for answers." Belafonte, interview with the author, 14 April 1993.

34. Dunham, interview with the author, 29 January 1993.

35. Unless otherwise indicated, all remarks by Katherine Dunham in this section are from her interview with the author, 29 January 1993.

36. Athan Theoharis, *Seeds of Repression* (Chicago: Quadrangle Books, 1971), 16.

37. Claude G. Bowers, *The Tragic Era: The Revolution after Lincoln* (Boston: Houghton, Mifflin, 1929), 309. Bowers (1878–1958) was the United States ambassador to Chile from 1939 to 1953.

38. Gilbert Bloch, *L'Humanité*, 10 January 1953; Dinah Maggie, *Le Monde*, 12 January 1953.

39. Katherine Dunham, unpublished letter to Bernard Berenson, 1 February 1953.

40. Ibid.

41. Dunham, interview with the author, 29 January 1993.

42. Ellis, telephone interview with the author, 8 June 1993.

43. Ibid.

44. Belafonte, interview with the author, 14 April 1993.

45. Ibid.

46. Ibid.

47. Ellis, telephone interview with the author, 8 June 1993.

48. Ibid.

49. Ibid.

50. The State Department incidents related by Dunham during her interview with the author are substantiated by Ruth Beckford in *Katherine Dunham, a Biography* (New York: Marcel Dekker, 1979), 58–62.

51. Dunham, unpublished letter to Bernard Berenson, 12 October 1955.

52. Ibid.

53. Ibid.

54. See Duke Ellington's "Notes on the State Department Tour" in *Music Is My Mistress* (New York: Doubleday, 1973), 305.

55. Dunham, interview with the author, 29 January 1993.

56. Dunham, unpublished letter to Bernard Berenson, 1 February 1953.

57. Katherine Dunham, *A Touch of Innocence* (New York: Harcourt, Brace and World, 1959), 66.

58. I am very much taken with James H. Cone's argument in his discussion of the blues that it is only through the "real" or "disclosed" in concrete human affairs that a community can attain authentic existence and that "insofar as the Blues affirm the somebodiness of black people, they are a transcendent reflection on black humanity," *The Spirituals and the Blues* (New York: Orbis, 1972), 113.

59. Dunham, unpublished letter to Bernard Berenson, 1 February 1953.

60. Katherine Dunham quoted in Joyce Aschenbrenner, *Katherine Dunham: Reflections on the Social and Political Contexts of Afro-American Dance,* Dance Research Annual 12 (New York: Congress on Research in Dance, 1981), 7.

61. Katherine Dunham, in Brian Lanker, *I Dream a World: Portraits of Black Women Who Changed America* (New York: Stewart, Tabori & Chang, 1989), 28.

11
The New York Negro Ballet in Great Britain

Dawn Lille Horwitz

In fall 1957, the New York Negro Ballet undertook an extensive tour of Great Britain, dancing in England, Scotland, and Wales. Their London season was canceled, as was a planned tour of the continent, but their performances throughout the English provinces represented a unique experience for their audiences to view what was then an equally unique phenomenon in the United States—a company of black dancers, all classically trained, with the women dancing *en pointe*. This chapter will detail that tour and its relationship to the emergence and eventual demise of the company.

PROLOGUE

The New York Negro Ballet began as a small group of black dancers, all of whom were studying with Maria Nevelska, a former member of the Bolshoi Ballet, who had a studio at No. 605 Carnegie Hall. The original group of six dancers—Ward Flemyng, Thelma Hill, Anthony Basse, Charles Neal, Elizabeth (Betty Ann) Thompson, and Cleo Quitman—would take regular classes six days a week and then rent a studio where they would rehearse on Sunday.

Ward Flemyng took charge of organizing their performances. Betty Ann Thompson recalls that a cousin of his owned a nightclub in upstate New York where they performed. She is not even sure they had a name at that time, although she recalls Doris Humphrey coming in to critique them.[1] Cleo Quitman remembers a performance at Brandon House, probably in late 1954.[2] Originally Mme. Nevelska either choreographed or reconstructed dances for them. By May 1955, when they were known as Les Ballets Nègres and performed at the Brooklyn Academy of Music (BAM), two more dancers from Mme. Nevelska's classes, Michaelyn Jackson and Theodore Crum, were added to the company. The program for this BAM "season" does not mention any one individual as being in charge, nor does it list an artistic director.[3] Four pieces were in the repertory: *Ballad No. 3,* choreographed by Mme. Nevelska for six dancers to music of Chopin; *Masquerade,* for seven dancers, also by Mme. Nevelska to music by Aram Khatchaturian; *Barbara Allen,* a long dramatic ballet choreographed by Anthony Basse to music by Howard Warren; and a piece called *Rompthru,* choreographed by Louis Johnson to George Gershwin. It is unclear when Johnson started to work with the group, but Quitman says that she personally paid him for this ballet, which she remembers as being "very pretty."[4]

Walter Sorell reviewed the program in *Dance Magazine.* Noting that the company was under the "leadership" of Mme. Nevelska, he said that none of the dancers was mature enough and that the group was "ill advised to present itself at this time."[5]

Although Sorell considered the performance amateurish at times, the inexperienced dancers were not amateurs. New York–born Thelma Hill, who was just twenty, had studied at the Metropolitan Opera school; she later danced with Alvin Ailey and became one of the founding members of the Clark Center in New York City. Betty Ann Thompson, also from New York, first studied at her local church with Sheldon Hoskins, a black teacher from Baltimore. She also trained under Oreste Sergievsky and attended the Juilliard School for two years, studying with Anthony Tudor, Margaret Craske, Alfredo Corvino, and José Limón.[6] Anthony Basse, from Cleveland, studied both ballet and modern dance at Karamu House in that city. He later co-founded the second Ballet Trocadero and became Tamara Karpova, the famed travesty company's "black rhinestone." Michaelyn Jackson was from Washington, D.C., where she had trained at the Jones-Haywood School.[7] She also studied at the School of American Ballet with Anatole Oboukhoff and Pierre Vladimiroff. Charles "Bunky" Neal was from Detroit, where he may have studied ballet there with Nicholas Tsouklas. Theodore Crum, from California, had danced with the Hollywood Negro Ballet and probably studied at the San Francisco School of Ballet; he was an old friend of Ward Flemyng's, and several dancers think their friendship began there.[8] Cleo Quitman studied ballet with Sofia Tsouklas, Nicholas's wife, in her native Detroit where Tsouklas taught black students in a separate class.[9] She came to New York in 1954 at the age of seventeen intending to enroll at the School of American Ballet; however, it was mid-year and the school would not accept her, so she went to study with Mattie Gabors and Alfredo Corvino at the Metropolitan Opera school. It was Charles Neal who directed her to Mme. Nevelska. Quitman later appeared as a guest artist with American Ballet Theatre in Agnes De Mille's *The Four Marys* (1961) and with the Joffrey Ballet in Eugene Loring's *These Three* (1966). Choreographer Louis Johnson, a product of the Jones-Haywood School in Washington, was an outstanding dancer as well as a choreographer. He had studied at the School of American Ballet and with William Dollar, Tudor, and Craske and had danced in the New York City Ballet's production of *Ballade*, choreographed by Jerome Robbins, prior to becoming involved with the group.

Last but far from least was Ward (Edward) Flemyng.[10] Everyone agrees that it was his sophistication, charm, and ability to find people with money that provided the impetus for the New York Negro Ballet. Born in Detroit, he too had studied with Nicholas Tsouklas and at the San Francisco School of Ballet before receiving a scholarship to the Katherine Dunham School in New York. Here, he also studied with Sonia Woicikowska at Ballets Arts before going to Mme. Nevelska, in addition to studying modern dance and jazz. He would later study in Europe and perform there widely.

FLEMYNG'S LEADERSHIP

Louis Johnson says that Flemyng had long dreamt of a Negro Ballet Company.[11] Kind, generous, intelligent, and "a fundraiser's dream,"[12] Flemyng enlarged the company and brought in more choreographers sometime in 1956. He was the group's catalyst as well as its coordinator and was one of its principal dancers, although others frequently had to substitute for him at rehearsals he missed while organizing the group.

Flemyng recruited two key people: Theodore Hancock and Lucy Thorndike. To date, little is known about either. Hancock, called "Theo," was an artist, possibly in his forties, who lived on East 82nd Street near the Metropolitan Museum of Art. The only description of him is that he stuttered. He had evidently inherited some money, and it is possible that he provided seed money for the company and introduced Flemyng to Thorndike.[13] Remembered as a lovely lady, Thorndike came from a wealthy Massachusetts family and was an old-fashioned kind of patron who paid for everything and attended several studio rehearsals in New York. Together, these two served as the producers of the New York Negro Ballet. Hancock, whose name, address, and telephone number were listed on mailings soliciting support for the company, was also involved in its daily business activities, and he is listed in all documents and programs as co-artistic director along with Flemyng, although his role was probably that of an administrator.

In a formal statement probably drawn up by a lawyer, Hancock, Thorndike, Flemyng, and Alexander Piner (an accountant) are listed as executive directors of the company, with Flemyng and Hancock being charged to implement their decisions. There was also an artistic advisory panel consisting of Bernard Johnson for costume and design, Perry Watkins for design and stagecraft, resident choreographer Joseph Rickard, Benjamin Steinberg for music, and resident composer Claudius Wilson. The company staff consisted of Flemyng as "Maitre de Ballet en Chef," Rickard as "Maitre de Ballet," Thelma Hill as "Regisseuse and Assistant" to Flemyng, and Charles Neal as the "Dancers' Representative."[14]

A solicitation for funds described the company as a corporation issuing debentures in sums of $500, $1,000, and $2,000 that could be purchased at "six per cent interest per annum" and were "redeemable within five years from October 1, 1956." The one-page appeal ends with the following paragraph:

The company exists and must have immediate financial help or we will lose this opportunity to show the world that out of these United States, in this exciting year of change, 1956, there can come a Negro Ballet expecting to be judged by the same standards as the great companies of the world—one that will take its place not only in the history of the Dance, but in the history of a People.[15]

In 1956 Flemyng invited the Los Angeles–based First Negro Classic Ballet (also known very briefly as the Hollywood Negro Ballet) and its director, Joseph Rickard, to join forces with the New York company. Rickard was of English German background and had danced with the Ballet Russe. He had taught ballet at Music Town in Los Angeles, where his students were predominantly black. This led to a few small concerts and, in 1947, to the founding of the First Negro Classic Ballet.[16] Although this was not the first black ballet company, it may well have been the first to have its women dance *en pointe*. By 1951, plans were afoot to bring the First Negro Classic Ballet to England.

"Cinders In Sepia" was the title of a two-page spread in the London *Illustrated* of 14 July 1951. The subtitle read: "Could there be a Negro Nijinsky? We may know, soon, when an all-coloured classic ballet crosses that Atlantic," and the article provided information about the company and its production of *Cinderella*. Also mentioned in the article was Rickard's ballet *Harlot's House,* which the New York Negro Ballet would bring to Britain in 1957. The West Coast group never made it to Europe. How Rickard met Flemyng is unclear, although it has been suggested that the two were brought together by Ted Crum (known as Theodore Duncan on the British tour)[17] and that Rickard agreed to come because he was chronically short of funds.[18] Rickard, however, did not go on the 1957 tour, but four of his dancers did—Guy Allison, Patricia Griffith, Carol Ann Wise and Graham Johnson—while a fifth dancer, Bernice Johnson, who was a bit older than the rest and Rickard's "star," rehearsed in New York for a while but then returned to California.

The company rehearsed sporadically in New York with Thelma Hill serving as rehearsal director. Delores Browne describes her as

Ward Flemyng and Delores Browne in Joseph Rickard's *Cinderella*. This ballet was rehearsed in New York but was not performed in Great Britain. (Photograph by Bruno; Photographs and Prints Division, Schomburg Center for Research in Black Culture, the New York Public Library–Astor, Lenox and Tilden Foundations; reproduced with permission)

having a "mind like a trap" and a "dramatic and kinetic intensity to her dancing."[19] George Chaffee, the American- and French-trained ballet master, gave the dancers a two-hour company class at his studio, where they also rehearsed.

The new arrivals, who ultimately numbered twelve, joined the eight dancers already mentioned. Barbara Wright, who came from the Jones-Haywood School in Washington, D.C., had studied at the School of American Ballet's summer program. Eventually, she took classes with Mme. Nevelska, and she thinks it was Michaelyn Jackson who brought her into the New York Negro Ballet.[20] Helen Taitt was from British Guyana. According to Louis Johnson, she was the only recognizably black student at the School of American Ballet when he arrived there in 1950. Remembered by many as a "lady," she is also described as being "old-fashioned" and "Pavlova-like" in appearance.[21]

Eugene Sagan (later Gene Hill Sagan) had studied with Michael Brigante in California and with Igor Schwezoff and William Dollar at the Ballet Theatre School in New York. However, it was from Mme. Nevelska, to whom he was introduced by his good friend Thelma Hill, that he receive the bulk of his training. Delores Browne started her training with Marion Cuyjet in Philadelphia, then took a classes with Antony Tudor at the Philadelphia Ballet Guild, Lisan Kay and Vladimir Doukodousky at Ballet Arts, and spent a year at the School of American Ballet. It was George Chaffee, with whom she also worked, who eventually gave her name to Flemyng. Bernard Johnson joined the company so early that some think of him as part of the original group. He came from Detroit, where he had studied with Maryann Baylor, Nicholas and Sofia Tsouklas, and Gertrude Jorry, a British dancer. Johnson came to New York in 1954 to study art and ended up taking classes with Aubrey Hitchins and Mme. Nevelska. Frances Jimenez was another Philadelphian who had trained with Marion Cuyjet and Antony Tudor at the Philadelphia Ballet Guild. Her friend Delores Browne gave her name to Flemyng, who auditioned her. Sylvester Campbell (who was Sylvester Briscoe on the British tour) had turned down a scholarship from the School of American Ballet because he lacked the funds for room and

board. Barbara Wright, his cousin, gave his name to Flemyng.
Candace Caldwell, a New Yorker, is remembered as being very
pretty and having a "spirited attack."[22] She was brought in to replace Barbara Wright, who had gotten into the Broadway show
Jamaica. Roland Fraser ("Rollie") later joined the Cologne ballet. Yvonne McDowell, another New Yorker who had studied at
the Ballet Theatre School and with Chaffee, was fifteen when
she joined the company. A powerhouse[23] of a dancer, she later
studied at the Joffrey School and committed suicide at the age of
twenty-three. Georgia Collins, recalled by her colleagues as a sensuous dancer, was later associated with Alvin Ailey.

This group—which included a large percentage of the country's black ballet dancers at the time—settled down to rehearsing at Chaffee's studio or, sometimes, at Mme. Nevelska's. Ward
Flemyng and Theo Hancock were busy locating backers; sometimes the group would rehearse for a couple of months and then
disband for a brief period. Chaffee gave a two-hour company class,
usually accompanied by Claudius Wilson, a composer and musician who had come from California with Rickard. Rehearsals,
which were mostly conducted by Thelma Hill, followed class. At
some point Janet Collins was hired as a "consultant." She came to
a few rehearsals, and Delores Browne remembers that she talked
about "arms and motivations."[24]

It was not long before Rickard began to be unhappy with his
role in the company. Despite his Ballet Russe credentials, he was
really second to Chaffee, a position he probably did not antici-
pate sharing. As Delores Browne put it, "Nobody knew who
Joseph Rickard was and very honestly treated him like a local
dance teacher from the sticks. He departed after that first summer."[25]

The company made only a few appearances before setting off
for the British Isles. One was at the Seventh Annual Choreographers Night presented by the New York Ballet Club on 19 May
1957. Ten members of the group appeared in Louis Johnson's
Folk Impressions to music by Morton Gould. At another point,
aboard the SS *Flandre*, Delores Browne and Guy Allison danced
the *Don Quixote* pas de deux, and Thelma Hill, Bernard Johnson,

and Theodore Crum performed excerpts from *Raisin' Cane,* choreographed by Graham Johnson to music by Claudius Wilson.

When the New York Negro Ballet left for London in August 1957, it numbered twenty-one dancers. (Two additional company members, Barbara Wright and Michaelyn Jackson, elected to stay behind.) The company was brought to Great Britain by Peter Daubeny, a well-known impresario who was later knighted. They spent their first four weeks in London where they rehearsed and took a daily class with Michel de Lutry. Born in France, de Lutry had studied with Lubov Egorova and had danced in Paris before joining the International Ballet in London after World War II. He later taught in Germany and Switzerland. Whether de Lutry was hired to bring an outside professional eye to the company or because the exchange law required them to have at least one teacher from the country is not clear. Although Frances Jimenez feels he focused on the strongest dancers and made others insecure and resentful, Bernard Johnson cites him as a wonderful teacher who gave them an understanding of the force and strength needed for classical dancing. For example, at the end of his class, the men reportedly performed thirty-two *entrechats dix.* They worked on excerpts from *The Sleeping Beauty, Giselle,* and other classical ballets they had never done before. De Lutry did not go on tour with the company because of previous commitments, and Jack Carter replaced him as ballet master. Carter had trained at Sadlers Wells, studied with Olga Preobrajenska in Paris, and danced with the Original Ballet Russe, Ballet Rambert, and London Festival Ballet (he served as chief choreographer for the latter from 1965 to 1970).

Through Mrs. Thorndike's generosity, this month in London, with full rehearsal pay, allowed the group to develop a working schedule, create a genuinely harmonious ensemble, and adjust to a foreign country. They had costumes and some new sets made. Funds were also provided for rehearsal clothes and pointe shoes. In connection with the latter, Frances Jimenez says: "The English mentality was very much like the Americans during that time. . . . We sent our shoe sizes and a cast of everyone's feet so that when we arrived there we could have our shoes made by

Freed or whomever we wanted. . . . They never made the first pair of shoes . . . because they did not believe that black girls were dancing on pointe. [To them] that was just on the photograph, but it did not exist."[26]

REPERTORY

The tour repertory consisted of six works: *Raisin' Cane, Folk Impressions, Waltze, Harlot's House, Theme and Rhapsody,* and *Mardi Gras. Raisin' Cane,* which had music written and played by the New Orleans–born composer Claudius Wilson, was a story ballet in three scenes. The choreography was by Graham Johnson, who also played the hero of the story, an innocent country boy named Tom, taken in by a cast of big-city characters, including a siren called Blossom, who steal his money. Scene One took place in a village outside New Orleans after the sugar cane harvest. The croppers elect Tom to go to the city to oversee the sale of the cane. Scene Two was set in a nightclub where the innocent Tom is taken after completing his business. Here he meets Blossom. Scene Three took place back in the village. In addition to Johnson, the cast of eleven included Yvonne McDowell as Tom's village sweetheart and Cleo Quitman as the seductive Blossom. Quitman's outstanding memory of the ballet is the wonderful costume designed for her by Bernard Johnson, which included a wide hat dripping feathers.

Folk Impressions, a ballet by Louis Johnson to music by Morton Gould, had also been performed by the company prior to the tour. According to a note in the Glasgow program, Johnson's inspiration was the "composer's impressions of American folk themes and [he] has created five different and symbolic movements."[27] Actually there were six movements: "Proclamation" featured a preaching soloist; "Sermon" was for eleven dancers; "A Little Bit of Sin," another solo, came third; "Shortnin' Bread," a comic duet, came fourth; "Protest" was danced by the ensemble and a "leader"; and the ballet concluded with "Jubilee," performed by the full cast. *Folk Impressions* was basically an abstract work shown on tour with new settings by English designer Richard Lake.

Waltze, a romantic ballet to music from the opera *Madame Angot's Daughter* by Alexander Charles Lecoq, was Johnson's second work on the program. An abstract ballet for twelve dancers in classical style, it had five principal roles danced by alternate casts. Its four sections were a pas de six for six women, a pas de trois for two women and a man, a pas de deux, and an ensemble finale.

Two of Joseph Rickard's ballets remained after he left: *Harlot's House* with music by Claudius Wilson, and *Theme and Rhapsody,* which had music by Brahms. *Harlot's House* was based on the Oscar Wilde poem of the same name, which Wilson had set to music. It seems to have been one of Rickard's earliest creations, since it is mentioned in the London article of 1951.[28] The story, set at the turn of the century, features two strolling lovers who stop before a brothel, attracted by the music and sounds within. The girl is mysteriously torn between entering the house or remaining with her lover. The cast of thirteen also includes three children, a blind man, the madam, a novice, and the harlot and her boyfriend.

Theme and Rhapsody, an abstract ballet in a neoclassical style, began with a theme for six followed by an all-male pas de trois, after which came a second pas de trois for two women and a man, a pas de six for three couples, and a finale.

Mardi Gras, choreographed by Ernest Parham, a member of the Dunham company, to music by Les Baxter, was a carnival ballet for the entire company that at least one member recalls as "classical ballet with overtones of primitive and Latin."[29] It included a prologue, with a bird as the symbol of Mardi Gras; a quadrille; a carnival scene, with a flirt; a love dance; and a ritual, led by an ancestral figure and featuring a group possessed.

One bona fide classical piece was added to the repertory in London: the "Bluebird" pas de deux from *The Sleeping Beauty,* which Michel de Lutry staged for Bernard Johnson and Delores Browne. According to Johnson, Peter Daubeny paid for the work, suggesting that the impresario himself had commissioned it. Johnson had earlier learned a version of the duet from Aubrey Hitchins, but he recalls that this new staging was one in which they were both birds and the woman really danced. He adds that

Graham Johnson's *Raisin' Cane*. *Left to right:* Thelma Hill, Guy Allison, Frances Jiminez, Theodore Duncan, Elizabeth Thompson, Eugene Sagan. (Photograph by Bruno; Photographs and Prints Division, Schomburg Center for Research in Black Culture, the New York Public Library–Astor, Lenox and Tilden Foundations; reproduced with permission)

Louis Johnson's *Waltze*. Cleo Quitman is in the center. *Back row (from left)*: Sylvester Campbell, Charles Neal, Graham Johnson, Theodore Duncan, Guy Allison, Gene Sagan. *Front row*: Elizabeth Thompson, Michaelyn Jackson, Frances Jiminez, Edna Philips (who rehearsed with the company but did not perform with them and did not go to Great Britain), Thelma Hill, Delores Browne. (Photograph by Bruno; Photographs and Prints Division, Schomburg Center for Research in Black Culture, the New York Public Library–Astor, Lenox and Tilden Foundations; reproduced with permission)

329

Sextet from Joseph Rickard's *Theme and Rhapsody* (Photograph by Bruno; Photographs and Prints Division, Schomburg Center for Research in Black Culture, the New York Public Library–Astor, Lenox and Tilden Foundations; reproduced with permission)

Bernard Johnson and Delores Browne in Ernest Parham's *Mardi Gras* (Photograph by Bruno; Photographs and Prints Division, Schomburg Center for Research in Black Culture, the New York Public Library–Astor, Lenox and Tilden Foundations; reproduced with permission)

Browne taught him to partner while they were doing it. "Blue-bird" was seen for the first time in Edinburgh, the third city on the tour.[30]

ON TOUR

An article in the October issue of the British monthly *Dance and Dancers* announced that Daubeny was presenting the company on a tour of the British provinces "prior to a London season and a continental tour." Negroes in ballet are not absurd, the author asserts; they have a greater sense of natural rhythm, and "there is no reason why it should not be disciplined into ballet form." Noting that the aim of the company was not to confine its work to classical dance but to combine it with the Negro heritage, and that the two directors planned to recruit well-known choreographers, composers, and designers, the author concludes: "The New York Negro ballet amounts to a sincere attempt at establishing the Negro as an important contributor to the art of ballet as a whole."[31]

The British public had seen many black dancers, beginning with William Henry Lane ("Juba") in the mid-nineteenth century. In 1946 the Jamaican-born choreographer Berto Pasuka founded and choreographed for the Ballets Nègres, which toured Britain and Europe before its demise in 1952. Notwithstanding its name, this company was not ballet-based, and its repertory was rooted in African and West Indian myths. In 1952 Daubeny brought the Dunham company to Britain for a highly successful tour. However, a classical company of black dancers was entirely new.

The tour that Daubeny arranged began in Glasgow on 8 September. Through reviews one can follow the group to Newcastle, Edinburgh, Sheffield, Liverpool, Leeds, and Cardiff. The company spent six days in each city (the seventh was reserved for travel), doing two performances an evening, at 5:00 P.M. and 8:00 P.M., plus a matinee on Wednesdays. Although Manchester and Nottingham have been mentioned as being part of the tour, no record has been found of appearances there. The program in each city was the same: it consisted of the entire repertory. The

"Bluebird" pas de deux was performed in Edinburgh and Sheffield, and there is no reason to assume that it was not repeated
for the remainder of the tour, although it is sometimes not mentioned. The performers were accompanied by a full orchestra, and
for *Raisin' Cane* and *Harlot's House,* by Claudius Wilson on the
piano. Surprisingly, *Mardi Gras* used recorded music.[32]

The reviews — and there were always several in each city — were
generally enthusiastic, stressing the vitality, energy, and excitement of this most "entertaining" and "exotic" company. Bernard
Johnson's costumes were universally praised, as was the musi-
cianship of Claudius Wilson; the orchestra was considered me-
diocre, as were Wilson's original compositions. The classical offerings were deemed successful, but they seemed to pale next to the
rhythmic and sinuous movement seen in the ballets more obviously based on black American experience. In general, it was the
performers, with their loose style and agility, who were appreciated, rather than the choreography. Their talent in mime was
observed by many. In Glasgow one critic wrote: "It is different,
not only as American entertainment, but as ballet. The choreographic art . . . seems to owe as much to the African ancestry of
the dancers as to the European ballet tradition they had assimilated, and while the coalescence may not be complete, the result is
something final."[33] Another critic observed that the dancers had
mastered classical technique "without being able to touch fine
spun elegance and without a prima ballerina."[34]

In Newcastle they were described as "a superb company . . .
[whose] joyous offerings brought many curtain calls and bou-
quets." Admitting that the sight of "Negroes in classical ballet
is disconcerting at first," the critic said the technical accomplish-
ments of the dancers caused this feeling to dissipate quickly, although the company "achieves its best work in the ballets which
. . . give full opportunity to the sensuous movements of the
dancers."[35]

An Edinburgh critic found the company exciting to see, though
lacking in technical perfection, and at its best in "items more
closely associated with their native traditions."[36] Another, while
admiring the dancer's technical skill, deplored the lack of good

choreography. One writer observed in the ballets as much mime as dancing and a "slight woolliness in some of the classical items" but concluded, "If the New York Ballet Company's [sic] aim is to show that negro dancers can perform in classical ballet then the production . . . last night proved that the experiment has achieved a large degree of success."[37]

Critics devoted more space to what they saw as typically "Negro" ballets: *Mardi Gras, Raisin' Cane, Harlot's House,* and, to a lesser degree, *Folk Impressions.* The dancers most often singled out were Delores Browne, Theodore Duncan, Cleo Quitman, Bernard Johnson, Thelma Hill, and Yvonne McDowell.

Mardi Gras closed the program, and judging from the critical reaction, this was a very wise decision. One review enthused over the work's "sheer spectacular agility . . . like a tribal dance from darkest Africa."[38] Another described it as being "as brilliant a colour spectacle as I hope to see [it] gives the entire company full scope for their dash, verve and vitality, the men in particular."[39] Everyone noted the exuberance and gaiety of this colorful work, with many attributing it to something particularly "Negro." In Edinburgh, a critic observed that although it resembled "African ballet" at times, the work showed the discipline of the classic style. Following this same idea, a Glasgow critic wrote: "To their classical movements they united Negro activity with rhythms inspired by Les Baxter's music, much of it sheer Africa. . . . If all had been as brilliant they would be high up in the ballet league."[40]

Raisin' Cane seems to have been the next favorite. Albert Mackie was particularly impressed by Frances Jimenez as the Lady of the Evening, a "lanky spider in black and yellow [who] is the sensation of this highly imaginative ballet."[41] Others noted the rhythm and flowing movements, the humor, the excellent miming, and the "wit and grace of the slender Cleo Quitman"[42] as the siren Blossom. In *Harlot's House,* the vividness of the mime was also noted. Claudius Wilson's music for both of these works was not generally liked, with one critic calling it "imitative, discordant and uninspired."[43]

The fourth of the so-called "southern" ballets, Louis Johnson's *Folk Impressions,* met with less overall enthusiasm. One critic noted that the "dull patterns and static poses spoiled what might have been an interesting experiment,"[44] yet this work, which was probably more subtle and less like a Hollywood movie (to which some of the reviews favorably compared the company), also received much praise. A Newcastle critic found it most impressive of all, making a tremendous impact even without a story line.[45] "Shortnin' Bread," the comic pas de deux, was singled out, and one writer observed that this work offered the spiritual of prayer, sin, and forgiveness without which "no Negro ballet would be complete!"[46]

The two "classical" ballets, *Waltze* and *Theme and Rhapsody*, received considerably less attention from critics, although the former was praised a bit more as a "pleasing" divertissement in yellow. *Theme and Rhapsody* was simply described as a well-danced, neoclassical ballet in blue. The "Bluebird" pas de deux, the one genuinely classical work on the program, was given attention in photographs but little in print, leading one to wonder if perhaps critics and audiences did not *really* wish to accept the fact of a black dance company performing the classics. One Glasgow critic wrote that the company was "without the rigid purity and negative restraint we expect of classical ballet . . . the jazz rhythms kept coming incongruously through" although "these apparent defects became virtues in the folk sequences."[47] Perhaps most revealing was the comment from an Edinburgh critic that "ably as these dancers can comport themselves in traditional classical ballet, it is a pity that they should waste their time on what is not really their element."[48]

In spite of several announcements to the contrary at the beginning of the tour, Peter Daubeny chose not to present the company in London, nor did it go on the continent. Instead the dancers spent an additional three weeks in London (possibly because the directors were seeking other presenters before returning to New York). It is unclear why Daubeny made this decision, since most of the reviews were good.

Reflecting on the experience over thirty years later, Bernard Johnson felt that in 1957 laymen were simply not prepared to see a company consisting of black ballet dancers, and that audiences and critics assumed that *Mardi Gras* was the kind of piece they *should* be doing. Hence, the popular audience did not come out, and the box office suffered despite the favorable reviews. Johnson thinks that Daubeny's decision was purely a financial one, and there is no evidence to indicate otherwise. What might also be added to this appraisal, however, is the fact that the original group had expanded rapidly and prior to arriving in London had not rehearsed for a month.[49]

AFTERMATH

When the company returned to New York, it was minus several of its members. Cleo Quitman and Bernard Johnson put together a blues and African act and toured the continent with it for two years. Roland Fraser joined the Cologne Ballet, as the first black dancer to do so. Sylvester Campbell started doing weekly shows for BBC television, danced with groups directed by Anton Dolin, and spent twelve years with the Royal Netherlands Ballet dancing in all the classics. Gene Hill Sagan briefly returned to the United States, then performed in Paris and Copenhagen and with several companies in Germany before spending ten years in Israel as a dancer and choreographer. Frances Jimenez got into a show called *Harlem Heatwave* immediately after her return to New York. It opened in London, where she studied for a time with Marie Rambert. Eventually, she signed with an agent in Milan and performed for several years throughout Italy as well as other countries. Ward Flemyng spent most of his career after the New York Negro Ballet in Europe. He danced in ten different musicals in Germany, did a considerable amount of television work there (as well as in France, Belgium, and Italy), performed in nightclubs in Paris and London, and choreographed several shows, including a *Carmen Jones* that toured Germany and Switzerland.

In November 1957 the company returned to New York. They continued to take classes and rehearse. Then one day they went to a rehearsal and were told the studio was not booked. The problem was money; their major patron, Lucy Thorndike, had died. Soon after, in early 1958, Graham Johnson and Carol Ann Wise returned to California and Frances Jimenez to Europe. About the same time, the Foundation for American Dance, a tax-exempt organization, sent out a large, two-page mailing, inviting recipients to become patrons of the New York Negro Ballet for sums ranging from $500 to $5,000. Theodore Hancock was listed as the sole company director and Howard Squadron as the lawyer.[50]

Although Ward Flemyng's curriculum vitae from a later date lists performances at several colleges and at the White Barn Theatre in Connecticut,[51] there is only one documented performance by the company in 1958. This was at the Ninety-second Street YM-YWHA on 22 June, where the company was identified as Ballet Americana, "formerly the New York Negro Ballet." The seventeen-dancer group had as its core twelve former company members plus five new dancers. Thelma Hill and Ward Flemyng were listed both as artistic directors and dancers. The program included *Divertissement,* choreographed by Louis Johnson to music by Lecoq (this was probably *Waltze* renamed); *Mardi Gras;* a Marvin Gordon work called *The Strolling Players* set to thirteenth-century music; the *Don Quixote* pas de deux staged by Anatole Vilzak; and Anthony Basse's *Barbara Allen,* first seen in 1955.

Doris Hering's review in the August 1958 issue of *Dance Magazine* praised the "landslide pioneering job" the company had done but found the repertory superficial and the company lacking in group cohesion. She found Basse's work "the most ambitious effort" and Johnson's ballet "charming," concluding that the company "danced with zest and high energy . . . yet to be cast in the careful mould of ballet."[52]

On 28 May 1959 a group called Coffee Concerts presented "soloists of Ballet Americana" at St. Martins on Lenox Avenue and 122nd Street. The seven dancers, listed as Guy Allison, Anthony Basse, Delores Browne, Don Dorsey, Eugen Sagon [*sic*], Helen Taitt, and Elizabeth Thompson, danced in nine ballets: five choreographed by Basse, one by Ernest Parham, one by Helen Taitt, one by Eugene Sagan, and one (a pas de deux from *Sleeping Beauty*) staged by Guy Allison. Thompson says that Basse was really the force behind Ballet Americana at this point.[53] By 1960 the remaining group had finally drifted apart.

Ward Flemyng's "dream" for a Negro ballet became a reality

when Arthur Mitchell founded the Dance Theatre of Harlem in 1969. However, the New York Negro Ballet came first.

NOTES

1. Elizabeth (Betty Ann) Thompson, interview with the author, New York City, 11 December 1989.

2. Cleo Quitman, interview with Constance Valis Hill, New York City, 2 November 1989.

3. Joe Nash Black Dance Collection, Schomburg Center for Research in Black Culture (hereafter, Nash Collection).

4. Quitman, interview with Valis Hill, 2 November 1989.

5. Walter Sorell, "Les Ballets Nègres at BAM," *Dance Magazine* (July 1955): 82.

6. Thompson left Juilliard to join the New York Negro Ballet.

7. Founded in 1940 by Doris Jones and Claire Haywood, this school still offers its students a rigorous classical curriculum.

8. No definitive biographical material has been found on either of these men.

9. Bernard Johnson, telephone interview with the author, 1 July 1991.

10. Several years later he changed the spelling of his last name to Fleming.

11. Louis Johnson, interview with the author, New York City, 19 June 1990.

12. Delores Browne Abelson, interview with the author, New York City, 17 October 1989.

13. Louis Johnson, interview with the author, 19 June 1990.

14. This statement is in the Nash Collection.

15. Sidney Offer is listed as the corporation's attorney, Alexander Pinter as its accountant, and Theodore Hancock as its president. Another flyer soliciting funds for a transcontinental American tour in the name of the Foundation American Dance lists the company lawyer as Howard Squadron. Both documents are in the Nash Collection.

16. James Truitte, who studied there for about a year-and-a-half, says that Rickard was not a great teacher. Contrary to what has sometimes been said, Truitte was *not* an advisor to the Hollywood Negro Ballet. James Truitte, interview with the author, 25 June 1991.

17. Thompson, interview with the author, 11 December 1989.

18. Quitman, interview with the author, 2 November 1989.

19. Browne Abelson, interview with the author, 17 October 1989. The second description is from Selma Jeanne Cohen, "Talley Beatty, Louis Johnson, Ernest Parham, Ninety-second Street Y," *Dance Magazine* 3 (April 1960): 29.

20. Barbara Wright, interview with the author, 8 July 1991.

21. Ibid.

22. Cohen, "Talley Beatty, Louis Johnson, Ernest Parham, Ninety-second Street Y," 29.

23. Sylvester Campbell, interview with the author, Baltimore, 23 May 1991.

24. Abelson, interview with the author, 17 October 1989.

25. Ibid.

26. Frances (Franca) Jimenez, telephone interview with the author, 4 November 1990.

27. Program note, Kings Theatre, Glasgow, Nash Collection.

28. *Illustrated* (14 July 1951): n.p.

29. Bernard Johnson, telephone interview with the author, 1 July 1991.

30. Theodore Hancock, telegram to Delores Browne, date undecipherable. Nash Collection.

31. "Negroes in Ballet," *Dance and Dancers* (October 1957): 9.

32. An unsigned, undated review in a Liverpool newspaper complains that the ballet was spoiled by the use of recorded music. Nash Collection.

33. "Ballet with a Difference," *Evening Times* (Glasgow), 10 September 1957.

34. Robins Milar, "Intoxicating . . . Tis Tom Tom Ballet," *Scottish Daily Express* (Glasgow), 10 September 1957.

35. "The Negro Ballet's Immediate Impact," *Northern Echo* (Newcastle), 17 September 1957.

36. "Exciting Ballet from Negro Company," *Edinburgh Evening News,* 24 September 1957.

37. Unidentified clipping, Edinburgh, 24 September 1957.

38. A. H., unidentified newspaper, Edinburgh.

39. Our Ballet Critic [*sic*], "Colorful Ballet Negro Dancers Provide Brilliant Spectacle," *Scotsman* (Edinburgh), 24 September 1957.

40. Milar, "Intoxicating."

41. Albert Mackie, "The Negro Ballet Can Win Friends," *Scottish Daily Express* (Edinburgh), 24 September 1957.

42. "Colorful Ballet Negro Dancers," *Scotsman.*

43. ADN, "Skilled Dancing in Negro Ballet," unidentified Edinburgh newspaper, n.d.

44. Ibid.

45. "Negroes Make All Ballet Exotic," *Journal and North Mail* (Newcastle), 17 September 1957.

46. Liverpool, unidentified clipping source.

47. D. McK, Glasgow, unidentified clipping source.

48. "Colorful Ballet Negro Dancers," *Scotsman.*

49. Bernard Johnson, telephone interview with the author, 1 July 1991.

50. A copy of the 17" by 22" flyer/brochure is in the Nash Collection.

51. Flemyng's curriculum vitae is in the Nash Collection.

52. Doris Hering, "Ballet Americana," *Dance Magazine* (August 1958), 57.

53. Thompson, interview with the author, 11 December 1989.

Contributors
Index

Contributors

SALLY BANES is Marian Hannah Winter Professor of Theatre History and Dance Studies at University of Wisconsin–Madison. She is the author of several books, including *Terpsichore in Sneakers: Post-Modern Dance* (1980) and *Dancing Women: Female Bodies on Stage* (1998), and is co-author of *Fresh: Hip Hop Don't Stop* (1985).

THOMAS F. DEFRANTZ is associate professor of theater arts at the Massachusetts Institute of Technology, and he directs the dance history program at the Alvin Ailey School of American Dance. He is author of the forthcoming *Revelations: Alvin Ailey's Embodiment of African American Culture*. He has published widely on the black body in concert dance, dance in the Black Arts movement, and hip-hop dance.

NADINE A. GEORGE earned her Ph.D. from Northwestern University. She is assistant professor of theater studies and African American studies at Yale University. She is the author of *The Royalty of Negro Vaudeville: The Whitman Sisters and the Negotiation of Race, Gender, and Class in African American Theater 1900–1940*.

VETA GOLER earned her Ph.D. in African American studies from Emory University and her M.F.A. in dance from the University of Michigan. She is associate professor of dance and chair of drama and dance at Spelman College. Her research focuses on contemporary African American women choreographers. She has published articles in *Choreography and Dance, The Citizen Artist: 20 Years of Art in the Public Arena,* and *EightRock*.

BRENDA DIXON GOTTSCHILD is professor emeritus of dance at Temple University where she taught performance history, theory, and criticism for more than twenty years. She is the author of *Digging the Africanist Presence in American Performance: Dance and Other Contexts* and *Waltzing in the Dark: African American Vaudeville and Race Politics in the Swing Era*, co-author of the most recent edition of *The History of Dance in Art and Education*, and Philadelphia contributor to *Dance Magazine*.

RICHARD C. GREEN is a Ph.D. candidate in the Department of Performance Studies at New York University. He has taught at the City University of New York, Duke University, and Stanford University and is co-editor of the anthology *Soul: Black Power, Politics, and Pleasure*. He is completing a study of the Venus Hottentot.

MARCIA E. HEARD earned her Ph.D. in dance history from New York University. She was a protégé of Dr. Pearl Primus. She has danced with Joel Hall and Joseph Holmes in Chicago and now dances with Sabar Ak Ru Afriq in New York.

CONSTANCE VALIS HILL is a dance historian and critic based in Albany, New York. She holds a Ph.D. in performance studies from New York University and organized the dance history program at the Alvin Ailey School of American Dance. She is the author of *Brotherhood in Rhythm: The Jazz Tap Dancing of the Nicholas Brothers* and has written extensively on tap and jazz dance as well as other subjects. She is currently at work on a history of African and Irish influences in nineteenth-century American vernacular dance.

DAWN LILLE HORWITZ holds a Ph.D. in dance education from New York University. Former director of the Graduate Program in Dance at City College, she is the author of *Michel Fokine* and essays on ballet and modern dance. She was co-curator of *Classic Black*, an exhibition about African American ballet dancers of the 1940s and 1950s sponsored by the Dance Collection, the

New York Public Library for the Performing Arts. She currently teaches dance history at the Juilliard School.

MARYA ANNETTE MCQUIRTER recently completed her Ph.D. in history at the University of Michigan. Her research is on leisure practices and urban subjectivity in the first half of the twentieth century. In addition to writing about dance, Marya teaches dance and is working hard to become a salsera.

MANSA K. MUSSA is a noted photographer who has been chronicling concert forms of African diaspora dance for twenty years. A former dancer, he has performed with Pyramid Dance Theatre, Djoulé African Dancers and Drummers, and Art of Black Music and Dance. His dance photographs are in the collections of the Schomburg Center for Research in Black Culture, the Newark Public Library, the Center for Cuban Studies, and the New Jersey Historical Society.

MAUREEN NEEDHAM is associate professor of dance history at Vanderbilt University. She graduated cum laude from Harvard University and earned her Ph.D. from New York University. Her honors include a National Endowment for the Humanities summer fellowship for research in Paris plus numerous travel grants for research abroad. Her publications include *I See America Dancing: Selected Readings 1685–2000* (forthcoming) and *Therapy in Motion.* She was chief contributor on dance for *Groves New Dictionary of Opera* and contributed to *American National Biography,* the *International Dictionary of Ballet,* and the *International Encyclopedia of Dance.*

P. STERLING STUCKEY earned a doctorate in history from Northwestern University where he was appointed associate professor in 1971 and full professor in 1977. He is currently professor of history at the University of California, Riverside. His books include *Slave Culture* and *Going through the Storm: The Influence of African American Art in History,* both seminal studies of African diaspora performance. His current projects include an extended study of slave dance.

JOHN F. SZWED is Musser Professor of Anthropology, African American Studies, Music, and American Studies at Yale University and is also a musician and record producer. His most recent book is *Space Is the Place: The Lives and Times of Sun Ra*.

Index

Abrahams, Roger D., 174
Adamczyk, Alice J., 15, 32*n29*
Aderemi, H. E. Sir Adesou, II, 120
aesthetics, 129, 137*n49*, 139*n69;* black,
5, 10, 14–15, 17, 96. *See also* blues
aesthetic
Africa/African: commonalities in dance
in, 44; European dance compared with
dance in, 239; influence on African
American dance of, 13, 14; influence
on American culture of, 181, 199–200;
and literature about African American
dance/black dance, 13, 14, 15; and research about African American dance,
19, 20; stereotypes about, 137*n48;* and
writing about black dance, 22. *See also*
specific artist or topic
African Academy of Arts and Research,
113
African American dance: and "being
black," 6–11; and "black dance," 3, 4–
5, 17; literature about, 11–17; and
locations for dancing, 27–28; nuances
and meaning of, 3, 4, 11–17; research
about, 3, 17–19; theories of, 19–21. *See*
also black dance; *specific artist or topic*
African American Dance Ensemble (Durham, North Carolina), 151, 152
African Celebration (Primus work),
136*n36*
African Ceremonial (Primus work), 105,
112, 115, 116, 116 fig., 117, 133
African cultural retentions. *See* Africanisms
"African Dance Festival" (Carnegie Hall,
1943), 113–14, 118
Africanisms, 14–15, 31*n25, 32n28,*
135*n13*, 136*n32*
Africa's Children (Hall work), 11
Africa Speaks, America Answers! (Warren
record), 146, 147 fig.

Afro-American newspaper (Balti-
more/Washington, D.C.), 22, 69–70,
96–97, 98, 270
agogo (instrument), 148
Aguga (dance of strength), 240, 255 fig.
Agunda (dance of joy), 244
Ailey, Alvin, 7, 8–10, 11, 30*n12, 34n49,*
149, 310, 312, 318, 324. *See also* Alvin
Ailey American Dance Theater
Aims of Modzawe (dance school), 147
Akan ethnic group, 44, 147
Albright, Anne Cooper, 21
Alexander, James, 115
Allan, Lewis, 112, 123, 126, 291, 315*n29*
Allen, Sarita, 35*n61*
Allen, Zita, 18, 19, 22, 212
Allison, Guy, 321, 324, 328 fig., 329 fig.,
337
Alston, Ovie, 276, 281
Alvin Ailey American Dance Theater,
7–8, 9–10, 30*n8, 34n55,* 149, 223
Americana (Dunham work), 294
American Ballet Theatre, 319
American Bandstand (TV show), 179,
201*n23*
American Dance Festival (ADF), 20,
34*n55,* 126–27, 133, 138*n60*
Amsterdam News (New York City), 97–98,
242, 270
Anderson, Charles, 280
Anderson, Marian, 267
Anderson, Sherwood, 247–48
Andrews, Dwight, 206, 227
Andrews, Ismay, 143, 144–45, 145 fig.,
148
"animal" dances, 171, 201*n22*, 202*n25*
Another Man Done Gone (Primus work),
137*n41*
Antilliana (McBurnie work), 112
Apollo Theater (New York City), 82, 226,
278, 286, 310